The Mark of the Cat

THE MARK OF THE CAT

Andre Norton

CENTURY
A Legend Book
LONDON SYDNEY AUCKLAND JOHANNESBURG

This edition published in the UK in May 1992 by Legend, an imprint of
Random Century Group
20 Vauxhall Bridge Rd,
London SW1V 2SA

Century Hutchinson South Africa (Pty) Ltd
PO Box 337, Bergvlei 2012
South Africa

Random Century Australia Pty Ltd
20 Alfred St, Milsons Point, Sydney, NSW 2061
Australia

Random Century New Zealand Ltd
PO Box 40–86, Glenfield, Auckland 10
New Zealand

The catalogue data record for this book is available from the British Library

Hardback ISBN 0 7126 3330 9
Paperback ISBN 0 7126 3399 6

Printed in England by Clays Ltd, St Ives plc

Introduction to
the Outer Regions

THE "OUTER REGIONS" were created by the artist Karen Kuykendall, whose book of paintings, *The Cat People,* and her justly
famous Tarot cards immortalized these fantastic lands and peoples. There exists among Ms. Kuykendall's records a complete
"Travelers' Report" upon which this book is based.

Each of the five queendoms—The Diamond, Vapala; The Sapphire, Kahulawe; The Ruby, Thnossis; The Topaz, Azhengir; The
Emerald, Twahihic—varies greatly. Each is ruled by a Queen, but
all pay full obedience to the Emperor. It is a carefully preserved
custom that these rulers come into power not by inheritance, but
through election, the Emperor through a series of severe tests.

The territory of these queendoms is mostly arid desert, and the
harshness of the environment has shaped both people and cultures.
What appears a frightening and barren world to stray travelers
from the hardly known inner regions is accepted as home and
a loved one by the five nations, the inhabitants so attuned to the
"essence" of the land that they are unhappy and adrift apart from
their roots.

The principal food of four of the queendoms comes mainly
from algae beds, for the whole region contains a vast shallow
thermal of briny waters in which live many kinds of these plants.
Only in Vapala, which is a mesa territory, is other vegetation
to be found—true plants—though some of these are grown in
the glass-bubble-protected oasis cities of Twahihic. Both people
and animals, however, depend mainly on the algae for food
and water.

Kahulawe is a land of slickrock isles which are pitted with caves
and crevices, crowned by weirdly carved sand spurs sheltering
the algae pans. Between these (most of which are owned by the
settlements of Houses and clans) lie stretches of barren sand. The

1

weather is very clear and sunny, so much so that most traveling is done by night. There are periods of death-dealing storms which may last for days. The people raise herds of oxen-like yaksen and the oryxen used as mounts. They produce fine leatherwork and jewelry and are a most prosperous and quiet folk. Their independent women are noted traders and often the leaders of the caravans.

Volcanic Thnossis is in direct contrast to this quiet neighbor. Quake prone, with rocky potholes and crevices which breathe out steam and gases, it trades in sulphur, pumice, iron, glass, and weaving. There are many noted smiths in Thnossis. This is the most unstable of queendoms, and its people are fiery of temper, moody, and fatalistic.

Most desolate of all is Azhengir, for it consists of wide salt flats and baked alkali lands. Its weather is very hot and clammy near the large salt pans, and as the other countries, it suffers from the sweep of violent sandstorms. Salt gathering is the main industry, though there is some manufacturing of limestone and gypsum products and glassware. The people accept their hard life fatalistically and find their main source of escape in music, singing, and playing on a wide variety of instruments.

Twahihic is known as the sand queendom. The terrain is undulating with great sand dunes. The glass-dome-protected settlements cover the oases. There is almost no rain. Smothering sandstorms and tornadic winds are always threatening. The inhabitants provide recreation for tourists from the other nations. Dune skiing and flying are very popular. Twahihic is also the center for fine glass and ceramics.

Vapala has the distinction of being the formal seat of the Empire. Situated on a huge mesa tableland, it has orchards, grasslands, and farms. There are two seasons, wet and dry. Farming, some herding, diamond mining, and the mechanics of solar energy provide work for the inhabitants. A profitable and stable country with the most advanced technology, its people are arrogant and inclined to consider those of the other four queendoms to be "barbarians."

Animal life has an important part to play in all five queendoms. The heavy-coated yaksen are both beasts of burden and sources of wool and meat. Oryxen, much lighter, larger, antelope-like creatures, equipped with murderous horns, are kept for riding. It is usual to clip the horns, though some expert horsemen and women are proud of mastering the more wild horned mount. One with clipped horns is known as a pa-oryxen.

Within almost all homes are kottis, small cats, independent of character. These choose the humans they wish to associate with and are highly esteemed. To deliberately kill a kotti is considered worse than murder and the offender is subjected to the death law.

The royal leopards have long been the symbol of imperial power. In fact, the Blue Leopard of Vapala is first guard to the Emperor and has a part in selecting those taking the tests for that position.

On the other hand, the larger sandcat is dreaded, as they dispute territories with human settlers. They are highly intelligent and have customs of their own. This species is distrusted and yet held in awe by the humans.

However, both sandcat and man have a common enemy in the packs of huge rats which prey upon all living things, befoul the algae pans, harry the herds, and are a source of death wherever they strike. Their hunger is never eased and they turn upon their own kind if no other prey is near. They breed continually and the litters are very large.

As to the customs of the queendoms: There are no formal marriages. Women only accept mates when they come into heat and not all of them ever do. Children are greatly desired but the birthrate is low. In Kahulawe, Vapala, and Thnossis a mating partnership is for life. In Twahihic and Azhengir polygamy is practiced and in those queendoms women who fail to come into heat are treated as servants and laborers. Children, being relatively few, are cherished and families are close-knit for the most part. However, unfit children and adults are put to death, since the community at large cannot support the unproductive. In Kahulawe and Vapala, where the normal deaths are fewer, the population of both people and animals is carefully monitored by a Minister of Balance and surplus of either humans or animals can be condemned. It is the quality of life rather than the quantity which is desired.

Belief is in the Cosmic Order and the Essence of the lands. Human sacrifice has been known in times of great drought. Often a ruler or person of importance volunteers as victim. But organized religion does not exist.

Only Azhengir practices slavery. In other countries servants have a firm social standing and dignity of person.

The solo—a rite of passage—is practiced in Kahulawe, Azhengir, and Twahihic. To be successful in this severe test, a young person must prove his or her ability to be accepted as a full adult.

In Kahulawe, Vapala, and Thnossis the Queens are elected by a council of representatives. The Queen has absolute power for life. In Azhengir and Twahihic the monarchy is hereditary; a Queen who does not bear children can be replaced.

Warfare used to be known between the isles of Kahulawe and in struggles between Houses of Vapala and mining towns of Thnossis. However, there has now been a long period of peace. Warriors still follow the traditional training but their only duties are the protection of caravans against the periodic raids of outlaws and the search for travelers lost in the harsh country. However, there is constant intrigue between the Great Houses of Vapala, with assassination and quiet murder often ridding some lordship of an enemy.

This then is land and people as they are in the here and now, but there are hints that all is not well and the future may be clouded as we come to the end of the reign of the Emperor Haban-ji. The waves of history are known for their rise and fall.

1

THE NIGHT SKY of Kahulawe arched over me. I had seated myself some distance away so that I could no longer see the lamps and torches about my father's house. But I could not close my ears to the songs and the drumbeat which inspired the lingering dancers.

There was no small furry body curled beside me, no gentle nudge of head against my arm, no low, crooning purr to assure me that whatever I might be to my family I did not lack at least one to whom I came first. There would never be that again.

The raw heat of anger gripped me as it never had before in my life. That I was a disappointment to my father, an object of disgrace to be bullied by my brother, a servant for my sisters—I had accepted, fought to accept. Many, many times I had come to this perch on the roof of my own hut with hurt, even some despair, inside me. Then that which is the very essence of my birth place had rearmed me, encased me, as a mother might welcome a hurt child to her arms.

I was Klaverel-va-Hynkkel, son to Klaverel-va-Meguiel, the last full commander of the Queen's forces before the proud regiments of the past shrank to the guards who now patrol the land against those who would prey along the caravan routes, or seek those gone astray from those same routes. I was his son and in his eyes I was a nothing. That I had learned to bear—or thought that I had. When I was younger I dreamed of accomplishing some act which would make my father turn eyes of approbation on me. But what deed could it be when I was not a bearer of weapons, one of those youths now strutting down around the house I refused to look at?

My brother Klaverel-va-Kalikku—now he— My nails scratched against the rock blocks fitted together beneath me as I drew two

5

deep breaths, fighting once more the rising rage which burned me as greatly as would the sun at full height— My brother was all in my father's reckoning that a son should be. It was he who skillfully rode the most vicious and hardly tamed oryxen, he who had hours earlier sent arrow and short spear to the heart of the test target, he who roared out the old war songs and danced the Advance of the Five Heroes.

I had accepted that, to my father, this is what a man is. And what am I? A servant, a caretaker of stock, a trader who goes to town when necessary, one responsible for things which no warrior considers needful—not unless all would suddenly cease to be done.

Once more I strove to put aside the unhappiness of others' judgment of me and strove to think of what I had which was my own. Whereas any oryxen would shy and lower horns to my brother, I could lay hand to its skin and fear no lash-out of horn or hoof. All our yaksen came to my whistle and made grateful noises deep in their throats when I groomed them, for none of my father's herd wandered matted of hair or needful of salve for hoof.

I was able to know with a single glance when those algae beds which supplied the major part of the food for ourselves and our herds needed to be double trimmed, and usually I was the one who harvested the major portion of the crop. Though at times my sisters would come with carry trays, to select for drying those bits which had special properties.

It was I who went to the market to trade yaksen hair to the weavers and select those needs which we could not supply for ourselves. The market— I shivered and leaned forward, resting my head on the arms I had folded across my knees.

No longer could I put off facing—and conquering in myself— what I must conquer. Let me then begin at the beginning, which lies with my sisters.

Melora-Kura— Her mind and her hands were truly filled with the essence of our land. I brought back for her such turquoise, agates, and other stones of color-life as she could use. She would sit and stare at such a piece for sometimes near a day and then her hands appeared to move of themselves, for many times she still looked only at the stone, to draw upon a sheet of cured skin that which she was moved to make. Jewelry from designs of Kura was greatly esteemed, so greatly indeed that outer traders from beyond our own marketplace would bring her commissions. She had never come into heat and I do not think that she regretted this, for she gave life with her mind and her hands and not her body. Not for her the wide-known feasting of a choosing such as occupied my younger sister Siggura-Meu this day and night.

Was Siggura satisfied now that she was engaged in something which Kura did not experience? That she had envied Kura I knew well. Too many times had I transported lopsided and strangely shaped pots of her manufacturing—such as she affirmed loudly were indeed works of art of a new kind—to market, where they were ignored or treated as a matter for laughter. No longer need she try to be as Kura: no, she would make her choice of those showing their prowess (if she had not already done so) and ride off to start a household of her own.

The market— No matter how my mind skittered away from the path of memory I would force upon it, I grimly returned to recall that. There I had always found a manner of acceptance. There was Ravinga, the far-traveling doll- and image-maker from Vapala.

And there was Mieu— My hand reached out to nothingness and there was a filling in my eyes, a tightnesss in my throat which were as painful as would be my father's 'epron whip laid across my shoulders.

The kottis are our friends, companions, our luck. They are much smaller than the wild sandcats which all men with reason fear, but they have that proud look about them, that independence of spirit which is shared by even the Emperor's great Blue Leopard, the very sign of imperial power.

Mieu had chosen me in the market of Meloa. She had but lately left whatever birthing place her dam had chosen, but there was already showing in her all the pride and intelligence of her kind. She came to me like a queen, her gleaming white, longish body fur jewel-patched by the black of onyx, the orange of fine agate. She was a treasure beyond all price and she made me hers.

From that moment we were as blood kin such as the bards sing of—comrades between whom there are no barriers. She took her place proudly beside what I had to offer in trade, even as she shared my sleeping mat and my food at home. It had been she—

I raised my head. For the first time I was realizing something I had forgotten, and I held to the scene in my mind. Yes, it was certain that Mieu had called me with her particular small urgent summons to Ravinga, running before me to where the dollmaker had her stand.

Ravinga was not in attendance at her sales place. That was occupied by a girl whom I had seen with her twice. She was very slender and her hair was the white flow of all Vapalans, though her skin was darker than Ravinga's as if she had spent more time in our hotter land.

Ravinga to one side was running her hands over the head of her great pack yaksen. For the beast was lowing and shaking its head. Ravinga saw me at once and signaled with upheld hand, stepping aside, for it was no strange thing that I tend a sickening beast.

It would seem that something plagued this one and I thought perhaps a salsucker had managed to embed itself in that thick covering of long hair. Such were sometimes to be found around the algae beds where the yaksen browse and they tortured an animal which could not rid itself from it, jaws gnawing into the skin.

I took my curry comb from my pouch and hunted, parting and lifting the hair. However, what I found was no dark green slug of a parasite—rather what looked like a tiny bag deliberately knotted into several strands. I changed my comb for a knife and sawed the thing loose. Once separated from the hairs it opened in my hand and I found myself looking down at a tooth.

The desert rats are the curse of our people and slain wherever they are found. I had killed many from my childhood on to keep clean the algae beds which they befouled and poisoned. Thus I was well aware what I saw now was one of the fore fangs of such a creature. It had been scored in several places and those markings filled with red paint but the lines so formed held no pattern I had ever seen.

I heard a hiss from the girl. But Ravinga struck my hand, knocking the bit of leather and its uncanny contents to the ground. Then she seized upon two rocks—flat pieces of yellowish stone which appeared so quickly in her hands that I do not know whence they came. These she clapped sharply on either side of that fang and ground them around as one would grind for paint powder. There had arisen a furl of what seemed smoke and a puff of noxious odor. When she pulled the rocks apart there was only a dead-white dust which she set her foot upon to tread it into the sand.

Having done so she stood looking straight at me. It seemed that there was a question in her eyes. I had questions also—in plenty. Yet it appeared I could not voice them. Now her hand went to her belt and she brought out something which gleamed.

"No!" The girl put out a hand. She was frowning and she certainly regarded me with no liking.

"Yes!" Ravinga denied her. She took two steps forward and I now saw that she held a round pendant swinging from a chain. At her gesture I bowed my head, then the chain was in place about my throat, and I looked down to see resting on my breast the finely wrought mask head of a sandcat fashioned from that ancient red gold which we seldom see in these times. I was well aware through Kura of good workmanship and had heretofore believed that no one could surpass my sister. Yet there was something in this which I had never seen before. The inset yellow gems forming the eyes almost appeared to have life.

"To you," Ravinga said. Then she repeated some words I could not understand. Once more breaking into the common tongue she added:

"This is for you alone and it shall be a key to that which is meant. Do not let it go from you."

When I protested that such a piece was worth a fortune she shook her head.

"It goes where it will. Now it is yours—I think—" She frowned a little. "No, the fate of another is not for my telling—take it, Hynkkel, and learn."

I had other luck that day, obtaining a very fine piece of turquoise which I knew would delight Kura, and I returned home, the cat head still on my breast, Mieu croon-purring on the top of my loaded yaksen.

However, I quickly found that I was wrong in believing that Ravinga's unexpected gift was a mark of good fortune. That I speedily discovered shortly after I reached the rock island which was home for my House. One travels best by night and certainly never under the full punishment of the sun, and so it was dawn when I passed the last of the towering carven sentry cats and saw my brother and Kura both heading towards me as I plodded wearily along.

Kura I expected, for my sister was always impatient to learn how well her wares had sold and what raw materials I had bought to build up her store. However, that Kalikku would pay any attention was certainly new.

As usual he was fighting his mount as he came. To Kalikku any animal must be harshly mastered, and most of his, so ridden, were so vicious that none other of the family chose to go near them. He felt always deprived because the days of war when one family or clan turned against another in open battle had passed, listening eagerly and with close attention to my father's stories of past engagements. Hunting and forays for caravan raiders were all he might look to, and who would become, he thought, a hero from such petty trials of strength?

I halted, waiting for them to join me, which they did speedily, Kalikku reining in with a swift cruelty which made his oryxen rear, sending sand showering. Mieu sat up and growled, turning a very unfriendly eye upon my brother.

"Foot padder"—that was one of the least cutting of the names my brother could call me and did—"make haste. Your labors are—" He did not finish; instead he leaned forward and stared, not eye to eye, but rather at the pendant I still wore.

The oryxen snorted and danced sideways as his rider urged the animal closer to me. "Where got you that?" my brother demanded. "How much of our father's store money did you lay out for it? Kura," he said to my sister, "perhaps it was your market profit this one has plundered."

Now he favored me with that ever-present challenge I had seen most of my life, silently urging me to retort either by fist or voice. And, as ever, I refused to give him the pleasure he had once taken, when we were very young, of beating me at will.

"It was a gift." Beneath my journey cloak my hands clenched and then by the force of my will loosened fingers again.

"A gift!" My brother laughed scornfully. "From whom could such as you receive that! Though I wager you certainly would not have the spirit to take it by any force."

Kura moved closer also. Seeing the interest in her eyes I slipped the pendant from my head and handed it to her. She turned it round and round, running her fingers over it. "No," she said musingly, "this is not from the hands of Tupa" (she mentioned one of the greatest artists of our people). "It is too old and also it is—" She hesitated and then added, "Truly finer work than I have ever seen. Whence did it come, brother?"

"From Ravinga, the dollmaker of Vapala, whom I have met several times in the market."

My sister held it as if she were caressing the fashioning of stones and metal.

"Whence did she get it, then?"

I shrugged. "That I do not know and—"

However, I had no time to finish what I would say, for Kalikku made a snatch for it, one which Kura was fast enough to avoid. "It is a treasure for a warrior, not for one who labors by his will." He proclaimed loudly, "Rightly such is mine!"

"No." For the first time I refused to be bullied. During all the night hours of my travel, that had rested not far from my heart. A belief had grown stronger in me with every step that it was indeed now a part of me. I did not really know what it portended nor why I should feel it now so but I did.

"No?" My brother showed his teeth in a grin like that of a sandcat seeing its prey at easy distance from it. "What is this dollmaker then to you that she gives you a treasure and you would hold it—your mat mate?"

"Stop it!" Kura seldom raised her voice. Ofttimes she was so intent upon her thoughts and plans for her work that she hardly seemed to be with us.

She dropped chain and pendant into my hand again. "If Hynkkel says this is a gift, then that is so. And one does not take gifts except for good reason, nor does one then surrender such to another. Hynkkel, I would like to look upon it again and perhaps make a drawing of it for my files, if you are willing."

"I am always at your service," I said. Among us we have no slaves—that is for the barbarians of Azhengir. Our servants are free to come and go as they well please—but usually as a caste they have their own well-earned positions and a different kind of pride. That I should be as a servant in my father's house was because I was a failure as a son, a son he thought was worthy of his notice. I was early a failure at those very things a warrior must know or do.

Bodily my strength was never that of my brother and I disliked all that went to make up his life. Though I had buried deep within me the pain—I always knew that my father denied me—I was content in other ways. I worked with our herds, I was careful as a tender of our algae beds, and I was always willing to go to the market. However, to my father's mind I was no proper one to inherit his name. It is true that I have always been something of a dreamer. I longed to make beauty with my hands as did Kura—but the one awkward figure of a cat guardian I chipped from stone was far from any masterpiece, though I stubbornly set it up beside my door, even as my father and brother had their "battle" standards beside theirs.

So, there being no middle way, I was a servant and that I tried to take pride in—making sure I served well. Thus I used a servant's response to my sister.

"You are needed." She drew a little away from me now as if, though she had taken my part, that was only in fairness and now we were back again in the same relationship we had been for most of my life. "Siggura has come into heat. We must have the feast of choosing. There is much to be done. Already messages to other clans have been sent by the drummers."

Kalikku laughed. "Do you not envy her, Kura—the feasting, the coming of many wooers?" His tone was meant to cut as might the lash of his riding whip.

She laughed in turn but hers was honest laughter. "No, I do not." She lifted her hands and held them out, letting fall the reins of her well-trained mount. "It is what these can do which gives my life meaning. There is no envy in me for Siggura."

Thus I had come back to pressure of hurry. Not all of our women are designed to wed. Some never come into heat. I do not know whether many of them regret that or not. But I did know that Siggura was one who would make the most of this chance to be the center of feasting and attention which might last for a week or more, until she was ready to announce her mate choice.

So it was that I got scanty sleep that day but hurried to oversee the checking of supplies, the dispatching of the others of our serving people to this or that task. The cat pendant I did not wear—I had no wish to stir up further comment. Rather I placed it in the small coffer where I kept the few things I truly prized.

To my surprise Mieu, instead of treading at my heels in her usual fashion, established guard there beside the box. So she remained for most of the time we took to arrange the housing of guests.

Siggura made her choice of the ornaments Kura spread before her, a collar of gold with ruby-eyed kotti heads, bracelets of fine enamel, and a girdle of shaded agate beads—the very best of her sister's stock, for she was always greedy. To match these she had new robes fashioned.

I saw very little of her though I offered formal congratulations. Words which she received with the smug expression of one who had achieved what was due her.

Our guests arrived, in both families and separate companies of youths ready to display their skills and their persons. There were dome wigs worn by men who had never seen any battle, even with the raveners of the trade trails, and much time spent showing off trained oryxen, singing and dancing. So our portion of the land was awakened from its quiet by the pulsing roll of drums, the lilt of flutes, the finer notes of hand harps.

I was heartily tired of it all on the night before Siggura was to announce her choice, when festivities were at their height. Also I had had several occasions to know shame, for there had been remarks made within my hearing about the disappointment I was. There was no brightly colored clothing for me, no jewels. Even my hair knot was held only by a small silver ring. But I had sense enough not to wear the pendant, for my showing of such a treasure would be questioned.

Wearily I came to my own small house. There was a glow light on and I expected to hear Mieu's welcome even though the singing was so loud. She always greeted me so.

Instead I heard a muffled curse and then a cry so full of pain that I threw myself within the door. My brother stood there. He was nursing his right hand with his other and I could see the blood dripping from what could only be bites and scratches of some depth.

He turned and saw me, and his face was the mask of a rat as he raised his hand to suck the blood from his wounds. My casket lay on the floor and—

There was a pitiful whine. I went to my knees and would have caught up that bundle of bloodied fur, yet was afraid to touch it lest I add to the pain which racked it. The small head raised a fraction and eyes which were filming with death looked at me. Under that head lay the pendant.

I already had my hand on the hilt of my knife when I swung around. Kalikku was backing out the door. Before I could move he hissed at me:

"Killer of kottis!"

"You—" My throat nearly burst with what I wanted to shout.

"You—there is but you and me—and who would Father believe?" He reached out his unwounded hand and caught up a flagon from the shelf near the door to hurl at me. I was not quick enough and it struck my head.

There was blackness and I do not know how long that lasted. Then I moved and was aware of the smell of the potent wine which my father had refused to have served at the feasting lest the drinking of it lead to quarrels.

I was dizzy and the world swung around me. Then I somehow got as far as my knees, holding to the stool for support. Still clinging to the stool, I edged about. My companion of little more than a happy year was only a fur bundle—unmoving.

Tears seemed to wash away the dizziness. I handled the body.

A blow, and then perhaps a kick— I felt my own lips flatten and draw back against my teeth. My tunic was wet with the wine and I jerked it off, for the fumes seemed to make my head spin the more.

I was able to think straightly again as I bunched together the sodden cloth and hurled it from me. As if it were as plain as an oft-told ballad, I knew what had happened.

To kill a kotti was death. Yet, for all his known harshness towards animals, my brother's word would be accepted. The story was very plain—I was drunk—I stank of that very fiery wine which was supposed to arouse men to the point of insanity. I was drunk and I had killed! Was Kalikku already on his way to tell his side of the story?

Or maybe he would tell it only if he were openly accused. That I would go into later and face it when I had to. Now there was something else.

I gathered Mieu to me. That pendant seemed to catch in her matted fur. I worked it loose and would have hurled it from me for the misfortune it had caused. Yet once it was in my grasp I could not force my fingers to loose it. Instead I wreathed the chain once more about my neck.

Mieu I rolled carefully into a scarf of green which was striped with copper glitter, a fanciful thing I had bought for its color on the very first day she had come to me. Then I carried her out under the stars, speaking in a whisper the while to her essence, even though that might have fled from her. There I laid her even as she had always curled her own body in sleep, and above her I built a cairn such as we erect for those furred ones who honor us with their friendship.

Then I climbed to this point on my hut and I tasted hate and found it hot and burning, and I tried to think what life would hold for me here now, with this thing ever in my mind. While below me the guests departed and the loneliness I craved in which to order my thoughts seemed not too far away. I watched the stars and tried to be one with that which is greater than any of us.

2

THE MORNING CAME with the rising fierceness of a wind. Afar I caught the warning boom of that nearest signal drum which was always to be heeded when a storm was imminent to raise the sand with such a flesh-scouring force that death was the answer if one were caught away from any shelter.

Below my father's spread of house the tall cat riven as a sentinel from the rock which formed our home territory throbbed in answer. I was shaken out of thought, out of my self-pity, if that was what had gripped me, and hurried about my duties of seeing the stock sheltered. Even my father joined in this, and Kura, who has a particular bonding with animals and could soothe and bring to obedience a contrary oryxen or fear-savaged yaksen, was there with the others of the household all aroused by the need for haste.

Working so, I forgot all except what was right to hand and drew a breath of relief when, at the time of the second heavy drumbeat, we had all secure.

I had not approached Kalikku, nor he me, during that time. Since my father had not summoned me to face his full wrath, I could believe that my brother had not indeed told the tale he threatened. Not that that betrayal might not yet come.

The storms are capricious. Often the warnings by which we live come to naught as the whirlwind-borne sand suddenly shifts in track. Yet never can we be sure that it will not strike. Thus we sit in what shelters we have waiting. We strive to be one with the essence of all about us, to be a very part of the slickrock islands which support our homes and settlements and of the treachery of the sand in between. For each has a place in the whole, rock and man, wind and sand—are we not all a part of our world? Storms may last, at their worst, for days, and those in tight-held

15

houses drink the particles which ably find their way in to film our water, grit it between our teeth as we chew on dried meat or an algae cake. It brings tears to the eyes, a gritty coating to the body, gathers in the hair, weighs upon one. Still we learn early endurance until the violent essence of the land is stilled.

This day our wait was not long, for there came the sharper note which was the signal from the distant drummer that we were not this time the chosen victims. I had spent that time of waiting sitting with the pendant in my hands trying to guess why Ravinga had gifted me with something which had brought such sorrow with it.

She had seemed to be grateful when I had discovered that foul amulet in the hair of her trusted trail beast. But her words had been cryptic, at least to me. Was I indeed not only awkward and clumsy with weapons, disliking all which seemed proper for my father's son, but somehow thick of thought, slow of mind into the bargain?

What did give me peace and contentment? To think upon what lay about me with curiosity, to have a warm rush of excitement when I heard some song of mine echoed back as I followed a stray from our herd, to examine the varied colors of the algae, marking the subtle difference in shade against shade, to look upon the handiwork of Kura and strive to find for her those desert stones, as well as those that traveling merchants brought, which would fit in some pattern of her dreaming. She had said more than once I almost seemed to borrow her own eyes when I went trading, so well was I able to fasten upon that which served her best. This was the inner part of me—as was the friendship of beasts, the companionship of Mieu—

I had thought around in a circle and was back once more to face that which had burned its way into my mind as a flame might burn determinedly its path. Almost I could see Mieu on her back, her four paws upheld, her eyes teasing me for a romp—or feel her soft, gentle touch of tongue tip on the back of my hand.

However, this time I was not to be left alone to chew once more on my bitterness. There was an impatient rap on the door of my small house and one of the herdsmen told me that my father wished to see me at once.

I was cold in an instant as if our sun had been struck from the sky. This then was the ending Kalikku had planned. Still I did not hesitate, but went to stand before my father's tall battle standard which already had been wedged back into place.

There I shed my belt knife, laying it in the trough provided for weapons. My brother's knife was there, the sullen red jewels on its hilt looking to me like the drops of blood he had shed. Also there was Kura's, bearing the fanciful design of small turquoise pattern which she loved most. My brother, yes, I had expected him, but that Kura had been summoned— Only, of course, as a member of the house she would be there to hear the sentence pronounced upon such a criminal as I would be named.

I whistled the small call and was answered by my father's deeper note and then I entered. He was seated on the chair fashioned of sandcat bones which testified to his hunter's skill, and it was cushioned, as the floor was carpeted, with the skins of those same mighty killers.

Kalikku was on his right hand, my sister on his left, but I had more attention for my father's face, for by its expression I might know whether I had been already judged and condemned. There was no heavy frown there, just the usual distaste I had met with for years.

"Hynkkel, there were words said among our guests which were not good to my hearing. Most were spoken behind the hand, but others more openly. You have reckoned some twenty full seasons—five since you man-banded your hair. Yet you have not soloed—"

"Let us name him ever untried boy and be done with it!" my brother said. "There is no spirit in him, as we all know." He gazed at me as if he dared his judgment to be denied.

However, it was not for him to say I was this or that—my father remained the Head of this House. And it was to him I spoke:

"Lord, none have spoken to me before of this thing, nor is it my place to do so."

Nor could I help but think of how this might go with us should that between father and son have been easy. My brother had soloed four years ago, Kura three. And each time it had been an occasion of feasting and joy, even as it had been for Siggura this day past. They had been escorted out into the unknown blindfolded, riding for a night beside my father and most of our kin and a greater part of the household. When there appeared one of the slickrock isles unknown to any and unsettled, my father had raised his hand and struck the honored blow rendering unconscious the one who must prove his survival skills to return home in triumph. There Kalikku had been left with weapons and some scanty provisions, and Kura likewise at a later time.

Triumphant had been their returns, proving that they had indeed been supported by their Essences, accepted as man and woman, adult and fit to choose their own way henceforth. So it was with all our youth. If they did not solo they remained always thought of as children, simple and of little worth, with no words of theirs ever listened to.

However, it was always those who were the House Heads who selected the time of such a solo, and my father had never so spoken of it to me. This being another thing which I thought he did that he might express his lack of feeling. Now—

"You will solo, Hynkkel. Though," he paused, surveying me from head to foot, "I expect nothing from you. Always have you stubbornly shown that you have no warrior mettle in you. Even your weapon—is it a spear, a sword? Paugh—it is a herder's sling—and a staff. When any other man's tool is put into your hands you are as awkward as your sister always was with those lopsided pots of hers—I trust she will not continue to inflict her 'art' upon her chosen Koolkan-va-Kastern in the future.

"Yes, you shall solo but I shall not expose this House to any more gossip or tittle-tell. There shall be no feasting where all can look upon you and see what is so woefully lacking. You may solo—but it shall be at my wish—and in my way!"

I swallowed and bowed my head. Even now there was no softening in him. He only wanted me out of his sight in a manner which would seem correct and leave him feeling he had done his duty, distasteful as it was. There were three of them, and me— but in my father's house I was alone.

So warned, I returned to my quarters and made my preparations: the sand-shedding cloak, the boots, the wide-brimmed hat against the sun. When I picked up that, a bit of fluff fell out, a pinch of Mieu's shedding, for when she was smaller she liked to sleep within that hat. There was my water container, and a packet of algae cakes, the rope coil and a few other things which, by custom, I might take. The last thing I did before I lay down to rest for the day was to gather those hairs of Mieu's shedding and weave them into the chain of the pendant before I set it once more about my throat. This was a symbol of the pain I would always carry.

I thought that I would not sleep but the weariness of my body subdued my thoughts and I went into darkness. Perhaps I dreamed; if I did, I did not remember. But at my awakening I found my cloak-cover twisted, my mouth dry, as if I had indeed fought some inner demon.

Forgetting for an instant, I looked about for Mieu, who always shared my sleeping mat. Then I remembered and rose to dress in the coarse journey clothing kept for travel. One of the herdsmen came even as I was latching fast my overtunic, bringing a bowl of thick soup, a small measure of the juice crushed from algae.

Thus again I was made aware of how my family considered me, that a servant and not kin brought this. Yet I was so accustomed to this usage that I ate and drank and, taking up my sack of permitted supplies, I went down to my father's house.

There were the three of them and in none of their faces did I see any concern. My father turned his usual mask upon me; my sister could have been one of the carvings she so patiently made and fitted into settings for her most elaborate jewels; only my brother showed in his eyes feeling and it was not such to warm my heart.

My father snapped his fingers and I went to him so that he looped over my head the blinding hood. Perhaps it was Kalikku who pushed me up so roughly into the saddle of the waiting pa-oryxen which I had seen to be the most worthless and expendable of my father's herd. Someone jerked the reins and the beast under me gave forth a cry, nearly a moan, as if it were being urged to do something beyond its slender strength.

There was no sound of any company gathering about us, no singing, no beating of drums to wish me fortune. I might be an outlawed one on his way for a ceremonial casting forth from his House. So meanly did they think of me then.

That same anger which had first arisen in me when I had witnessed Mieu's death became a steady fire. There is in all my race this need to be one with the homeland, with kin, yet my need was not acknowledged in the sight of all by this shabby exit on my solo. I held to my anger, for if I did not keep that as a shield, I had no strength to battle that great feeling of loss which was like a stone resting on my heart.

Kalikku talked, but never to me, or of anything concerning me. Instead he set himself, as I had known him to do many times, to interest my father, draw to himself the full attention in which he basked. He spoke of a prospective sandcat hunt which the youths had planned, of an expedition to the city to see and perhaps buy some of the weapons new come from Thnossis which were rumored to be of better metal than men had seen before.

At length my father was wooed into answering him. But I did not hear the voice of Kura, though the drift of her own spicy scent reached me now and then in spite of the blinding hood.

We paused for no nourishment nor rest, but plodded on. I was more used to tramping on my two feet when I journeyed to market and I felt stiff in the saddle. Nor, without seeing the stars overhead, could I begin to guess in what direction we were now headed.

There could not be too many unoccupied rock islands, for my people ever search for more land where we may build. This is an anxiety that occupies the mind of the Head of each House, for the Master of Measures and Balance stands always ready in the imagination of even the most steady-hearted of our people.

When it would seem that we occupied too much living space, when we began to outgrow the resources of the land—then there could be an accounting. And that was a ritual I think even such as my father feared to face. Flocks could be decimated upon the command, even people given to the sword's edge, that their fellows might have living room. There had not been an accounting of that kind for many years, yet the thought and threat of it always overhung us.

I had much time to think as I rode so. Though I had taken merchant roads many times, had fought off the attacks of the rats which preyed upon every algae bed and the other life that had to gather there, yet I was not one to count myself a seasoned traveler. I had listened to the accounts of those who had undergone this same challenge and now I found I remembered best the disasters rather than the triumphs.

Our small party came to a halt at last. There was a quick jerk to remove my hood after I had been dragged roughly from the saddle. I had barely time enough to see that there was a dimming of the stars overhead before the blow caught me and I was enclosed once more in the dark.

I was in a furnace—one of those they tell of which are parts of the mountains of Thnossis where they use the inner heat of the earth itself to aid in the shaping of metal to their will. With all my might I strove to free myself from the bonds laid upon me to hold me to such torment and opened my eyes.

My head and shoulders lay within a shallow hollow of rock but the rest of my body was positioned in the full heat of the sun. I speedily drew farther back into my small shelter. My head ached and before my eyes both rock and sand were in sickening motion. Slowly I was able to raise hand to my head. Back of my right ear there was a place where touch brought instant pain. And that pain cleared my mind so I knew where I was and why.

My pack lay in the direct rays of the sun. I lurched forward to grasp and pull that to me and as I did so something glittered and fell into view. My fingers closed upon an armlet of burnished copper such as my sister often chose to work with. On the wide band there was set a pattern of turquoise twined to glistening yellow stones such as are those set in the eyeholes of the guardian cat statues.

I held the gift, turning it round and about in my fingers. Its color and fine workmanship would raise pride of possession in any beholder. Yet to me it brought a chill. Resolutely I slipped it up above my elbow, thrusting back the sleeve to view it against my skin. It was such an ornament as would be worthy of several well-trained oryxen if offered in the city. A thing made to please and honor yet with that chilling message of its own—for I was sure I read it aright—this was my sister's farewell to me.

Did she believe that I was going to my death? Perhaps that was also true. Yet I lived now and that new stubbornness within me said that I would continue to live in spite of all the omens against me.

So I made fast the ties of the bag which held my supplies, shouldered that, and looked about me. By the width of sun outside my crevice night was not far away. And night would bring stars. None who ever ventured on the merchants' trails lacked knowledge of those as guides. I would see what lay above me and then I would move—and keep moving—

3

OURS IS A LAND of great color and beauty. The slickrock islands are rugged, baring jagged fangs to the sky as if some sandcats lay upon their backs thrusting up their well-clawed paws. Many are the forms of these rocks also, beside such spires. There are even domes which might mark homes, yet no man's hand carved them so. Others take on the shape of strange beasts from the ancient tales. The winds sound with voices of their own, sometimes with the mocking notes of speech or song one cannot understand.

Under the full sun the rocks blaze forth hues of the colors of Kura's gems. At nightfall their splendor is not fully quenched, for then there lies a silver glimmer over the drifts of sand, glittering at the slightest shifting of grain against grain. This world is a part of my kind even as are the smaller bits upon which we build our homes.

I scrambled to a higher point on the island where I had been left. There was still a streaking of grayish purple and muted gold in the sky, but already some of the stars shone palely. As I looked around to view all that I could before dark took over, I saw that this place of temporary exile was larger than I thought it might be. That such a stretch of available homesites had not been colonized was a puzzle.

Throwing back my head I drew several deep breaths. There are three scents one may pick up on slickrock formations, two of which may mean death, while the third is just the opposite, being rather a promise of existence.

Two species protest the rulership of my own kind. Firstly there is the rat. Though these run in packs they have no real kinship with each other even for the dams which bear them. Much larger than the kottis, they are personified avid hunger given legs and the freedom to hunt down what will fill their ever-empty bellies.

23

They can live on algae but do so stupidly, wasting and befouling the bedding pools until they poison the whole of the crop so it may take years before it will recover from their visitation. Being able to burrow deeply and rapidly under the ground, they can shelter so from the sun and emerge only when the worst of the day's blaze is gone, issuing forth to kill and eat, kill and eat. If they cannot find aught they turn upon each other—even the young upon their dam or the dam against her own offspring. There is nothing but evil in them and their stench is enough to bring vomit into the throat of those who must face them.

Our yaksen with their thick coats of long hair have some protection against any small party of such raiders but a large pack can surge over them in a space of breaths, even as the full wind can bury in sand anything alive. The oryxen, on the other hand, though vicious fighters themselves when their horns are not clipped, can be easily slain.

Rats have two enemies—my own species and sandcats. We have our long-practiced strategies, our spears, swords, sling-pellets, hunting knives, knife-staffs—yet there have been unfortunates pulled down and left only well-gnawed bones.

The sandcats, which we also fear (it being a test of manhood to go hunting such and to bring home a trophy of teeth or hide as a matter of praise from family and kin), have not only a wily and clever form of battle, but jaws and talons which they put to excellent use. Like the yaksen they possess a thick fur coat which is an aid against all but the most well placed and forceful bite. It is probably their presence here and there which keeps down the possible fateful ravages of the hordes of the rats. For the latter are moved entirely by their hunger and will keep fighting rather than retreat because of the constant gnawing of their bellies.

The cats, also, have their scent—a muskiness which is not unpleasant, and a sharper odor with which they carefully mark the boundaries of their hunting territories. They do not gather much together, there being perhaps only one mated pair to a single rock isle, and they have but one cub at a time, that one striking out for itself when it reaches a certain stage of growth. There is fighting between the males for both territory and mates, and the loser often becomes a roaming rogue, always a danger.

Tonight I smelled neither rat stench nor cat trace, but rather the third scent—that I wished for. That was the one which might mean my own survival. The algae pools and pans mean just that to those of my race. For it is on those waterlogged plants that our principal food depends. We have the product of our herds also, but those beasts themselves feed only upon the algae. The only thing else which grows on our brackish soil is the fus-melon, which must be harvested just at the right time or is too hard to be edible.

If this islet on which I stood had an algae pool, I might also encounter some wild yaksen which could furnish sun-dried meat for future traveling.

Traveling which way or where? I looked up to the stars which were growing steadily brighter. Each of us who travels the trade trails is familiar with those points of light which mark the passages we use. However, we are not a wide-roving people, being too heart-bound to our land and our homes to venture far afield. I knew the position in the sky of those which would spell out my own road from home rock to the market at Meloa and return. I could not mark those from where I stood now, nor did I expect to.

It certainly would make the solo of no purpose if he or she who was to make it were placed so as to find their path of return an easy one. But there were other guides and if fortune favored me I might well find one of those.

Among our people one who has been given certain benefits by fortune or who has escaped some dire peril, or wishes to honor an ancestor, might order carved some place along any known trail, where there stood rocks more than life high, the likeness of a kotti—to be supplied with gem eyes to glint in the sun, or a collar of stones which served the same purpose. Many of the main trails were very well marked along their lengths with such sentries, but even lesser known ways had one at least at some important point.

Could I sight one of these— I sighed. There was no firm belief of future fortune left in me.

My eyes adjusted enough so that I could see something of what lay ahead. It would be best I decided to move along, as best I could, the edges of this island until I was able to see how large it was and whether it had—

At that very moment there came a sighing of air which is sometimes born of the evening, and what it brought to me then was the very welcome scent of algae! Nor was there any taint to suggest that this was a poisoned pool which had been deserted. The footing was rough and I went slowly, never knowing when a crevice could confront me suddenly. Also the surface might turn treacherous and a wrenched ankle or broken bone would soon put an end to not only this venture but me.

I was able to follow the scent, alert to any faint stink of rat or the acrid odor of a cat marking. So far it was only the wholesome breath of growing things which reached me.

At length I came out on the edge of a drop and, in spite of the roll of shadow, beneath I knew that I had indeed found the pool, and one of some size. Which added to my puzzlement that this was not already colonized or rat-haunted.

I found a cave of some promise and shifted my pack from my shoulders to store there before I essayed the climb down into the pocket of the pool. Though I was no master of sword or spear, there were two weapons with which constant practice during my duty with the herds had made me expert. Even my brother had never challenged me to a duel with a sling—he professed to find this not befitting a warrior's warrior but rather that of a servant. The sling I had with me as well as that herder's stout staff, which a twist of the wrist equipped with knife edges protruding halfway down its length. My knife I loosened in its sheath before I swung over, hunting foot- and handholds. I made it only partway down so prudently, for then one of my footholds broke loose and I slid, to come up with a painful slam against rock.

The algae had a night glimmer of its own, some varieties of it giving forth more of the pallid light than others. So I could see that I was not far from the beginning of the bed. However, as if my jarring fall was a signal, there was a boiling up out of the ground not too far away of a slavering pack, red eyes agleam, the fangs in their gaping mouths a faint green. They squealed with ear-punishing shrillness and the stench of their bodies and breath near made me vomit.

I was not foolish enough to have made that descent unprepared. The staff slung on my back seemed to flit of itself into my hands— the knife edges extended as far as possible.

With my back close to the wall down which I had come, I made an outward sweep with my staff. Two of the rats were caught near in mid-air and sent sprawling. In a flash the laggers among the pack were on their fallen fellows, but I was busied with those who came at me. There was not enough room for me to use my sling. I had to make do with staff but that use I knew well.

I swept away two others and snarled myself as my staff was seized in the jaws of one that was larger by half than its fellows and whose red eyes promised full vengeance. Quickly I released my grasp on the staff, now knife in one hand. Use of that I also knew well. This was not the first time I had faced the fury of a rat pack but never had I been alone. Before, when I had defended the home herd, I had given the signal and knew help would be there speedily. While the yaksen, well aware of their longtime enemies, had lowered horns and trampled with sharp hooves. There was a sudden sharp pain like the bite of a sword at my thigh. I stabbed down with my knife. Luck had provided me with a place to make my stand where I was sheltered in a crack between two projections of rock wall. The rats could only approach me two at a time and those I could meet. However, there was only one of me, and my enemies numbered more than I could count as they whirled about, moving with the speed which was part of their nature. One came from behind the two which were engaging me, leaping across the backs of its fellows for my head and throat. I flung up my hand and the impetus of its leap brought it smashing into the knife. The force of the meeting sent me back, my hand numbing, but not before I had felt the smashing of bone.

The attacker fell with a squealing shriek at my feet, striking about it dazedly, and so bringing down the attack of those two that I had been holding off.

There was a flurry of battle which kept the others of the pack away from me. My shoulders grated against the rock and I breathed heavily. Such a respite could last but a moment and then they would be at me again— For all the strength I had learned in my own way as herdsman and trader-traveler I knew that I could not hope to last out against another determined attack.

I was afraid, yes, but I also knew anger that I would lose my life to fill the bellies of these monsters. As many as I could take with me, or feed to their own, that I would. My staff lay there but the fight of the three rats before me raged over that and I had no chance of retrieving it.

There was a shifting of the pack. In this light they were only black shadows with those fire coals for eyes. I stiffened, waiting for the last rush to bring me down.

They were backing away! I could not believe that—though the rats were thought to have little or no intelligence, these might almost be withdrawing to take council how best to attack me without so much loss to their pack.

However, more and more heads were lifted, not toward me but to the sky overhead. Then there rang out a single shrill cry, to be picked up and added to by a second and third. Those three rats entangled before me still gouged. One lay beneath, trampled upon, but its fellows were at each other's throats for the privilege of consuming it. They alone did not display the strange behavior of the pack.

Once more the cry arose. I thought I read into it not an urge to battle but a warning. I found myself also head high, listening, trying to scent more than the stench of the pack. There was a whirl of breeze and I knew what had altered the behavior of my enemies. We who are a part of the land, and live close to it, are readied to catch its changes.

Storm— I had heard no warning drum, none of the far-carrying vibrations picked up by the road sentinel cats to be relayed. Instead there was that strange prickling of the air itself which sent a tingling of the skin down one's body.

The pack, squealing in chorus now, were gone. Even one of those in the struggle before me tore loose and went limping after. They were seeking the shelter which all life must have if it were to survive the coming blast—as I must have.

I leaped over their two bodies so near my feet and sought the side of the algae pool. Such storms had been known to last for days and I must have some provisions to supplement the few rations I carried. With a sweep of hand I gathered algae, storing it in my jerkin against my body for want of better carrier. Only three such garnerings dared I allow myself.

The cliff down which I had so unceremoniously descended had to be faced and climbing was always far more difficult than descent. Yet I schooled myself against such haste as would deposit me once more at the bottom of that drop unable to find shelter before the menace born of wind and sand struck.

Panting with the effort, I did regain that small cave where I had left my gear. Dumping the soggy mass of algae I had managed to bring up with me onto the rock therein, I set about making my cloak into the partial shelter which a traveler could depend upon. The cave was cramped but I was lucky to have it at all.

Now I formed a protection with the cloak, wedging my staff to hold it as secure as I might hope to make it. Then I huddled down, a handful of algae in my hand to suck upon, waiting for the storm to strike.

Strike it did. There was no escaping its fury. My preparations were as nothing against such constant blows. Sand as fine as grit reached me. My skin was scoured raw by that. I was deafened. And I was blind, binding my scarf over my eyes so that I would not lose them to the ever-present torture of the sand. When I was driven by a hunger which seemed as demanding as that of the rats, I strove to choke down bits of the algae, only to feel within each bite the grit which shifted through my poor protection to coat everything within.

One loses count of time when one becomes a prisoner of a storm. I must have slept because I remember one wild dream wherein I confronted a sandcat and felt the slashing of its claws, the rasp of its rough tongue. It was playing with me as a kotti plays with one of the vine beetles. There was no welcome escape, no death—only darkness. Into that I sank thankfully, no longer able to summon up the strength to fight. Still in that darkness the roar of the storm deafened me and there was no peace to be found.

Was this to be the end of my attempt to prove myself before my kin? No, something in me would not accept that! There was a part of me which endured through darkness and pain—which held stubbornly to life.

4

THERE CAME AN END in time and with the deafening howl of the wind out of my ears I awoke out of the darkness which was not true sleep, only to lapse again into the slumber my tense and aching body craved. All I realized in those moments before I fell asleep was that I had survived by some chance such fury as could wipe out a caravan with ease.

It must have been a dream—certainly I did not in truth act out what was so vividly real to me. There was a room lighted by lamps which gave off an amber glow like unto the eyes of giant cats, so that I seemed to stand before some judge who held as much right over me as one of those dreaded masters of the desert.

There was movement and into that area of light came two I knew, Ravinga, the maker of dolls, and her apprentice. Ravinga held in her hands, with the care one carries something precious, a doll whose like I had never seen before. Such was the art of its making that it might indeed have been a man in miniature. Then I saw that indeed it had the likeness of a man and that man was me.

She came two steps forward and held the doll out and her eyes went searchingly from it to me and back again as if she would so make sure her likeness was correct in every detail. Then she nodded and spoke.

But the storm might have indeed rendered me deaf, for though her lips moved I heard no words, nor did she address me, but rather her companion. The girl moved forward also and it was plain to me that she came reluctantly and that whatever was happening was against her will. Still she came. She put out her hands, palms flat and up, side by side, and Ravinga laid the doll which was me across them. The girl bent her head, and her tongue showed forth its tip from between her lips. With

31

that she touched the face of the doll three times while Ravinga's lips moved again as if she sang or spoke. Like a snap of the fingers they, the lamplight, all of it was gone. I opened my eyes.

Clawing away the scarf I had bound above my face, I saw that I lay in darkness and when I tried to move there was a heavy pressure against me which brought a start of fear. The driven sand must stand high against my frail protection of cloak and it was as if I were sealed into this crevice.

When I struggled to free the staff which had pegged that down from within, I could feel a sliding and some of that pressure lessened, setting me to quicker action, to be free of what might have been a grave.

I worked out into the night. There were no ominous clouds of whirling sand. The stars hung as well-tended lamps. Trembling and moving stiffly I got to my feet to look around. I smeared my hands across my face striving to free it from the caking sand dust and there followed pain from my blasted skin.

The algae pool! Not only should I find there the food and moisture my body needed, but there should also be some of the growth meant for healing.

It was then that I felt that other, that I was not alone here. Yet when I steadied myself and looked about I could see nothing but rock where runnels of sand filling every depression were sifting across the edge of the ledge beneath which lay the pool, as might a trickle of water drain away. I had never seen such in my life, for free-running water would be a marvel almost past believing— though I had heard that such did exist in Vapala.

I did have one gift which I cherished but which had never impressed my father, that of being able to sense something in trouble. That impression was with me now, sending me wavering along, not down to the pool which my own body demanded, but rather on the edge of the depression which held it.

There was pain in that sending, strong enough to make me wince in spite of my own raw skin. Pain, and a suggestion of fear.

I lurched on, leaning on my staff, striving to avoid those dust-filled cavities which might bring the careless down with a broken limb. Then I halted, for the scent came clearly. The musk of a sandcat overlaid with that of blood and the beginnings of infection—a wounded animal? But how had such been able to survive the storm? And a sandcat—

The tales of their ferocity and cunning were a part of our lore. We honored any man who slew one. By all we knew there could be no peace with such.

Still the pain lay heavy in my mind. If the creature were badly wounded and suffering—would it not be better to put it out of this misery of life? I have had to cut the throat of a yaksen that had served me well when I found it rat-torn and in agony. Pain—no living creature should be left to face such a slow descent into death.

I passed now the end of that cavity in which lay the pool. The scent of the sandcat was heavy; still I could not sight any trace of the animal. There was a sudden low growling. I faced around, to see a dark opening in an arching rise of the rock.

With my staff grasped in both hands before me, ready to forestall any leap as best I could, I crept forward. Unbidden by any thought, I found my voice as if some instinct I had known nothing of before now spoke through me.

"I come in peace, Strong One— Peace—" Then I fell to humming softly as I did when I tended some hurt of one of the herd— having early learned that such seemed to soothe any fear of me.

There was movement in the darkness. The night glimmer of the sand pools about gave aid to my night sight. Indeed within that hollow was a furred body, and the smell of pus-filled wounds was foul. Pain—but with it now menace—defiance—

I strove to balance my own thoughts, to subdue any of the fear that this one's kind arose in me, as I went to my knees before the mouth of the cave.

"Great One, I come to help—" As I leaned forward the cat pendant fell outward from the folds of my thickly sand-powdered travel shirt. It startled me, for it gleamed and with a greater life than did the shimmer of the sand. My hand went to it, but there was no heat as a lamp might give forth—only the light increased.

That rising snarl from within the dark cup stopped. Pain I could still sense, but there was something else now which I could not define. I only knew that if I crawled forward I would no longer need my staff, nor the knife at my belt. So I laid aside my shaft and went ahead.

Great golden discs of eyes met mine.

"Great One—" I said slowly. Then I caught that other smell— the stink of rat—and my hand rattled away a well-gnawed bone. The light of my pendant had increased and I could see that this was a male, with mangled paw, now swollen and giving forth the stench of corruption. It might be too late to offer anything but a clean death but I could try and that, I knew deep within me, I must do.

Those same water plants with which I had thought of relieving my own scored skin—could they draw the infection out? At least I could offer the animal water and something which might lighten a little of its present torment.

"Great One—I go for that which will comfort—" I spoke as I might to an injured kotti. If my fear had matched his, so was it now decreasing.

The descent to the algae pool was difficult. My sore hands were as if burnt by the time I reached the pool side. For the first time I remembered the rats which had been driven away by the coming of the storm. I listened, drew deep breaths to pick up their smell. There was no sign nor scent of them. So I got to the pool, plunging my own hands and arms deep into the mass of growth there. There was no strong light to show me the graduations of color necessary to tell one type of plant from another. I merely gathered all that I could within reach and, with that bundle, won once more to the surface of the rock and so to the cave.

The wounded beast must have scented what I carried. He growled once but then was still. Carefully I squeezed some hand-fuls to the stone where he might lick it off, and then turned my attention to his wound.

To my relief, from what I could see by the light of the pendant which had obligingly flared up again, there was only one wound. Moving quietly, again humming, striving to project to him that I meant no harm, only good, I crushed another mess into a paste, and, with all the care I could to spare the pain of a wrong touch, I began to spread it across the wound.

The paw twitched, I saw those wickedly sharp claws show. He raised his head from where he was licking up the last of the algae and once more stared at me round-eyed, unblinkingly. I refused to be so easily cowed, finishing my task as deftly as I could. Then I settled myself not too far away, sitting cross-legged and eating avidly what was left of the store of algae. Part of it was bitter but I was sure that it was no different from the crops grown in our own home pool, and the moisture it carried to my body was as soothing in its way as the touch of it was to my skin. The rats had had no chance to befoul and poison this bounty.

The sandcat finished the rest of the algae. With his good paw he pushed at one of the gnawed bones and I knew that he craved more than the stuff from the pool, but I carried no dried meat with me. To deliberately seek out and kill rats was a test I was not yet ready to face. Though I was very sure that it must come sometime.

I had withdrawn to just outside the cave space this strange new companion was using for shelter. My body ached with fatigue. The pounding of the storm and my exertions since then had brought me close to exhaustion. Already the lights of dawn showed along the horizon I faced from the place where I had dropped down onto the rock. Those supplies, my cloak, all the rest I owned and had left behind when I had sought out the source of that unvoiced call for succor were some distance from me.

Still I could not just leave this creature who had given me an unusual portion of trust. Judging by my past knowledge of animal tending, his wound would take some time for the healing, if heal it was going to. To leave him here unable to find food, a prey to the rats whose scenting ability when it came to any living thing (and all life was their prey) would speedily bring them seeking him when they issued again from their safe burrows— No—

"Great One," my hand had gone unconsciously to the pendant, "I must go but I shall return. This I swear by—" my fingers closed about the mask, "by this which is a thing of power." And when I said that, I knew that I spoke the truth. Where this had come from, for I was sure it was not of the craftsmanship of Ravinga, I did not know. Kura had said it was of such workmanship as she had never seen, and my sister was always one avid to collect any new pattern or design which she did sight; also that it was old.

Somehow I pulled myself to my feet. At the pace my body would allow me it would take me some time to reach that crevice which had saved my life and I must do so before the sun was up enough to be a menace. I leaned heavily on my staff as I went. There was a querulous sound from behind me and I looked over my shoulder. Those eyes were fastened upon me. They did not hold the glow they had showed in the dark yet they compelled. Once more I offered assurance:

"Great One, I shall return."

It was almost as if my words were a message he could understand. His large head dropped, rested upon his good paw, he blinked, and his eyes closed.

So I made a toilsome way back to my own place of refuge, taking good care as I went to sniff for any taint of rat. The rocks around me were taking on day color now, yellow, red-brown, here and there some point like a small cliff layered with a hue nearly red between two dull yellows.

There is a beauty in our land which travelers may call harsh. But there is born in us a feeling that we are a part of it. Even as our skin is bronzed like unto some of those shades of red and rich brown, we choose to wear colors which are brilliant. So we may even feel that we have indeed been hewn from the very stone which forms our dwelling places. It is our custom to open our hearts and minds when we are alone to the land, the sky, all which may be about us.

At this moment as I so painfully trudged back to my camp I paused now and then to look about me, breathing deeply of the air which was now free from any trace of sand powder. However, each time I surveyed the sand which lay beyond this perch there was no sign that any of my blood had been here before me. There certainly were none of the rock-hewn cat markers to be sighted.

The heat of the day was already up when I reached the crevice. My stiff, sore body protested as I made as swift a business as possible of folding my small store of possessions into the pack and lashing it so with the rope.

I went to the edge of the rise and looked down at that portion of the pool which lay below and then I changed my plans and decided that to follow along the shore of that, close to what moisture the pool exuded, would be a better plan than to keep to these sun-baked heights.

Though the descent was a cruel test of my body, I made it and came almost immediately upon the body of one of the rats which I had killed during the attack. Perhaps it was the fear of the storm which had kept it out of the stomachs of its fellows. Save for some torn flesh it was almost intact. Remembering the gesture of the cat, reaching for the tooth-stripped bone, I stayed long enough to butcher the dead thing, taking legs and haunches from it.

These I lashed together with the end of my rope and added to the weight of the pack. At the edge of the pond I stopped once again and ate of the algae I recognized as the most nourishing. Later I could harvest such and dry it into cakes so that when I would move on again I would have fresh supplies. When I would move on again—

I hesitated over the thought. Prudence would suggest that I do so as soon as possible. Still something, perhaps the stubbornness which had been born in me so that I could not be the son my father wanted, told me now I had a task before me whether I wished it or not.

Men said that there was no greater enemy to us than the sandcats. They prey upon our flocks, and, it was widely believed, upon such of my own people as they could take. Teeth, claws, and hides of them were proud possessions of the hunters among us. There was an insurmountable enmity between my species and theirs. Yet now I could not leave this one to certain death.

I stirred algae with one hand and tried to sort out my thoughts, to understand. The pendant in this light had lost all its glimmer of the night before. To any eyes it would seem merely a finely made piece of jewelry, a little strange perhaps— I began to remember that odd dream or vision which had been mine during the storm— of Ravinga and the doll which had been made in my likeness. My dripping hand went up, not to my mouth, but to touch my face, as I remembered the action of the girl, the unwilling action.

Had that only been a dream? Or something else? Dreams could seldom be recalled as vividly as I did this. Suddenly I knew that if I came through this time of solo and was free to go my way, I would seek out the dollmaker. I wanted to know more, not only of the mask I wore but the meaning which lay behind it. That there was such a meaning I was sure.

Having eaten my fill and noting that the sun was now near a period when I *must* seek cover, I started on around the edge of the pool, my staff ready. Heat of direct sun might well not keep the rats from my trail, they were always too avid for flesh.

Walking here was more even and I was able to make good time until I came to that portion of the wall which I recognized as had been my path when I had sought out food for the cat. I made the journey up and then hoisted the packet of my belongings by the end of the rope.

There was a muted growl. The cat raised his head. His lip drew back a little to expose those fangs which are so fearsome a weapon for his kind. Then his head dropped again upon his paw as if in weakness.

I freed the rat meat and brought it to him. He lifted his head a little and his tongue licked at the offering. For a moment I was afraid that he was indeed so near death that he could not eat, but it seemed that that licking aroused him, for he planted his good

paw on a portion of the meat and started tearing at it, seeming
to gulp it down without chewing. While he so disposed of the
food, I searched through my scant belongings and brought out
a small leather bag which held some yaksen fat into which had
been worked certain strains of algae I knew were healing. This
I kneaded until it was very soft and once more I approached the
cat, humming again as I did so.

"Great One—" he had finished most of the meat and had been
licking at a leg bone, "give me leave to tend your wound."

His stare was a measuring one and then he actually moved, as
if he did well understand my words, pushing forward a little his
wounded leg. As carefully as I had applied the algae poultice, so
now I pulled it free in flakes. I was sure that the limb was less
swollen than it had been last night, yet I could not altogether
depend upon that.

Now I could see clearly that the wound was a nasty tear, almost
as if a portion of the flesh had been detached from the bone, and I
thought it was a rat bite. That it might well be infected was the
problem. I could only hope that the small knowledge I had gained
concerning the hurts of animals would be of help.

Once more, as gently as possible, I covered that expanse of
angry-looking flesh with the salve. When I had done he dropped
his head to sniff at my handiwork and I feared because of the scent
of the grease he might set to licking it off again. But he did not.

Meanwhile I set about making a resting place of my own. I
envied my companion his cave, for I had to make do for a shelter
with my cloak stretched between two upstanding fangs of rocks.
However, there was a third, higher pinnacle which did give me a
dark shadow for cover, at least for now.

One of my final preparations was the finding and choosing of
stones suitable for my sling. Those I piled in three places where
I might have to take refuge if the rats did come sniffing along
the trail.

There was little more I could do and I curled within my own
cramped shelter, hoping the cat would give warning if we were
attacked. Though the full heat of the day was now upon us and
perhaps that would be our greatest defense.

5

I HAD GOOD REASON to be glad that I had chosen ammunition for
my sling and had that within reaching distance as a growl from
the cat—one which heightened to a roar of defiance and rage—
brought me sharply out of uneasy slumber. The stink of rats was
strong. In spite of the fact that the sun was still high enough to
light fire heat on the rocks, the creatures were on the hunt.

That they ventured out into the full day to do this was sur-
prising. It must have been that they had picked up not only my
scent but that of the cat so altered by his wound as to make them
think that he would be easy prey.

I brought down two and sent a third howling and stumbling
back, one foreleg dangling. As was usual their pack mates closed
in upon the injured as well as upon the dead. But there was something else which surprised me above the natural heat of battle.

The pack milled about the foot of a taller spur of rock and on
the top of that there was a black spot which in spite of the sun's
glare I at length made out to be another rat. But this one was
different from the others. The shape of its head, as I made it out
against the red of the rock, was too large and almost misshapen.

Even as I was able to see that much, the creature raised its
head and howled, a sound different also from the squealing of
its fellows. It was on its feet and I could see that the thing was
at least twice the size of the pack members below, formidable as
those were.

As if it had voiced some order the pack surged forward towards
us. Still that brief pause had given me a chance to use my sling
to good advantage. Two more of those attackers went down, one
snapping at its own side where my rock had thudded home, as if
to bite at the thing which had hurt it. This time those who fell
were not set upon by the rest. So that small advantage was lost.

I had already moved so that my back was to the cave wherein the roaring cat was fighting to get to its feet. I had jerked with me the cloak I had set up to use as a sunshield and this I swirled out with one hand, to engulf the first of the rats coming within reach.

A moment later I had thrown my knife, taking a desperate chance upon something which was just a suspicion. It struck deep, not into one of those upon whom I was now using my staff in the sweep which was the best answer to their charge, but into the neck of that thing on the rock point above.

Its peculiar cry was cut off, as I was busy with the rest. One of them would have taken me from the side, but the cat, as handicapped as it was, smacked that down with a single blow of its good paw.

The whirlwind of their attack was finished as quickly as it had begun. Dark forms, their skin patched with the green muck from the pools, drew back. They once more waited at the foot of that spur where the larger creature had taken its stand. Only, the body of their leader (and when had any rat pack known a leader?) was flopping until it rolled from its perch to fall among them.

Then the remainder of the attackers acted in the true style of their kind, throwing themselves upon the larger form, tearing and fighting among their kin for a chance to devour the swiftly dead. However, then I saw a strange thing indeed. Those who were nearest to and even had their jaws in the flesh of the dead suddenly flinched back from the body, fighting each other to get away. Moments later they all turned and slithered off, quickly concealed among the spurs and tumbles of rock.

There were left the bodies of the two killed nearest to the cave, a third dragging itself away uttering cries of pain, apparently its spine broken, and the partly tattered bundle of skin and bones of the one that had watched from above.

For moments I crouched where I was, unable to believe that the rats had given up so easily. I surveyed every blotch of shadow, sure that at least some of them lurked there ready to jump again if I relaxed my vigilance.

However, such a maneuver was foreign to them. Though they might indeed have swept men and animals from many of the islands by sheer might of numbers, they had never been known to show any such signs of intelligence, only the blind rage and hunger which brought them out in rush attacks. I looked to the cat. His senses were more acute than mine. I longed to be able to communicate with him, to discover what he thought of this strange withdrawal.

He still growled, but his battle cry was stilled. Then he reached out his uninjured paw and drew towards him the body of the rat he had slain and began to eat avidly. That he would do so in the face of the enemy was something I did not believe. So to the sound of crunching bones I made my way across the sun-heated stone to look down upon that one which I had knifed.

To the eye its torn body seemed no different from the others I had seen all my life, save that it was so much larger—almost equaling the size of the sandcat. It was the head which showed the greatest difference, as I saw when I used the end of my staff to roll what was left of the body over so that it lay more straightly stretched upon the bloody rock.

The skull was domed to a high level, and, though that had been crushed in its fall, there was something else, a glint which flashed from the shreds of torn skin. I had no desire to touch it, yet I needed to get my knife which, I saw, to my satisfaction, was buried in the neck where it joined the shoulder.

It was not the knife which had glittered. I knelt and now used the tip of that knife as a probe, lifting forth a thing which was certainly not native to any rat.

It was well smeared with blood. I tipped it onto the rock. What I saw was an oval of what could only be worked metal and in the center of that a stone or perhaps another bit of metal which was a dead black in color.

From where I had lifted it there came the knowledge that it had been embedded in the fore of that oddly shaped skull. Surely the creature had not so encumbered itself. I fumbled in my belt pouch and sacrificed a piece of dried algae to clean it, handling the thing very gingerly.

There was that about it which made me wary of touching it, even when it was clear of blood and spattered brain stuff. Nor did I want it to be with me even to the extent of being bundled into my pouch. Instead I hooked it up with my knife point and returned to the cave, turning it out on a stretch of rock under the sun which was now well towards the other horizon and so less of a menace.

The cat stopped his meal to look from me to the stone I had laid in sight. Once more he growled.

"We have here a mystery, Great One," I said. Though he might not understand me, still it seemed good to express my thoughts and perhaps fears aloud. "That one which fell to my knife had this embedded in its skull. Yet this is of the making of another and not any badge of true rat."

I thought of my father's Leader banner which stood proudly beside his house. It is true that my species were given to such badges and sign posts of position and honor. Yet it was also true that for generations there had been no story of any leader rat that would impress its will on the remainder of the pack. Each was an enemy to the others and always had been. That they traveled together might also be their way of life but it meant no cooperation among them.

"Great One, why should a rat one wear such? Do they now change their way of life? If so this is an ill thing for all of us who dwell in this land. It—"

I stopped almost in mid-word. For I had been watching that thing I had taken from the dead. The center stone which had been shiny black, its setting which had glinted like red gold, had lost color as if the heat had leached it. And under that touch, light as it was, the piece crumbled as might a bit of sand which had been temporarily shaped but could never hold for long. Powder it became, with a twist of thin metal also crumbling into nothing.

Metal I knew, stones I was well aware of. At times I had watched Kura at her work fashioning that jewelry which was a source of pride to all our House. Nothing I had learned of her, and she was always ready to talk of her art to a serious listener, had suggested that there was such material as I had just watched fall into nothingness.

"Great One," I said now very slowly—though the sun still could reach us, I felt within me a chill—"this is of evil—" Of that I was very sure. But what kind of evil and whence it came, who knew? Were I to travel to the Emperor's court with such a tale, who would believe me when I could bring no tangible evidence?

The cat growled again. Its eyes were also on that pinch of dust. I suddenly got to my feet and swept out my staff, sending the remains of that dark object away from us. Then, to keep my mind away from speculation which was of no value, I set about butchering those rats which had been untouched by their fellows. I had no liking for rat meat but a man needs to feed his body, and strips of flesh, sun-dried, would be welcome to take with me when I moved on.

That night I climbed to the higher pinnacle of rock which had been part of my shelter and tried to trace the star paths overhead.

There was nothing I could identify, but I settled myself, staff across my knees, striving to put from my mind all the tumult of the day, and open the inner part of me to the essence of the land about, as is the custom of my people. Thus there came a measure of peace though one part of me never relaxed sentry duty.

We had driven off the rats which had come by day but they had been acting out of nature doing that. It would be more likely that they would make another try, under the usual cover of darkness which they favored.

Though I had good reason to expect so, there were no more attacks in the dark. I came down from my high perch and spread out the skins of the slaughtered rats. I had neither the time nor the materials to do any curing; still I scraped them as best I could and spread them out on a level rock where the sun's heat in the morning could produce a manner of very crude drying. These I would need to patch my boots.

No footgear had a long life for anyone on foot in this land. It was the custom for any traveler to carry several pair of boots in his luggage as well as tough hide for repairs. To the best of my ability I worked with what I had, and every time I glanced up I could see the glowing eyes of the cat watching me closely.

So as I worked I talked, though there came no answer. But I put into words what lay in my mind, addressing the cat as I would some very old and wise one of my own species.

"In my father's house, Great One, I am the least of those under the protection of the kin. Perhaps it is that I have carried with me some curse from my birth hour, for my father takes no pleasure in my company, and my brother—"

The heat of that anger I had buried deep within me was stirring a little though I would not give it room to grow.

"Is my unfriend, though the reason for that I do not know either. Save that I have no wish ever to be a slayer—"

Then the incongruity of that struck me as I rasped the knife over the skin. Who was I to speak so who had fought and brought to death that very creature whose hide I now claimed for my own?

I settled back on my heels. The glimmer of the sand, the light shining from the cat mask which swung free outside my overshirt, fought the dark, though nothing could reach within the many shadows, for I had no lamp.

"Great One, how does a man learn in truth what he is? I say I shrink from taking life, I have laid hand and voice upon beasts and soothed them into peace. Yet since I have come to this place

I have killed and killed. Though no man can stand with empty hands against the rats and it may well be that in the end, should one's own life be at threat, one takes up the nearest weapon—"

I turned to look straight at those unblinking eyes. For all I knew, the cat might be an instant enemy, more deadly than any rat, to be slain lest I be slain. Still within me there was no wish, no fear, to act as would my father, my brother, any of warrior stock.

All this time the feeling had grown in me that this wounded warrior of another sort was far greater than any beast. He presented more and more of a riddle and one I was drawn to solving.

At last, putting aside my work on the hides, I went downslope to the pool to collect more algae and returned to dress again that wounded forelimb. There was no growl now, in fact the animal stretched out his leg though I was sure that that gesture caused him pain, in order that I might work the better on it. When I put a portion of the algae down where he might lick it I heard a rumble which I realized in surprise was a purr.

So encouraged, I put out my hand and laid it for a moment on his head, feeling the soft thickness of the fur there, even thicker than that Mieu had worn, and longer. However, I did not take any further liberties. I leaned back to eat my own portion of the growth I had harvested—as well as smearing some on my still tender skin—though that also was healing.

The night went swiftly. I was ever on the alert for any move from our enemies. In my pouch there was a twist of cloth which held certain stones which I had found when I had been hunting for ammunition for the sling. There were two lumps of turquoise, which made me think of Kura—though they were of inferior color, and my sister would doubtless scorn using them in any of her work. There were some agates also, and those I had set aside for the color—for they were boldly striped in several hues even as were the rocks about. I had seen such in which those lines, were the stone to be skillfully enough cut, seemed to make pictures of sand and rock.

All these offered in a market might bring me food. In a market—did I then plan to return to Meloa where I was known? Rumor flies from rock isle to rock isle, from market to market. Those who were servants to my father had tongues in their heads. I did not in the least doubt that many times our affairs had been a matter of curiosity-led discussion. That I had gone on this solo in such a shabby manner would be a matter of comment which would well reach afar—before I had the chance of even discovering any marked trail. And if I went to Meloa, then it was certain I would be expected to return to my father's house.

My father's house, where there was no longer any place for me!

So close are kin to kin among us that such a thing was hardly known. In fact when I even thought of it now there was a sickness in my throat as if I must spew forth the food I had eaten. What place was there for me?

I was fingering the stones I had harvested, passing them from hand to hand. What could I do? That I had a good hand with herd beasts, that I had trained oryxen so that even my father had accepted mounts I had gentled without question, that I knew was perhaps my only gift.

In Meloa I had once seen an animal trainer. She had been out of Vapala, sent to bring back some high-bred oryxen for one near the Emperor. Her I had looked upon with respect and longing—longing that I might hold such a position.

It was the custom for a younger son to be apprenticed to some trade—or such was true in families which were not of the ancient warrior blood. Could I by myself arrange such an apprenticeship to some beast handler? Though that could well mean leaving all that I knew—even this land—for such a chance would be quicker found in Vapala than in Kahulawe. Again that sickness was sour in my throat. To leave—turn my back on all which had been a part of me—I—surely I could find some other way of survival—

Survival! If I were to survive the immediate future, and there might be little chance of that, it was better to fix my thoughts on what was immediately around me and not strive to read the future as certain women were supposed to have the gift of doing.

Dawn came at last and there was light enough that I could look upon the wound of the cat and see it well. The swelling was down. In two places the ragged tear was knitting, I noted, as I replastered the hurt for the second time.

I had emerged from the cave and was standing, striving to set in place once again my cloak and staff shade against the coming heat when I heard it—and from behind me—the menacing growl with which the cat had announced the coming of the rats—and yet this was not from the animal I tended!

6

I SCHOOLED MYSELF against any hasty action, knowing well that such might bring attack at once. Why had I accepted so easily that the beast I tended was the only one of his kind on the isle? It was well known that the sandcats lived in small family groups.

Very slowly I moved and at the same time I hummed that soothing sound I had made when I had first found the hurt one.

Crouched on one of the higher lifts of rock was indeed another sandcat. Now I heard growling, was sure I saw a tenseness of shoulder and leg which suggested that the newcomer was well ready to spring and bring me down. My staff I had just wedged into a crevice to support my improvised tent. I had only my knife—my opponent was too close for me to use my sling.

This was a female. Rounder of body, amber back in striking contrast to the white spots, the clump of white fur growing longer between her ears and along her spine, about her broad muzzle and underparts, she was majestic. Her club of tail was held spear straight, and her great eyes centered on me. She was but slightly smaller than her mate.

For what seemed to me far too long a time we faced each other eye to eye. Then my senses were acute enough to see that tenseness begin to leave her. If she would attack, it would not be at that moment.

Still humming and continuing to face her, I sidled around until I could reach for some of those strips of rat meat I had laid out for the sun's drying. With several of these in hand I edged back towards her.

"Great One," I kept my voice as low and as even as possible, "to your lord I mean no harm, nor any to you. Accept this guesting gift."

Suppressing all my unease I ventured to the very foot of the short height on which she was still in crouch and there laid down the meat, edging once more well away. She had growled warningly when I approached her but she had not sprung.

Now, having eyed me intently, she did leap lightly from her perch to sniff my offering. She took a long time at that as if she were still suspicious of my good will and distrusted the gesture. Then, apparently having satisfied herself that I had indeed presented her with no more than it seemed, some meat, she took up two of the pieces and in a bound was at the side of her mate.

As he bent his head to sniff at the meat and then bolt it, she in turn dropped her nose to only inches from his hurt and then put out a tongue to lick at the poultice I had smeared upon the wound. From that examination she raised to tongue her mate's head, grooming his fur between his ears. I could hear again the rumble of his purr.

The feeling grew in me that they had some form of communication. Yet when I took a step towards them she was instantly on her feet, her lips drawn back to show fangs, warning me off.

She was well away from the path I must follow down to the algae bed and there was a need to gather more of the crop there, shape it into cakes to be sun-dried like the meat. I felt it safer to have a supply of food to hand than to continue to risk more and more separate descents. We had certainly not accounted for all the rats, and their knowledge that we were here would bring them again. Of that I had no doubt at all.

The female cat watched me go towards the cliff. She did not stir from the side of her mate. Still I felt as one might when trying to slip by a horned oryxen, as if I dared my way past an unsprung trap.

Two trips down and up I made, transporting masses of algae. The second time I came to my improvised camp I saw that the female was stretched out beside her mate, but still she watched me with what I believed was a lively suspicion.

I set about fashioning cakes of the algae, separating that which I had brought for the tending of the other cat's wound. Selecting a fairly flat section of rock I spread out my supply. Though I kept some for this day's food.

As I leaned forward to pat the last of these cakes into shape, my cat pendant swung free into the sun. There was a brilliant spot of light dancing across the rock near the mouth of the cave, the sun reflected from that metal.

The heads of both cats turned, were watching that dance of beam. From the female came a sound which was not a growl, rather something close to a mew. Her eyes were now on me as she sat up, or rather fixed on what I wore that gave that ray of light birth.

Now she arose. I made myself remain where I was as if any fear of her was forgotten. Those great paws, either of which could tear the very features from my skull, as had been done with some unwary hunters, were lifted and replaced deliberately.

However, she was not heading in my direction but rather for the rock where lay the already leather-stiff meat. One strip she picked up by its very end, then she did turn in my direction. Coming to within a distance which would allow a blow of her powerful forepaw to flatten me, she sat again, and with a slight movement of her head tossed her meat so that it fell half across the toe of my nearest boot.

So—

Almost I could not believe. From all that I heard about the sandcats, I knew that they were wily opponents and that they could match men often by some act of intelligence which caused the older people to whisper of demons and the like. For generations beyond generations my kind and this beautiful beast before me had been enemies to the death. Now of her own wish she had made the same peace offering to me that I had earlier made to her.

I picked up the strip of meat and set tooth to the toughness, striving to worry off a mouthful which had the consistency now of a dried melon vine, almost beyond my dealing with it.

Grimly I chewed and swallowed and hoped that the brittle fiber of it would not abrade my throat as it went down.

"My thanks, Great One, so we share upon share—" Of course she could not understand me but I hoped that the tone of my voice would make clear that there was peace between us. On impulse then I slipped the chain of the cat mask over my head and held it out, letting the pendant touch down upon the rock not too far from her.

Instantly her attention was all for the mask, now a blaze of fire in the full sun. She inclined her head and her tongue came out. Delicately she touched the pendant with its tip.

Memory came to me of that dream—of how the girl who shadowed Ravinga had made something of the same gesture towards the doll her mistress held. There was no resemblance between that slender girl and this massive cat form—save they were both female—but somehow my thought linked one to the other.

The sandcat drew away, back to the side of her mate. Him she nuzzled and then, without warning, she leaped outward from the mouth of the cave, was past me like a stream of bronze fur. To the top of the same height from which she had first viewed us she went, but not to linger—instead she disappeared almost instantly from view.

I went to pick up the pendant and restore it to its place. The heat of the day was advancing quickly; it was time to take to such shelter as I had. And that I did. The sandcat had withdrawn farther into the cave and I thought he was asleep, an example it might be well for me to follow.

I did not dream and I awakened quickly to sound—the growl of my companion. There was no need for explanation—rat stink was heavy on the air and it was evening. Yet the enemy did not come boiling out at us as I expected. I could indeed pick out forms slinking from place to place and they were ingathering. To dismantle my shelter in order to free my staff for battle took but an instant or two.

After, I made my way quickly to the edge of the cave. For both our sakes it was better that we stand together against the surge when it came. The fact that they had not already struck at us began to add to my uneasiness. All my knowledge of the creatures was being questioned and the tactics I had been taught to use perhaps would not now be of much service.

Was there out there somewhere another of those giants wearing that evil thing the other had borne? Rats answering commands—it was unnatural and so doubly threatening.

I could hear low squeals now, picked up by some chance of the rocks about us and echoed back. There was no telling how big a pack we might be facing. The other cat—we could well use her strength and fighting ability if she had only stayed with us.

Out of my shirt I pulled the cat mask and instantly the light it had shown of itself before was there. From slightly behind me my companion gave a howl, surely a challenge. And that the rats answered. They slipped and slid around and over rocks to come at us, a vicious dark flood of death.

Again we fought and this time the cat had drawn well towards, even a little before, me, swiping out with his good paw and smashing the brutes away, sending their bodies back to crack bones against the rock. While I swung my staff, fighting with what was to me a new assurance and strength. I began to note that the rats would not face me squarely, that whenever I moved and the light from the mask touched any one of them, it would squeal and leap away to darkness.

It was to my utter astonishment that the attack suddenly withdrew, for this was completely out of rat nature. I remained alert listening intently to the noises out of the night. The hissing of the drifting sands was a monotone but across that came a series of squeals and to my mind they seemed to make a pattern. There was the skittering sound of rat claws on rock and I braced myself for another wave.

It was gloomy within the chamber. Ravinga had ordered the curtains drawn at dusk. Not only did those, thin as they were, keep out all the lights of the Vapalan city but much of the air, so one could no longer smell the flowering qutta trees in the garden. Instead there arose curls of aromatic smoke from the brazier placed on a tripod in the exact center of that secure chamber.

I sat straight-backed on the stool my mistress had indicated, holding in my hands the box she had pressed upon me. This was not the first time I had assisted at such a ceremony nor would it be the last if I were to achieve my purpose and gain the knowledge I desired, for such wish was as an ever-eating pain within me.

Ravinga herself crawled across the floor, pulling with her the square of painted oryxen hide. That design had occupied her for many nights, sometimes with long pauses between one touch of a paint-thick brush and the next. It was as if she must drag the pattern from very far depths of memory.

On that hide now rested small figures. These were not the dolls which we sold in the markets to gain our bread but were far more elaborate ones. The small face on each had been molded over and over until the features suited my mistress. Some I knew well—

There was the Diamond Queen of Vapala with all her crown and formal robing. And the Topaz Queen of Azhengir, that most barren and forbidding of lands. Here was also the Grand Chancellor of the Outer Regions with the Sapphire Queen of Kahulawe.

All were fashioned of Ravinga's secret clay mixture which gave the appearance of living flesh to heads and hands. And they were all garbed in fine bits of fabrics, miniature jewels so perfect that one wondered indeed at the maker's great skill.

By each Queen stood her Minister of Balance, his features rock hard as if he fronted some period of a weeding of flocks and perhaps even of people.

There was also Shank-ji, who was not one of such an exalted company by any right of office. Son to the Emperor he might be, but our lord took no formal wife and any get of his held naught but a position of minor nobility. I looked upon Shank-ji and I remembered—my thoughts straying from the pattern I had been set to hold. Old hatreds run deep and cannot always be kept under control, at least not by one who has not followed the rituals into the Higher Plane.

Ravinga glanced at me with anger. She, being who and what she was, could read emotions, if not minds. Resolutely I made my eyes move on from the doll which was Shank-ji; the next was the Emperor—not as he had appeared at the last great court, a curiously shrunken figure with a hand which shook when he held the leopard staff of authority, as if that shaft was too heavy for him. No, this was a representation of the Emperor as we had not for years seen him. And beside him his Chancellor.

The four remaining figures were not human but animal. There in all his majesty of office, first bodyguard of the Emperor, was the Blue Leopard, and with him two of his own following. But the last certainly had no place in any company save that of death itself, for it was a faithful representation of a rat.

That did have meaning of a sort, for it was a symbol not only of death but also of evil, which could not be touched nor in any way governed by even those who held to the old knowledge and were such as Ravinga.

She reached the other side of the brazier and there three shadows awaited her, Wa, Wiu, Wyna, the black kottis that had been a part of her household ever since I had taken refuge here. They sat erect now, their eyes upon Ravinga while she began to place the figures upright on the floor as if they might indeed march off about their business.

Emperor flanked by the two Queens and they in turn by the Chancellor and their Ministers of Balance, before the Emperor the Blue Leopard and the guard that one commanded.

But the rat remained lying upon the hide, under its carefully fashioned body a symbol drawn in a red of fresh-spilt blood. Ravinga did not reach for it, rather she snapped her fingers. I answered at once to her signal.

From the box I brought her she took out two more figures, each rolled in a fine silken cloth. The cloth covering one was the gold of clear citrines and there was a wandering thread wreathing through it of the rust red of certain rocks, such as I had seen in our travels to Kahulawe. This she drew away to display that doll which she had showed me before when she had begun this ritual days ago.

A youth—yes, I even knew his name—Hynkkel—and I had heard of him, too, and not only from my mistress. What she appeared to approve, others found a reason to disparage. Second son of a gallant warrior, he refused to follow the trade of arms. In his own family he became a servant, and not even one of prideful background since he had not gained that position (as most of the low-born may) through his own efforts.

He was a herder of beasts, a runner of errands, one who bought and sold in the market, one whom those of his own rank would pretend not to see.

Yet Ravinga had dressed his representation in the fine robes of a great lord and had by some magic of her own given him the look of one who would rightfully wear such.

Now she placed him directly facing the Emperor. There was also a staff of honor in that small hand of his but the insignia topping that was a sandcat. Seeing what she did I wanted to decry it all. This youth was no leader of men, no bearer of the old blood of Vapala—no, he was a barbarian and held by his own people to be of little worth. Ravinga—what strange fault of thinking had made her shape him thus?

She was already taking out the other figure. This was one wrapped in a dirty white, the shade of the sand of the Plain of Desolation. Here and there was a pattern in black of small skulls, both those of men and beast. She did not unwrap this one and I knew the reason for that.

What lay within that coil of cloth was no body, no carefully fashioned replica of a living person. For Ravinga knew not as yet the person of the one whose existence she could only sense. That stranger kept about him a barrier which no dream search could penetrate. We had even tried together, I uniting my smaller strength to hers, to find the presence of the enemy, spy out who or what that was.

Now Ravinga set the shrouded doll up and placed it beside the rat on the pool of scarlet. Sitting back on her heels she began to sing. I squatted opposite her and my tongue also shaped words, the meaning of which neither of us knew—old and old and old was that chant. Only those who had the true gift could even mouth them, so twisted awry they were from our normal speech.

The doll things answered—that is, all did save the rat and that which stood by it. The Queens raised their arms and held forth their scepters, the Emperor took one step forward but only that, for Shank-ji strode about until he faced his father, his head up arrogantly. Now the Chancellor moved in from one side and the Ministers from the other, all of them turned so they faced Hynkkel and the Emperor's son.

Ravinga's voice soared and quickened until I found it hard to match her word for word. I saw her hands knot in the folds of her robe as she leaned forward, as if she would bring about some other movement in the small people she watched so intently. But those now were frozen in place.

What did move was the rat. From lying on its side it scrambled up, baring fangs and moving at Hynkkel. Shank-ji stepped back to make room for its coming. The doll Hynkkel swung his cat-topped staff and the rat withdrew step by step. Then that muffled thing which had shared the creature's stand shifted awkwardly and the rat came to it and lay down at its feet (if feet were hidden there). Hidden one and rat were still and as I watched, that illusion of life left all the dolls.

There came an instant dawning of weariness to Ravinga's face. Her hands were now clasped loosely in her lap.

"So be it," she said and there was deep unhappiness in her voice. "One can only do the best that one can. It rests now upon the land and those who dwell here. We must have strength against what comes. But the strength must declare itself and that I cannot force."

She raised her eyes from the dolls. They trembled as if all strength had been removed from their small bodies, then they tumbled to lie face up or away as they had fallen.

"You have seen, Allitta?"

"I have seen, Caller of Shadows." I made the proper answer.

"And in your time you shall see more." As so often before, she ended some ritual with the same words.

Did I want to see more? Did I want to drink of all the knowledge this woman could offer me? Yes—for I had a purpose of my own. In spite of all of Ravinga's warnings I would seek that purpose in the end and that I knew past all doubting.

That which was in the brazier had nearly burned away but Ravinga made no attempt to gather up the dolls. I knew that her energy was now at a very low ebb, yet I could not help her, for with these dolls only her hands could deal. I went to the nearest window to draw aside those muffling curtains, to let in fresh air to banish the last scent of the burning spice wood.

At that moment there came a chime from overhead. Someone in the shop? But at this hour? The curtain twisted in my hand and I saw that there was sun without—what had begun in the proper darkness which would nourish the power had finished with the coming of day.

Ravinga paid no attention to that summons but I went swiftly.

Our servant, Mancol, would have opened the shop for the day and usually all simple sales could be left to his management. He got around very spryly for one of his manifest age and he treasured the dolls with a fervor, taking delight in showing off the most clever and beautiful of them.

However, when I entered the shop room I found that there was a customer, or a prospective one, who would indeed not deign to deal with any underling, though she would with me, as I would not disturb Ravinga for this one.

The First Maiden of the Household of the Lady Yevena stood there, her sandaled foot tapping an impatient tattoo which echoed the lighter sound of her long fingernails as they ticked against the counter which ran across one side of the shop. Above were the cases of dolls, new-conceived ones directly in a middle one. Mancol had come from behind the counter, was dragging a cushioned chair intended for our most profitable visitors towards the Maiden though she had so far not taken any note of that suggested comfort.

In the doorway lounged two shield men, an escort for which there was certainly no need here except for purpose of display.

I bowed my head in courtesy as I would to any except Ravinga—for her I would have made the bended-knee salute if she had ever allowed me to. That curtailed gesture I knew would irritate our caller. She was frowning and there was a flush of red under her clear skin. She gave a little toss of her head which sent a-tinkling the nodding, stemmed jewels of her headband.

"Where is Ravinga?" she demanded harshly.

"This morning she is indisposed," I returned. "Does the lady desire some new treasure for her collection?"

I took Mancol's place behind the counter and pointed to the glass-fronted shelves in the prime place. "There is, as you see, a new Topaz Queen, she who ruled in the days of the Emperor Tampor and was accredited the most beautiful woman wearing a crown in that time. And here is a fanciful one of Ravinga's own dream design—" I indicated a very lifelike (in miniature) sandcat, but this one wore a necklet of rubies and opal agates and had emeralds for eyes. Also, it was sitting up and between its forepaws it held a Kifongg harp. I snapped open the case to take forth this temptation and touched a small button at the cat's back. Straightway it began to play and there was a thin yet pleasing music to be heard.

The Maiden's attention was taken for a moment. When I set the small wonder down she put a finger to its head and I knew she could feel the outer covering of fur which made it seem all the more lifelike.

Then she snatched her hand back and once more there was anger in her face. "Behold this," she was sneering now. From a wrapping band in her hands she shook out with no care a doll, but one which had lost its head. Though the head rolled out with it.

Though it was not as perfect a resemblance to Shank-ji as the one I had just seen Ravinga put away, it did look close to that arrogant young warrior, fully clad in all his trapping, from fuzzed-out silver wig to small, perfectly fashioned sword.

"Broken. Three days only has my lady had this in her hands and when she would bring it forth to show his lordship she found it broken! An ill omen and if he sees or hears that it has happened so—" She drew a deep breath— "My lady is not one to be made to look foolish or worse!"

She glanced across her shoulder at the two guards who had accompanied her here. "Those of the Six Families have their ways of attending to such problems."

Her suggestion might be one of pique. Only one who could recall certain events in the past would understand just what a person of the Lady Yevena's type might be moved to do. The old families were jealous of their distinction and city-backed power. They sometimes held themselves even above the Emperor, chosen as he was by chance, in family and breeding.

"Maiden, I shall take this straightway to my mistress and let her see what is—"

"Let this maker of dolls come to *me*!" That was almost a snarl. Again there was the sign of that touchy need for difference which was ever a part of one of close intimacy with the Six Families.

"I am here." Ravinga did not address this messenger with any honorifics. She was outwardly her usual self and I hoped that inwardly she had recovered from the ritual.

I moved away to let her see fully what lay there. Because I knew Ravinga so well, had been ever alert to the small changes in her features, even the little tension of her hands when she was deeply aroused about anything, I now could read that she was moved.

She touched the head and then picked it up and surveyed carefully where it had broken away of the neck. In turn she examined the body closely.

"The Lady Yevena was warned that these must be carefully handled," she said. "These are not dolls for the pleasure of children such as those," she waved to the right-hand case, "but things, one each of their kind, and to be kept carefully. This cannot be repaired—for a treasure once damaged loses its value to all. The Lady Yevena is collector enough not to wish any repaired piece in her display. We can offer to make another—"

"She wishes to have the saying of that! She has ordered that you attend her at the fourth hour."

Turning her back on us, she walked out with as near a stamp as her flat sandals would allow.

Ravinga nodded to Mancol and he hurried to draw the door shut. She was already bending closely over the doll, running her finger back and forth across the broken neck, then she gathered it up quickly and went off to her workroom.

When I would have followed to give what aid I could, comfort even, for her dolls were indeed treasures to Ravinga, she made a quick gesture for me to remain where I was.

It was true that no two portrait dolls were ever made alike. Some of them were fashioned as copies of deceased members of the House. There were even several past Emperors on display in the palace. Some were made for love gifts—had the Lady Yevena intended this to be such a one?

Mostly they were made to order, unless they were historical like the famous Queens on the shelf above, or as some fantastical object such as the sandcat who played its harp.

I put this back in the case and snapped the lock. But I was thinking more of Ravinga and knew some uneasiness over the whole affair. Little troubles could lead to disaster, just as it had for me when I was so small I could not have seen the top of this counter. Ravinga saved me then. But could there be anyone to step in and speak for us if the House lady wanted to cause trouble? A merchant said to sell imperfect goods got short shift in any market.

7

A RAGING FURRED BODY sprang over the rocks. Beside me the female cat took up position. The rush attack I waited for did not come. Nor did the cat make any effort to go seeking it. Instead she backed against her mate, though she did not relax at once. I could no longer hear the scrabble of nails after her war cry died away. Then there arose a second squall. But not from either of the cats which were with me.

Sounds of battle and that too died away. The female snarled and turned her head to wipe her tongue across her mate's ears as if in assurance. He was growling deep in his throat, still facing outward, trying to rise to his feet although the female, flanking him, threw out a huge paw and, as she might to some disobedient kitten, rested that on his shoulders, pushing him down once again. From her now issued a series of small sounds much like the "talking" of the kottis, as if she was reassuring him.

Then she faced outward. It would seem that I was wrong in hoping our ordeal was past, for both cats were alert. I reached for my sling and the supply of the rocks I had garnered as ammunition. At least I might be able to take out one or two before they reached close enough for staff work.

However, what crossed the rocks towards us now was no wave of rats, but rather another sandcat. Open jaws showed that one of this male's great fangs was broken off. His fur was clay-colored and ragged. There was a bloody tear on his flank where one of the rats must have bitten him.

The male beside me roared a challenge and again struggled to get to his feet. I realized that what we confronted now was a "rogue" who had been driven from his own holding and wished to fight both for this rock isle and the female. Against my companion he might well triumph, for he was at least steady on all four feet and the rock ruler was still weak from his wound.

Once more the cat beside me challenged. Now he was answered with a deep-throated roar of pure rage. I whirled my sling and sent the stone flying, aiming as best I could.

My missile thudded home not as I had planned, for the great rogue had flattened in preparation for a leap. Instead the stone struck on the beast's shoulder and he snarled, turning his head to bite at his own flesh where the blow had fallen.

Then a newcomer went into action. The female stalked stiff-legged towards the rogue, a beginning hiss rising into a screamed threat. He hissed in turn. She leaped, bowling him over so his body struck against a spur of rock and he yowled in pain and fury. The surprise must have been great, for among their kind the females and the males do not fight each other. It appeared that she was intent on taking on the battle in place of her wounded mate.

The rogue squalled and appeared to be trying to withdraw from battle. Claws had raked him viciously and now he shook himself free and ran, the female bounding after him. Her mate was still growling deeply and had completely arisen as if wanting to follow. While that plaster I had put on him shifted.

"Great One, Warrior of Might," I went down on one knee beside him, "not yet are you healed enough to do battle. Let me tend your wound again."

That I speedily did as he lay down and stretched out the injured leg as if he understood perfectly what must be done.

The rest of the night I stayed on guard, having dragged the rat bodies within reach to one side. The air was foul with the stench of blood and the natural stink of the creatures. However, I felt that I could not take them out of sight lest some of their kind still lingered below the rocks waiting for our watchfulness to falter.

I had expected the female to return and began to worry. Could it be that the rogue, once he had gotten over his astonishment at her attack, had turned on her with the full ferocity of which he was capable? Yet there was nothing I could do, except hope that we would see her again and soon.

It was near dawn and I again made my way down to the pool and harvested for the day's food, restored my rough camp. The soothing aid of the dressings I had applied to my own sand-scored skin had done its purpose. I kept on exercising, so that the new skin forming there would stretch fully. I fed my companion and brought two of the corpses from the night's battle that he might also restore himself with the flesh his kind craved. There were the skins to be taken and worked upon.

Certainly I had never expected to settle on this isle but I could not walk away until I was sure that the cat was able to care for himself. At least he had the female—but now that there was a rogue ready to do battle was another thing.

I slept away much of the day. Again before I awoke at the sun's descent I dreamed. It is said that in the very ancient days, before our five countries drew together under the Emperor, there were those born with certain powers and talents. Yet these had been hunted down, and their whole family lines wiped out after the last great battle so that no one might again arise to use such gifts—or curses—in the name of some leader.

The last and greatest of these had been driven into the Plain of Desolation and that was so many generations ago that only the keepers of the records could count them. Nor were any ever welcomed to even study those ancient accounts, they being under seal.

So, though there were vague stories of such things, powers and dreams, even those tales were not the subject for any bard, nor teacher, to mention.

Yet this night I dreamed.

There was a darkened room where a single lamp gave light to what lay on a table. There was a pair of hands which came out of the shadows beyond the tight focus of that lamp, handling, with delicate fingers, what the light showed very clearly. It was a manikin or a doll, and it lay in two pieces, the head snapped off at the shoulders.

It was the head which interested those hands the most. With a knife hardly thicker than a large needle, the puffy silver wig was worked loose to display the coiled hair beneath. That also yielded to the probing of the knife point, and the top of the skull, if one might deem that so, came off.

Now the knife was set aside for a pair of fine pincers such as my sister used for her most important work of setting the smallest stone. Those were inserted into the cavity of the head, to emerge holding a tiny ball which flashed like a diamond in the light. One of the hands disappeared and returned in a moment with a small metal box into which this bead was dropped and the lid clamped down with a force which seemed to say that this was a very precious thing, perhaps one to be kept secret.

Swiftly the doll head was restored to what it had been, and the hands withdrew, leaving the broken warrior lying where he was, still headless.

So strange was that dream that it remained vivid in my mind and I was surprised when I opened my eyes to find that I lay in my rude tent. What had it meant? I had nothing to do with dolls—no, those were Ravinga's. But never had I seen among the stock she had brought into the market any such fine product as this, smashed though it was. That was no lifeless doll face which had been turned up when the hands were busy with the head— rather I might have been looking at the small figure of one who was alive, or had been so. I remembered that other dream which had been of Ravinga and her apprentice and another doll.

I put my head in my hands and tried to think clearly. Certainly I was caught in that which I did not understand. The very fact that I had been able to establish a fleeting relationship with a sandcat and his mate was something I had never heard of and many strange things are always eagerly told and listened to in the marketplaces. Cats were deadly enemies—yet I no longer saw them as so. Last night I had even known something of pity for the rogue—like me he had been driven from his proper place and sought his old life again. Would I come to seek my own return after this venture? That thought I pushed sharply away as I crawled from my shelter to welcome the cool of the night and see to my charge.

I was greeted with a throaty sound from the sandcat, who was clearly awake, instantly aware of me. However, though I had expected to find her there, his mate was still missing. And I felt uneasy. Though a male might not attack a female, yet when she had carried war to the rogue, it might well be that he had turned on her and she lay somewhere on the uneven surface of the isle in pain and torment just as her mate had earlier done.

"Great One," I had gone to my companion to examine the dressing on his wound, "is there trouble in this place which has taken your lady?" I tried to open my mind, to sense if there was any uneasiness in the male, even as I had done when I served as herdsman and had striven to seek out some disaster among the beasts for whom I was responsible.

There was nothing of tension about him. When I uncovered his now closed but still tender wound, he set to licking it after the manner of his kind when they tended their own hurts. I left him to his own treatment and once more went to the pool.

A shadow moved, took on a slinking form. No rat but the rogue, one ear half gone, a visible tear along his shoulder, was slipping down to the pool on the opposite side. I saw a lift of lips, heard a rumbling growl. Then he looked to me no more but pulled himself forward to the moist edge of the algae bed and mouthed torn masses of the stuff as if his belly was completely empty.

Looking upon him so, I knew that there was no danger to be feared from him. Clearly he had forced himself here for what succor the pool offered but he would not try to dispute it with us again, keeping to his own side.

I watched him feed and then he withdrew but no farther than a slight distance. He moved with such labor that I thought he was badly hurt. When I had climbed above again with my own gleanings I took up two of the rat bodies and passing along the edge of the rise near to where the animal now sheltered, I tossed them over. They did not fall too far from his chosen shelter. His blood-smeared head came up and he looked at me. But his eyes were empty of any expression I could read.

Once more I skinned rats and tore meat apart for the drying. The scraps I tossed down a narrow crevice in the rock for which I could see no bottom. The skins I had scraped earlier were hard-dried now and I began clumsily to stitch them across and around my boots.

As I worked so in the twilight I spoke aloud, for I felt very much the need of hearing speech in this vastness, even if it were my own.

"Great One, there is much in the world which is beyond understanding. Why has it come to me that I must be a part of something which—" I stopped the punching of holes in hide with my knife point and looked out at what lay about me.

There was a change. I slewed around, my hand going for the staff which I had laid close to hand. Another form came out of the dusk and I greeted the female.

"Lady, your lord does well." She crouched beside her mate and first sniffed the wound I had left uncovered after sponging it off with the algae, then began to lick it.

She raised her head for an instant to gaze at me and then went back to her licking. The male was purring, the rumble of his sound attune, it seemed to me, with the peace of the night, perhaps perilous and short-lasting as that might be.

However, we perhaps had proven ourselves to be too much of a danger even to the rats. For it was not us they attacked this night; rather I heard their squeals from across the pond and the roars of the rogue doing battle.

The female was instantly on her feet and her mate struggled to stand beside her. I ran, staff and slingshot in hand, to that place from which I had tossed the meat earlier. There was still a portion of twilight and more vision of what was happening below than I had thought. I used the sling and saw two of the things fall. Then I turned to the throwing of stones.

Halfway I feared that they might turn on us at this attack, yet I could not leave that other to be savaged, enemy though he might be. A clean death by hunter's spear or knife was one thing; to see a helpless beast eaten alive as the rats handle their prey was more than I could allow. Now I was hurling rocks with my hands and saw a third one of the attackers fall. There was movement beside me and the female went into battle, taking the descent in one great leap and landing full into the middle of that pack where she used her claws and teeth in a whirlwind of well-delivered death.

The squealing of her prey rose to a high point and through that sounded that same strange howl I had heard in the battle wherein the great rat had died.

On the ground the rogue was rolling, his jaws fastened on the scruff of a rat's neck and surely the creature he was striving to pull down was a near match to him in size.

I lifted a rock with my two hands and, running forward to the very edge which hung nearly above that struggle, I hurled my crude weapon out and down. By some chance of fate it actually struck the rat which had just torn free from the rogue, not fair, but well enough to make the noisome creature stagger. In that instant the rogue reared up and closed his massive jaws on the neck of his enemy and gave a sharp swing of his head. I could not hear above the clamor of the pack the sound of the snapping neck but I saw the thing go limp.

Again the pack, upon the death of this one, withdrew, scrabbling away, some of them actually plowing through the algae pan. There was a silence as if the night with the complete fall of darkness had swallowed up all their company.

The rogue was panting heavily, the sounds he made close to whimpering of pain. He strove to crawl out of the algae into which he had rolled and had made such an effort that he did draw himself free of the growth only to collapse.

Nor did he pay any attention now to the female, who was licking down her fur. As far as I could see in this dim light she had suffered no deep hurt, a guess which was proven when she came clambering back up the slope to join us.

I listened for any return of the rats. The suffering of the rogue troubled me. That he would be minded to tear a hand from anyone who strove to touch him I well knew. But I could not leave him there untended. Also I must know more about the last of those things he had killed—whether it was like unto the other we had found.

Thus I descended to the pool and, with care and wariness, rounded the end of it to the side of the animal. There was a faint snarl; he lifted his head a fraction and showed his one fang now dyed with blood.

"Great One." I held out both hands and in the swinging light of the pendant he could certainly see that they were empty of any weapon.

His eyes picked up the gleam of the cat mask and followed that to and fro for an instant as it swung.

"Great One, mighty have you been in battle. Now you are hurt, suffer it that your wounds be tended."

His untorn ear flattened to his skull and his body writhed in a futile attempt to get to his feet. Then he fell flat once again and I could see that there was a great gash across his back and he could not move his hind legs.

There came a sigh from him and his head dropped forward to rest upon one paw as if, worn by the roaming of a day, he would sleep. His eyes closed and I felt at that moment that his essence was at last freed, and, for all his lonely wandering and his many wounds, he was now one with the land and all that is about us even as we all wish when the final end comes.

In his time he had been a warrior and— I stood to look about me. At the last he had been searching for a home. It was not in me to leave his body to be devoured by those filthy monsters upon their return—and that return I did not doubt.

In the wall of the cliff to the north was one of those gash openings, not quite a cave, for at the top it was open to the sky. This could be a place of burial for one who deserved honor.

I found it hard to move the body. Worn by privation as he was, he was still a load more fit for a yaksen and I had to take the task by degrees. However, at length I had the body well within the opening. Then it was a matter of gathering stones to wall it in and that I did also, though my shoulders ached and I was gulping great gasps of air by the time I had done with it

all, unable at first to summon even enough energy to reclimb
the wall.

When I looked up I could see the glint of four eyes watching
me and I knew that the other cats had witnessed all I had done,
though that they might understand why, I doubted. If I should die
by rat fangs or starvation here, there would be none to raise any
monument to me. As I sat there in the night I thought of that
and what I could do to make sure my body did not lie scattered
bones.

Once more I searched the stars overhead for some sign I could
recognize. There was little use in my staying on here. The sandcat
was healing well, and, with his mate, could hold his own against
the rats, once more ruler in his own place.

What place remained for me?

I got wearily to my feet, believing now that I had the power
to reclimb the cliff. The night was surely far spent and tomorrow,
tomorrow I must make my preparations for moving on. I had been
caught in such a venture here as few men would believe—one that
I could not voice lest I be declared a braggart and a liar.

Taking a step forward I nearly stumbled over a contorted
body—that of the giant rat. I made myself do grisly work upon
it—to find once more the same evidence that this was no common
desert menace.

Having exposed to the destroying air that ball of stuff I had
picked out of the skull of the rat, I was remembering in detail two
hands which had plucked forth from the head of a doll a similar
implant, save that had been a brilliant diamond, rainbow-endowed
piece and this was dully evil, so I was careful not to touch it with
my flesh.

What further mystery might hide here I did not know and at
the moment I was too tired to care.

8

THERE WAS THE THUD of a heavy body landing close by. I lifted my head and saw that the female cat was watching me with curiously narrowed eyes. There was something about that gaze which I found measuring, making me uneasy—wary— As if the truce between us had worn thin.

Before I could move or defend myself she was on me and her great jaws closed about my left wrist bringing such a thrust of pain as made me cry out. My throat next, I thought dazedly—but why—now?

Blood spurted out of my torn flesh. The cat drew away from me and I crawled to the algae pool. I must staunch that bleeding if I could. Though through the haze of torment I hunched my shoulders, waiting now for the full weight of the beast to flatten me, claws to find my throat and shake the life out of me as if I were the giant rat.

I rose to my knees and pitched forward, my mangled hand plunging into the smarting water thick with the plants. I thought I had known pain many times before in my life but this blow dealt me out of no reason seemed to sap my strength almost in moments. I met the cushion of algae with the forepart of my body and then there was nothing.

How long I lay so I did not know but there came back to me a kind of hazy consciousness which sent me crawling once more. How I made the way back to the cliff foot I will never know, but once there I knew that I could not manage any more. Still the cat had not put an end to me. However, to even turn my head now to look and see what she might threaten was beyond my strength.

There was the heat of the red-streaked stone about me and that heat sank into my body, became a part of a fire which seemed to seek to destroy me. The nothingness which had held me earlier was gone and I had not even that escape.

My head had fallen sidewise so that a stone bruised my cheek and that small torment seemed to make all the rest worse. When I opened my eyes I saw no pool, no green and orange of algae— only the long stretch of red which could be some plain as great as that of Desolation.

Then across that something moved, coming in bounds. The cat! I tried to move my arm in some feeble defense which would be nothing against her attack.

Yet what came to me was another. Mieu leaped towards me and from her mouth swung the mask pendant. I felt her paws heavy on my wounded arm, and again cried out as she dropped the mask on my breast. Her tongue came forth and I could feel the rough rasp of it against my cheek: she might be washing a kit in reassurance.

I talked with her and she answered me, but what we two said to one another I could never afterward remember. However there came a quiet into me for a space and it made the pain recede to a bearable distance.

There was more movement on that plain of red sand. Fine as dust the grains spurted up to clog the air behind a rider. There my brother pulled up his oryxen and sat at ease in the saddle though the beast bucked and fought his control as always, until he aimed a heavy blow behind one of its tender ears.

He struck his mount almost absently, his full attention was for me, and I saw his lips curve in a smile which became sneering amusement.

"Weakling!" He leaned forward a trifle, as if to view me the better and gloat over what was left of me. "No man—child always—accept what you are and leave true life to your betters." And his laughter was as loud a roar as that of the cats offering battle.

I could not rise to any challenge now. He was right—I was a weakling and even my body refused to obey me.

Once more he laughed and then urged his oryxen closer, now coming to me spear in hand until I thought that he would do what was unknown even among the most brutish of barbarians, put kin to death.

However, it seemed that what he strove to do was hook the point of that spear into the chain of the mask, to make that finally and undisputedly his own. Mieu was on her feet. Hissing, her small body swollen to nearly twice size, she struck at the metal point with a paw, only to have him make a sudden sweep with the spear, send her tumbling away with a cry of pain and defiance. Then I struggled to rise, and still laughing, my brother rode away. Yet the mask of the cat was not yet his.

Though that metal still rested on me, yet I also saw it rise through the air until it crowned a staff as might the Honors of a House. Still no House would bear such a device.

It was past the hour of nooning. Even here in Vapala, where nature dealt the easiest with humankind, these few hours were a time when merchants put down their shop curtains and fortified themselves in the shadows those barriers gave to the full heat of the day.

Mancol nodded and dozed on his cushion behind the counter, now and again waking himself with a snort of snore to look bewilderly around for a moment before sinking back into the languor none of us could avoid.

We had an inner court where green things grew—such as were found nowhere else in the five lands. That was Ravinga's storehouse wherein were rooted many plants which were not even to be seen, except perhaps in the gardens of the Emperor where gifts from the eastern lands, more than half legend to most of us, grew, though not easily.

Small winged things swung from one bright patch of flower to another, and there were others which crawled upon the ground, or hopped. These, too, were only known in the mesa land. Under the sun spicy odors were drawn from the growth. Seated now on her padded mat, my mistress looked out over her small domain. Yet there was no satisfaction in her expression. She could instead have been reckoning up omissions and mistakes for which a strict accounting might be well demanded later.

Before her was a small lap table hardly larger than a tray for mid-day food. On this were several rolled scrolls and one which had been spread open. Its curled edges holding so because planted on either side were two of her delicate tools. While by her knee a carbon box, yellowed by great age, showed beneath the flung-back lid rolls of sewing thread, as rainbow in its many shades.

I had my own task and I kept to it. Though when I had come to Ravinga I had not been too handy with a needle, for in those days I had ridden and hunted, and knew freedom beyond what

was given most of my caste. Yet I had set myself to the learning
of what would be a part of my craft from now on—and I had
mastered with dogged effort most of the intricate stitches which
Ravinga taught—briskly and sometimes impatiently—for she had
to school her belief that all could be as accomplished as was she
if they would only try.

What I dwelt upon this day, being very careful to match colors
and setting the slant of each stitch just right, was a patch which
might have served for the shoulder bag of some highly placed
servant in one of the Six Houses. Yet it had no connection with
any that I had ever seen or heard tell of, for it was the head
of a sandcat so perfectly designed as to seem that the mask of
an actual cat had been stripped from its skull and reduced to
miniature size.

While such heraldic beasts, for the purpose of badges, are
usually shown expressing defiance, each after its own way, this
was calm as if the cat were all-knowing and observing which lay
about it, not yet ready to take part in affairs.

The eyes were gemstones, very well cut—those we call citrines
for their clear yellow. These were not faceted as such usually
were, but smooth, and when I studied them closely I was almost
sure I could see, deep within them, a hair-thin line of black set
as a pupil.

I had finished most of my work upon the head of the animal
and was now dealing with a frame of sunstones and bits of filigree,
so fine and pure the gold that one might inadvertently bend them
during the task of making them fast. These made a frame for the
mask and, as elaborate as it was, still it did not subtract from the
forcefulness of the less ornate head.

When I set aside one threaded needle and reached for a second
I saw that my mistress's eyes were closed. Her breathing had
slowed until there were unnatural pauses between each lungful.
The signs were unmistakable. Though Ravinga had made no
preparations for an outseeking, she was indeed caught in the
forestages of one such.

Slower and slower came her breaths. Her hands had fallen to
the surface of the small work table and there were clasped lightly
together. Ravinga now walked shadow ways which I had taken
once or twice, knowing full well the terrible fatigue of body and
mind one must expend thus.

She drew a last sighing breath and then it was as if she had
done with all outer life. I moved uneasily. To anyone who watched

another in this state and knew exactly what dangers it entailed, this was always an uneasy business. I, too, allowed my work to slide out of a tight grasp.

It was my part to play guardian. Ravinga usually retired into her bedchamber, behind a safe locked door when she went far questing—that she had not today was a matter for concern. I reached slowly into my belt pouch, made sure that no gesture or sound I might make inadvertently would break the spell she was weaving tighter and tighter. My fingers touched a slick smoothness which was the result of time's long use and I brought out a herdsman's flute.

Back and forth I followed the road of soft notes, watching Ravinga. We had played these roles before and I knew what had to be done: still there could always be a first time of failure. To those who gather power that brings awe and fear and if it does not—then that dabbler in forbidden things is a lackwitted fool.

Ravinga's skin was darker than that of the usual Vapalan, which I thought came from her many travels across the five nations. She was no fine lady to go veiled against the sun. Now I saw a flush creeping up under that brown skin. Her lips parted a fraction and her breath came pantingly as if she struggled for air. I watched her very closely. No, it was not yet time for me to take my part in any awakening. Did I so too soon, I would rightfully earn her wrath.

There was a shadow of change in her features also. Her face looked a fraction leaner, wearing small signs of some past struggle. I saw the darkness of a thickening shadow on her upper lip beginning to bracket her mouth and then I was almost startled into some bitter mistake. Before my very eyes, as one would assume a traveler's cloak, my mistress was drawing on another identity— and this masculine!

Hynkkel! Why? My grip nearly broke the flute in two. I had seen such shadow masks worn by Ravinga before when she locked herself into deep seeing—but what was so important about this cast-off son of an old army officer, a family which had lost its importance long ago and had with this very son (if rumor spoke true) come to an ignominious ending?

There was more than the heat of the day walling in the two of us. The fire was of the body, as if my mistress was consumed by some flame of disease. For the first time her hands arose from that limp clasp on the table and moved as if she were pulling towards her something of vast importance. So would a healer—

I had the flute to my lips though I still did not send forth its summons to the wandering spirit. This Hynkkel suffered some ill and my mistress was striving to turn it from him!

Ravinga coughed, her upper body arching a fraction as if that came as a painful stretching. Her hand groped outward as if she sought something she could not see. I caught up a goblet standing to one side, my quick motion disturbing its contents so that the liquid within swirled around and gave off a strong scent of herbs. This I pressed into my mistress's hold and she, still unseeingly, raised it to her lips and drank. One long draught near emptied the goblet as she swallowed.

I knew that what she did was not for herself alone and that the medicine which that container held was meant to pass farther in the way of inner healing from her to Hynkkel.

There was no trace of blood on that thin green robe which was all she wore. Oftentimes a famed and blessed healer could project upon her own body any hurt or wound which marked the one seeking help. No blood—except—she had dropped her left hand once more to her knee and turned the wrist outward to show dark, puffed lines, a wound which might well have gone bad.

I did not need to be prompted now. This had I done twice before when I had learned how to sever the power of Ravinga. I took the goblet from her. There still remained a mouthful or so of the drug at the very bottom of its bowl.

My own work skipped unheeded aside, I snatched up a small bit of soft cloth and sopped up that remaining liquor in the cup and then, holding Ravinga's hand with force against her own knee, as for a moment or so she tried to jerk away from me, I wiped the sodden rag back and forth across the lines of a wound another truly wore.

Twice Ravinga hissed and attempted to free herself with a jerk but I held on and she could not be free of me. The mark there had been a welt raised above the skin it disfigured. I was able to feel that upthrust of the very red flesh.

In my own throat rose the hum which was part of this treatment. My flute I could not use as long as I held the cloth to her arm.

I vacillated between two opposed beliefs. One that I wrought for good, the other that I sustained what was better left alone. Now the welts were subsiding, even as they paled in color, that dangerous darkness fading.

Out of nowhere came words I could not translate as I mouthed them. The strange wound on Ravinga's wrist was being banished. Nor did I believe that it would again threaten my mistress.

Her skin bore only a scar. I put aside the cloth which I had used. The slender length of the pipe slipped easily through my fingers. I raised the flute to my lips and began to play.

Nor did I stretch or seek for any notes, rather such came to me, following fast one upon the other as if I unconsciously held to some pattern of music I had once known so well that I need not think on what I played.

As I played, so that pressure of which I had been so aware eased. Ravinga's head fell forward on her breast as if she had worn herself out at a task which had been nearly beyond her.

The flute was quiet. I dropped it from my lips and sat with it between my fingers. Now there was no mark on Ravinga's right wrist, but the wide bracelet she always wore as a cuff on the left had slipped and beneath it lay a scar—an old one not unlike the one I had seen. Her eyes were closed and she breathed evenly as might one in refreshing slumber.

I looked down at the cat head which I had been fashioning. The citrine eyes—almost I would swear those were alive! For me there was no explanation of what we two had done, save that Ravinga had carried to its end some ritual of great strength.

Heat and pain—save that the latter was now less, a lash which fell only lightly across my body to bring back the memory of what I was. I stared straight up. Over me was the night sky. There was the rasp of a great rough tongue across my cheek and I saw that on my right crouched the female sandcat. Only her eyes were clearly visible in the night's dark, but those held me as I strove to lift a hand.

"Great One." My voice was a harsh whisper.

"Friend—" My head ached as if I had spent time striving to make sense out of sounds alien to me. I gave a cry of wonder, for I was sure that this was no dream, that I had indeed sorted intelligible sounds from the noise issuing from that furred throat.

Only this was a time I could not rise to take in wonders. I was still prisoner to all which had overtaken me when the cat's teeth had closed upon my wrist.

But I seemed also to hear a pattern of music I had known so long that it had been a part of me.

They rose, they fell, those notes, and it was almost as if I saw water falling in droplets as might a trickle poured from a jug into a basin.

There followed silence at last, and I slept.

9

I LAY ON MY BACK, the folds of my cloak wrinkled about me. The pain had been leached from my wrist. I felt light, content to be where I was. Another dream? No, I was sure that was not so. Certainly I had heard and understood moments earlier the exchange between the sandcats when the female had gone off and left her mate to play sentry.

Klaverel-va-Hynkkel—I was him. My eyelids were heavy. It was hard to clear the haze which seemed to wall me in. There was a wind against my desert-dried skin. I blinked at puffs of sand carried by that breeze in arcs against the darker rock. It was a place of desolate loneliness, I thought—for a space—

"Myrourr—" I twisted my speech as best I could to form that name.

A lazy, questioning sound answered. The great head lifted from its position on forepaws, and golden eyes surveyed me critically. This was as one might feel on the weapon practice ground of my home isle—just as that huge body of gold-grey fur could have matched the broad shoulders and well-trained body of my father's marshal at arms.

I could talk, be understood, be answered. Sometimes it was as if I shared camp with one of my own blood. Death crawled below— there had certainly been no wiping out of all the rats. Still I pushed the thought of these from me for now.

"—Metkin of Rapper's Way—" I caught those words clearly. The cat had been doing some inner shifting of my memories.

"That one was a hero of many battles. On the days of remembering he is called and from him came stories that his clan stood proud of reckoning." The deep-throated rumble of speech was akin to a purr. "Before him Myart of blood of the Five who fought for the many." The great cat drew his paw towards him leaving

75

parallel scratches on the rock surface. "Behind that one Maslazar—and others—many others. Myroe—Meester—" He yawned as if reciting these scraps of history brought a need for slumber.

"And did these heroes company with my kind?" I had to feel my way word by word, unsure as to whether my alien voice could shape these names which held a slurring difficult for me.

Myrourr's head moved in the negative, his sleepy eyes half closed.

"Our clan far from roads of others. Myfford went to death where blow winds of great harshness. He spoke with one living apart, asking for knowledge. Only able to remember a small part of that told him. But as was the beginning, so the end."

Now his slitted eyes closed. Mine followed, for what he had given me in fragments whirled in and out and made no strict sense. Nor had I any desire to probe the deeper.

My sleep was a drifting in strange places where there was always one beside me, striving to pressure me to do something, though I slipped aside and evaded easily the control which would have kept me at labor.

I was aroused at last by another sound, the grate of claws on rock. So I levered myself up on one elbow to see the better. Not too far away was the female cat. And she was not alone. Copying her solemn stance, watching me with the round eyes of inquiring childhood, was a half-grown sandcat. Its mouth hung a little open and it was panting.

Though he was colored like his elders, his spots were more indistinct, his fur was less thick, and his feet oversized as is the case of many cublings. But he gave full promise of equaling his sire in time.

Maraya, the female, used one paw to urge him forward.

"Murri—" Her voice was hardly more than a purr. "This one is of our get, smoothskin. As is among your kind we also have a time when the young go forth to learn. Murri will be as a little brother, lifting claw and fang for you."

She paused and again I strove with the word sounds of the furred ones.

"Great lady, do you entrust your cub to me, who am one with those who hunt you?"

The Great Cats might not laugh but there is humor in them and that colored her answer to me.

"Entrust him to you, youngling? No, rather we trust you to him."

"But—"

"It is thus, youngling," Myrourr spoke. "In this place strange things have happened. I lay open to your knife. Yet you took no life, rather worked to save me. We fought side by side, foul things of the inner dark."

"And the old one," Maraya cut in. "You felt for him and did not leave him to the foul ones to worry."

"Nor are you any longer what you were," Myrourr continued. "For in you now is blood of our blood. To our kind you are sealed."

I glanced at my wrist. There was a scar there but the wound had closed cleanly. I had heard traveler's tales that some people afar signed adopted kinship so. But that any had sworn a pact with others than their own species, that had not been told.

Myrourr and Maraya exchanged a long look. If they communicated so, I could not follow. The male arose, stretched, his huge body nearly as large as that of a bull yaksen. Then he leaped, as lightly as a grain of sand upward borne by the wind, to the top of a rock spur. There he stood, facing outward over the sand beyond the isle, so still he might have been carved from this stone. His head went back and he gave voice to such a roar as might well challenge a storm in fury, once, thrice, and yet again, each time turning a little to face in another direction.

What he sought I soon learned. Across the distant sands, sometimes so much the color of the land that they could not be detected save that they moved, came sandcats in scores beyond my counting.

There were those as great in size as Myrourr, there were females coming in pride, bringing with them young. All approached the slickrock isle and made their way up it to where Myrourr and Maraya waited with the dignity of rulers among their kind. The visitors touched noses lightly with the two who waited them and then scattered out, forming small family groups, waiting—

With the coming of dusk they gave tongue. My people have a love of song—the bard is ranked high among us—but this wild music was to no pattern that I knew. Yet the longer it continued the more it sounded right to me, so that I raised my own voice, timidly at first, to join in their ululating wails. There were some who led the singing, perhaps selected the songs. Maraya was one of these and twice all other voices died away allowing hers to echo to the sky, as proud as any challenge.

Singing was only the beginning. Now they danced. First one and then another leaped upward. By some trick of breathing they were able to draw air into them. Their fur fluffed out until they looked like great soft balls as they leaped and floated for distances I would not have thought possible had I not seen it. They rolled, they twisted, as might cublings at play, in the air, as they arose above the crags of the isle.

Their exertions had another result, for the fur of the airborne ones gave off sparks of light. I watched and I longed, too, to so float in the wind. I could leap, yes, and twist somewhat, but there was no escaping the pull of the earth on my body and I could only stand, panting from my vain efforts, to watch the whirl of the dance. Now those aloft singled out one another and spun together, dipping above or below their partners. Once more they sang. I saw cublings try to climb the sky but with hardly better success than I had had. Twice Murri came to me, short club tail switching, striving to pull me into the midst of the youngsters' wild circling on the ground.

I did what I could, for my childhood was not so far behind me that I could not remember certain tricks I had learned from entertainers in the marketplace, somersaults and leaps. My clumsy, probably foolish, efforts appeared to excite Murri and led him to more attempts at soaring, rising to the point where he could circle my ground-bound body.

Soon I was the center of a circle of cublings and they watched me with unblinking eyes as if I were some marvel. However, I was soon panting heavily and the strength drained from me so at last I seated myself just to watch.

I was not the only one tiring from that wild revel as more and more of the larger cats touched surface and settled as might kottis before a fire. Though their bush tails were too short to curl about the forefeet as did those of our home companions.

Myrourr and Maraya threaded a way through their resting kin and came to me, to stand one on either side. From Myrourr there came an order that I show this company the mask pendant.

Straightway when I pulled it into the air it took flame, as if it drew from those about the sparks of fur light. It blazed forth brave as any torch, save there was no heat in it. I held it up so it could be clearly seen.

For a moment there was complete silence, no scrape of claw on rock, no pant of breath. Then from all that company arose a hum which could be reckoned a great purring—and the sound shook me. They moved in upon me, marshaled as if they were warriors in review before a Queen. Each halted but a moment directly before me, head a little forward as if to sniff at what I bore and then at me. Even though I had shared, in my very small way, their dance and song, I found this a little daunting. To be surrounded by the cublings had been one thing, but to be encircled now by those I had been trained from childhood to consider prime enemies of my kind, awakened uncertainty within me. And still they came.

It might have been that they wished to store in memory a scent to recall again in times to come. They were accepting me as one of their own, something no one of my species had ever known— at least as far back as our bard songs went.

For three suns that company remained. The pool algae was shared by all, and there was a determined night hunting for rats. For the first time I witnessed that the sandcats would seek those out even in their burrows beneath the surface of the ground. There was a concentrated digging and runways were laid open, nests of the vermin uncovered, those within being speedily taken care of.

On the third night the first of the gathering began to drift away, followed by more and more. They made no formal farewells to their host and hostess, nor did any of them seek me out.

During the meeting the cublings had engaged in mock battles of their own with much snarling, hissing, and even flying tufts of hair. Murri rendered good account of himself in two such encounters and his trot took on something of a proud roll when he came to me afterward that I might smooth his fur and hail him as warrior.

Once the company left and the silence settled once more on the isle, I helped the family sweep the debris of the meeting into deep cracks and fissures. Again I took up scraps of rat hide, softening it from the stiffness of sun drying by pulling it back and forth across the edge of the rock.

I could delay no longer. The future I had refused to meet must now be faced squarely. Where I would head when I left the safety of this isle I had no idea. We were not too far, I believed, from that stretch of death-dealing land—the Plain of Desolation. But I still lacked any guide.

As I worked packing sun-dried pats of algae, more strips of rat meat, whatever I believed I could carry that might mean my life later on, Myrourr came to me.

"There is a road." His speech was easier for me to understand the longer I listened. "Masca Broken Tooth said it lies so—" He lifted his head and pointed outward from the isle.

"Where does it lead?"

"Who knows?" He made it very clear that the trails of my kind were of little account to a sandcat. "But some pass along it. Twice has Masca had good hunting from their beasts. Murri—!"

He summoned his young son, who squatted before him. I received a jumble of thought impressions and knew that the cub was being instructed by his sire. Since the sandcats were rovers of the desert lands, certainly they must possess powers of direction which were more than even the knowledge of our far-ranging patrols.

When Myrourr had done, Maraya followed with more warnings and instructions, ending that her cub was now to be the comrade and protector of another and one who was not properly taught.

How long it might be before we found another such refuge as the one which had served me so well here, I had no idea. The more supplies I could carry with me, the better our chances.

I made up two packs, one containing my own few belongings and all I could cram into it of the dried food. The second pack was not a heavy one for neither the algae cakes nor the meat strips were of weight. I enfolded this in a crude covering of skins lashed together and showed it to Murri.

He backed away, looking at me and uttering sounds of refusal.

"To travel," I told him with what authority I could summon, "one must feed. Thus we bear food in case we stray days from new supplies. I can not carry two packs. On the trails comrades share burdens."

Murri's measuring gaze went from me to the two adult cats as if he expected them to back his proud refusal to carry a burden like a yaksen. But neither of them moved nor made a sound. Then he looked back to me and I nodded.

Showing by every muscle movement of his lithe body his distaste for what I asked, he advanced a stride and stood while I made fast the pack, settling and securing it as best I could to accommodate his movements. I took up my staff and then it was my turn to face the older cats. Farewells come hard. My people are clannish and find it difficult to cut any ties. This rested upon me now even though I fronted sandcats and not kin of my own kind.

I bowed my head, as I would to the Head of some House and spoke the words of going forth—as I had not been encouraged to say them by any of my blood on the night I left my own home.

"To Myrourr and Maraya, this visitor within their land gives thanks for hearthright and homeright. May the Great Essence of all enclose and keep you, and may the end of the trail be that which you most wish."

Myrourr answered me:

"Smoothskin, I have taken the gift of life from your hands—as none of my kind have done. Between us there is no claw nor fang, no knife, no spear. Those are for ones who have no understanding. Go in peace to follow the trail set for you—there is more than chance in what you do."

Then, with Murri trotting confidently in the lead as if he followed a visible marking of foot and hoof prints, we left the isle of Myrourr and Maraya. I looked back once over my shoulder, but so akin were the marking of their fur to the color of the rocks that I could not see if they still watched us, or if they were already about business of their own.

Murri appeared to be entirely certain of the way, and I could only accept his confidence in hope that he knew what he was doing. The coming of day found us passing out of the sand waves onto a bone white land where there was only a spread of sharp pebbles under foot. Our pace slowed as each step brought with it pain, for those pebbles could be felt even through the boots I had cobbled over with dried skin. Murri began to limp well before the coming of morning.

There was no sign of another isle where we might be able to find shelter or food. From our two packs, my cloak and staff I devised a limited cover from the glare of the rising sun and set about treating Murri's bruised and torn paws, smearing them with algae salve. Over them I then tied foot coverings fashioned from rat skin, making sure these were tightly lashed into place. Murri aided me as best he could by the stretching of paws.

We ate very little of our supplies and then huddled together within the shelter knowing we had the fire blast of the day to get through.

10

"ALLITTA!"

I set the square of black-painted hide carefully on the table so that the beads laid upon it in intricate pattern would not be shaken from the lines upon which they were to be firmly attached. There was the scent of incense in the room and I turned down the lamp under the basin where the tree gum from the far east simmered. I was purposefully deliberate in all my movements, having learned long ago that haste was the enemy of many of the tasks left for my hands.

Now I passed from the workroom into the shop. Mancol was gone, having his list of errands for the morning. So the outer curtains were still pegged into place, leaving the interior in shadows.

Though I knew very well all which was about me, I felt as always that uneasiness which plagued me in any half light in Ravinga's house. I had seen all, or most all, of those tiny bead eyes, set in place to give a lifelike appearance to the ranks of dolls. Still the skillful fingers of my mistress appeared to have awakened all images into life so that they stared at me, weighed me. Almost I could believe that I was the object of gossip among those eyes' owners when I was not present.

There were times when I was sure that Ravinga's skill was far too good—that now and then a doll passed out of her hands which was so akin to a living person that it might have been an illusion projected from flesh and bone.

During the past four seasons a new, macabre demand had arisen among the Vapalans to keep Ravinga busied—a fashion for portraits of the newly dead. Even to being clad in scraps from the favorite robes of the deceased, these foot-high figures had been fashioned as permanent records of friends and kin lost

to their Houses. The making of these had not been introduced by
Ravinga. In fact I was certain that she made such against her will.
Yet she had not refused to accept a commission no matter from
whom—grieving lifemate, sister, brother.

I remember quite well the first of her making—it had been
of Wefolan-ji, one of the elders of a House now prominently
represented at court by Giarribari, the Grand Chancellor, and the
customer, Ravinga was informed, was from the far eastern inner
lands which are legend to us.

Since then Ravinga had wrought a full dozen more, and I heard
that such were now on display in the halls their models had once
known in life.

Very recently it had not been only the dead that friends chose to
honor so—but upon the coming of anyone into fame, those of the
House would order such a figure, to be clad in full court dress.

Two such lay even now in boxes behind Ravinga on the shelf,
well wrapped and sealed against any jar. Now her hands were
busy shuffling through a packet of dried and beaten tav leaves
on which were drawings in color, plainly the specifications of
another such representative of the living, or the dead.

She did not look up as I drew closer, only fanned the last of
the leaf pictures out upon the counter where a low-trimmed lamp
banished the shadows immediately around.

"Haban-ji." Her voice was very close to a whisper.

I shivered. There was that in her tone, in the tense stance of
her body, which was a warning.

"Who brought this order?" I kept my voice low to match her
own hiss. "And why?"

"Who—the confidential clerk of Giarribari. Why—?"

The Grand Chancellor was not one to draw upon Ravinga's
skill in a need to flatter her lord. All knew her for what she
was, a shrewd, somewhat calculating autocrat, true servant not of
Haban-ji—rather sealed in loyalty to the office she now filled. To
Giarribari the laws, rights, very life of the Empire were infinitely
greater than any one man.

"She does not wish to flatter," I spoke my first thought aloud.

"There is no need for her to do so. She knows her own worth
and weighs well the worth of him whom she serves—"

"Haban-ji has been more than thirty storm seasons on the throne.
There have been no speeches against him."

Ravinga nodded. "Nor has there been much speech for him.
There has been no true testing of him."

"But truly there was! Otherwise how would he carry the leopard staff?" I protested.

"True—he won the crown testing. However, matters change through the years. He who was a bold young hunter becomes, when lapped in power, another. There has been much coming and going lately between Vapala and the far eastern inner lands. Their merchants make journeys hither lately in large numbers. And each of those pays two tolls—"

Now she was repeating a rumor of the marketplace. Though the Six Houses were long established and among them controlled most of the trade, still they might well be complacent now, not too quick to follow up some whisper that one or another of their kind had sudden access to luxuries unknown in the outer lands.

However—the Emperor! One who had passed through the great trials to reach the throne—what need had he of foreign merchant favor or greater riches than his office gave him?

"There was a difference in the past," Ravinga continued. "Then an Emperor did not gain the throne and forget he might have to struggle to hold it. For there was once a set period of seasons and then he knew the challenge might come. We of Vapala now speak of such action as barbarian and not for us to follow. Yet it was once the law that the Emperor was to be the nourisher of his people—he was to give all himself to the land, strengthening the Essence in a free surrender. Now he is not the sacrifice but rather makes token offerings and such are accepted."

A token offering! I looked to the patterns she still shuffled back and forth as one might treat papers which carried ill news, wishing to throw them away and yet unable to do so.

I need not ask the question in my mind—she had caught it.

"A token? Perhaps. If so—" she shook her head slowly, "that is sensible reasoning. Yet I wonder. There is Shank-ji."

Our rulers, the five Queens, the Emperor, do not take lifemates. Though that did not mean that they live celibate lives. However, any children born of such matings had no standing above any others of noble Houses, nor were such ever recognized at any of the courts, unless they won to high place by their own efforts. For the past three seasons we had heard much of Shank-ji, the Emperor's son in all but formal name.

He was said to have openly vowed, before the great ones of the court, that when the time came that his father died he would enter the contest for Emperor and that he fully meant to take the High Crown.

"This is," Ravinga's hand curled into a fist and she brought it down upon the lined leaves, "an honor doll for which there is no honor to celebrate. Therefore it can become—"

"A death doll!" I clapped my hand over my mouth even as I said that. "But there is no talk of the Emperor ailing—more than the general ills of age."

"Just so," Ravinga agreed. "Yet this is also the season of fevers. Haban-ji is interested in curiosities from the east. There have been reports from the sentries at the far border that there is grave sickness beyond. One caravan was discovered with all the traders dead about their beasts. Though they did not die of any sword or knife thrust—their killer was a thing unseen. Let Haban-ji be given some toy from such an infected camp—or seem to be given such—and there can well be good reasoning for a death doll."

"And the Grand Chancellor?"

"Who are such as we to know the intrigues of the court? They have little to do, those noble ones, and thus they may play some odd games such as we commoners would not try. Yes, there are changes coming. Have you not also foreseen it so?"

"And if I have? I tell you, mistress, I will have no part in such! Have I not been life twisted already, and by none of my own doing, because there are those who clutch with greedy fingers? There is no longer any House of Vurope."

I was angry. She was pushing me into paths of memory I had no wish to travel—paths I had worn so deep over the past seasons that they were only too open to entrap my course of thought.

Ravinga had put together in one packet those leaves and now she placed them in a flat envelope. But that did not join the rest of the patterns in a side drawer, instead she pushed it into a seam pocket of her robe.

"You will make it then?"

"What excuse can I rightfully raise to refuse such a commission?" she countered. "I delay by this much. I have asked for the proper jewels with which to fashion a crown of state. Outwardly, Allitta, this must be accepted as any other order. However, there is also this—"

She half turned to pick up from the shelf immediately behind her a box of some dull black substance. There was a strange look to the surface of that container, as if it could swallow light, a devouring shadow, so that any color or gleam of metal, even warm lamp glow, was dimmed in its presence.

Ravina had jerked from a crumpled mass of dust-laden cloths such as Manol used each morning to rid the counter of debris, a square which was streaked with black back and forth. Some artist might have used it to wipe a brush upon it.

She used that to handle the box, spreading out the dirty cloth beneath it. We often received oddly protected materials in the shop, and this was not the first time my mistress was so very careful about how she handled some such container.

Ravinga now pressed at either end of the tightly sealed lid. There came a whiff of vile odor, like the stink of a waste pit under the sun. When she raised her thumbs again the lid adhered to them, was so carried up.

The inside of the coffer was splattered with red which had thickened in some places into gummy bubbles. Amid this rested, not such a doll as I had more than half expected to see, but rather the representation of a beast.

We of Vapala might not be threatened by the desert rats but I had seen their carcasses enough to know what this was. Still keeping her flesh covered, Ravinga levered up the creature and dumped it on the counter between us.

It had been made of some material I did not recognize—seemingly of a bit of real skin stuffed, but it was manifestly too heavy for that, for it landed with a heavy thump. Save for its size it was complete in every detail, even to the bloodlike spots which glistened as if it had been recently slaughtered.

The head of the creature moved! There were sparks of yellow-red fire filling the eye cavities and which I sensed were aware of me, of Ravinga. What I thought of was the skitter of clawed feet on stone, many such.

I watched my mistress pinch together where the cloth lay beneath the monstrous thing. There she held a grip which made her knuckles stand out.

"So—so it is—" I said and then I moved. From my girdle I jerked a short rod carven from fire-born rock such as gushes out of the mountain crevices in Thnossis. And I flailed out with that, the end of it catching the creature on the side of the head even as it lifted lip to me in threat.

At the same moment I armed that blow, Ravinga also jerked her hands. The touch of my rod rocked the figure, and it fell back into the cloth. Then my second blow followed the first. The beast's body jerked—simulating life which I was sure it did not have before it crumpled into small crumbs.

I stood, rod ready for a third blow, staring down at the broken mass.

"I was right! I was right!" I said and my breath seemed to hiss between my teeth.

"It was no dream—but the truth!"

Anger as hot as the stuff of my wand had once been surged in me. Behind me arose all the times I had heard a story, only to be told—soothingly by some, angrily by others—that I had fastened on some dream and claimed it for reality.

I had learned through pain of both mind and body that the truth of one is very often lost by the will of many.

Now, once more, I saw the mat bed—and the woman who lay upon it, the struggle of childbirth and pain twisting her. Imposed upon that scene the half-seen face grinning, grinning with a second mouth which opened wide inches below the one nature had granted him. I saw once more the vicious gleam of those eyes, which only I had seen alive then. I heard my own voice, a much younger voice, cry out protests and pleas as he held me in a grip which near tore my skin with its savagery, and I felt the flash of red-hot fire about my shoulders again and again!

So beaten had I been that there was hardly shred of life left to me when I was thrust into a place of darkness and knew, through the pain, that this was only the beginning of suffering to come.

However, I did not meet that death. Though I never knew whom I had to thank for that. A spark of stubbornness, of the growth of that need for vengeance, had set me crawling through a place of shadows. I sensed that there was that also crawling through the dark which was even worse than he who had attacked me.

I looked to Ravinga again and her eyes met mine. "What and who?"

It was true that my hot-tempered father had had the two rights over me—life which he had given me and death which was his for the asking. He had many enemies—which one of them had devised such a scheme, one to attack me past any hope of either belief or forgiveness? Yet it was not the battle of kin which I had ever fought, but more my own. Nothing dampened my wrath but I had learned to bury it deep for a space.

"Who—why?" My mouth was so dry those two words came as croaks.

"Who—why—?" she echoed me. "Someone tried now a variation of a game played so well before. There is an order for a ceremonial figure of Haban-ji—then comes this filth secretly.

Mancol found it on an upper shelf of the store room this morning. Tongues wag freely—an Emperor ages—perhaps dies. In my hands there is an honor image—with something far worse to be found if the guard comes to search. Was it not something of the sort before, girl?"

I was not too overwrought by memories of the past to see the dark and threatening logic of what she said. A web woven.

"Someone fears—" I said slowly. "But why me? Power is yours, but who has anything to fear from me?"

Ravinga swept the stained cloth together and thrust it into the box which had held the rat. She pulled towards her the brazier meant to scent the air with burning powers. Into the coals which still existed in the heart of that she slammed the cloth and the now empty box.

There was an explosion of raw light, a noise which hurt through my ears far into my head. The upward blaze of the flames obscured the box at once.

"There may be two who play—one may be a searcher into lost knowledge who strives to turn bits and pieces into weapons—the other—the other may also be a seeker—of other things. For this time what can we do but watch—listen—sense— We must be the guardians of our own lives and freedom."

11

FOR AS LONG as I can remember I had heard tales of the Plain of Desolation, a heat-blasted land closed to all life forms save bands of rats. These seemed to have become adjusted to its lack of any water except algae beds so minerally poisoned as to kill the wanderer with the first mouthful.

Even the most desperate of raiders would not venture therein and there were accounts of outlaw bands turning at bay on the edge of the Plain to face a death they knew, rather than a worse one than any sword or spear offered. Traders made lengthy trips to north or south to avoid that death trap.

Where Murri and I now traveled was the very edge of that ominous waste. It was not speedy travel as the sharp pebble footing slowed us. The stores we had started with I stretched as far as possible. Murri might outlast me, for the great predators were better used to going longer without food. Yet there would come an end to strength for both of us unless we could find some sustenance in time.

Murri's pack was exhausted first, though he was clever enough to take no pleasure in that loss, knowing how much we needed every algae cake, every scrap of rat flesh which each day we divided into smaller and smaller rations.

I was losing my confidence in him as a guide. After all, though the cats did roam outward from the isles each pair claimed, yet I could see no sign of any heights ahead, or any break in the baking enormity of the Plain. Our journeying was by night. Always Murri seemed certain of the way. The parched white stretch of land about us had the starkness of bone, and, while there was no night-awakened glimmer of sand, yet we were not altogether without a ghostly light which sprang here from the pebbly ground.

We were five days out from the isle when there showed a promising break on the skyline ahead. Within an hour after we started on the fifth night, we came to traces of some who had dared this path before us. Bones of both beasts and men had been dragged apart and splintered by teeth. Three wagons still stood roped to the shattered remains of yaksen carcasses. Some traders' party had come to an end here. I moved among the dead unable to tell one set of remains from another so hardly had all been used.

Without very much hope I dragged open packs from the wagons. These had been near torn to tatters. I could guess food supplies had been in some. But two were intact and when I unrolled them there were inner pockets full of rough gemstones, unpolished and showing little color. Still I had been schooled well enough by Kura to recognize the worth of what I had found. There was a bundle of notes of sales and that I took. Were I ever to escape this deathway, what I had discovered might be returned to the heirs of those who lay here.

There were in addition two knives and a sword—trade goods of high value—and those I gathered up eagerly. What small training I had in sword play had given me far less skill than that of my father or brother, but a good blade in the hand was in a way heartening and I was more than pleased with my find.

Murri had been prowling around the scene of the disaster and now he came to me.

"Cat—smoothskin—other—"

"Other?"

I let him lead me to a place where there were five of the skeletons huddled together. The glint of jewelry showed among splintered bone. However, that was not all—two skulls lay with their empty eye pits pointing up to the sky. And the very center of each was blackened and turned to crumbling ashes as if they had been in a fire.

I squatted down on my heels to view them but I did not put forth my hand, even my staff, to touch them. The bones were clean, the death about us one I could understand.

Sandcats could well strike so, even though there were no traces of any of their dead—

"Here one!" Murri had taken two long strides and there lay another skeleton, plainly one of his own species. The massive skull of that was charred from behind as if the animal had been brought down as it fled the scene of the other deaths.

Who killed with fire? We could tame that into lamps and torches to carry with us, lanterns even, to set up for night guards along the trade roads—though those signals are carefully imprisoned in cavities in the heads of the carven cats, the light to shine through their eyeholes.

I could imagine some desperate traveler of my own blood using a torch as a last weapon. A cat could have been so felled. Yet here, too, were the fallen of my species showing the same traces of grisly wounds.

"Other cats?" I asked of Murri.

"We honor dead," he returned shortly.

"Why then—?" I nodded to the skeleton he had found.

My night sight was good enough to see the rising of hair along his spine. He growled.

"This is of evil." He turned aside and picked up in his mouth a long tatter of one of the supply bags. With a flick of his head he sent that flying so that it fluttered down across the bared bones. One tip of the torn hide falling across that blackened hole.

Flame is red, yellow, many shades of those colors, as anyone who has watched the dance of fire tongues can tell you.

The hide drew something else—it was grey, as if this country had even bleached the life from fire itself. But that strange flame leaped into being as the hide curled, giving forth the stench of its burning. When the last of it was ashed there was only the blackened hole and no sign of anything which might still lie in wait there. I had seen that happen. Such was totally beyond any traveler's tale I had ever listened to with the greed of one who wished to know yet hesitated to venture forth to learn for himself.

Now I went back to those other two skulls which bore the brand of the strange burning. This time I impaled a tatter on the end of my staff and gingerly shook it free so that the stained ribbon might fall upon the human skull.

There came fire again—only this burned with a sickening greenish hue—and was as quick to finish off what I had fed into it. Two kinds of fire? Or only one which answered in different ways because the prey differed?

What had happened—

I started back, tripped over the bones of a yaksen, and fell on my back, as helpless for a moment as one of those brilliantly colored beetles the traders from Vapala offer from time to time.

Again—

Sound, a moan of sound—then pattern of notes—as if someone lost in this desolation was singing his own death melody.

Murri snapped around but with care for his footing. He was facing outward, away from the ill-omened battlefield.

Again—now there was a continuous background hum from which came notes, or even sounds like a much repeated refrain aroused. And since the first shock was over I realized what it was—that there was one playing a Kifongg harp and with it singing a dirge which was only rightful for this country.

"Life!" Murri's whole body stiffened into a point.

Had someone escaped massacre? The law of the trail was plain: it was my duty to hunt for that survivor.

Or—I glanced once more at the blackened skulls—was this a trap?

Murri picked up that thought. Perhaps it had already occurred to him.

"No trap—life, cave, food—" He was impatient.

I had stored my finds into my pack. Now more than ever were I to reach some authority I must report our discovery. Leaning on my staff a little as the ever-crunching and moving gravel cut at my boots, I moved on into the night after Murri.

As suddenly as it had sounded out of the night, so that dirge ended. We had passed out of the treacherous footing that lay on the edge of the Plain and once more faced the rise and fall of the glimmering sand dunes. Here the wide, furred feet of Murri made better time than mine and I had dropped a length or so behind when I sighted a spark of light ahead. It seemed so high in the sky that first I thought it was a star, yet it seemed too bright for one of those dim beacons which had so far not served me at all.

We came upon our first-seen spur of rock. And a moment or so later, I was sure that this was not altogether the work of nature. Rather it was a part statue of a way cat, the head and shoulders of which had been snapped off to lie as a partly shattered mass to one side.

Not far beyond that a second way marker reared, and this one was not only intact but within its head a small fire had been kindled, for there were yellow beams to mark the eyes. It was a work of cunning art and it wore also a necklet of dullish jewels, certainly so eroded by the sandstorms, as well as rings at the tips of its well-shaped ears. Yet there was that in its outline which suggested the sandcat rather than the harmless kottis with which we were always so glad to share our shelters.

The statue was faced partly away from me so that I saw only the one eye clearly. As we passed it the land began to slope downward and we had to fight our way through shifting sands, which, in places, were like to swallow Murri to his belly fur and me to my knees. It was the sloping of this way which had hidden, by the aid of the night, the fact that we had entered a great basin. Nor was the cat with the burning eyes the only one who was set there on guard. There were three others, and a second of these also showed the burning night eyes.

We won through the slopes of the dunes and came out upon a more level space. Here there had been erected a whole clan of cats, some showing signs of wear, and others standing as straight and tall as if they had just been set in place. While not too far away that was a line of darkness blotting out some of the sand glitter—surely the outermost shore of one of the isles!

Murri held high his head, his ears pointed a little forward, his nostrils expanded. My senses were so much the less than his but I knew that scent too well to be deceived—there were yaksen ahead! Though that did not mean that we had come upon some outpost of a holding here—for the thick-coated beasts of burden roamed free in many places.

We came to where rock sprouted upward from the sand. Murri uttered a small sound. Water! Somewhere not too far beyond us now was an algae bed and there lay what we needed the most.

Still we were not utterly disarmed by our need. Murri yet took the lead with a spring which carried him up into a shelf extension of the rock and I followed with greater effort.

I heard the snorting of a herd bull that must have picked up our scent. Murri was inching along an ascending ledge, his claws unleashed to make sure of every small advantage to come from hooking them into the seams and crevices.

"Saaaaaaaaaa!" It was almost the snarl of a cat and there bounded downslope, only inches away from my defenseless head, a rock, full double-fist large. I flattened myself until my cheek ground into the stone.

The musky smell of the yaksen was strong. I could almost hear the click of their hooves.

"Saaaaaa!" Again the rising cry of a guardian herdsman. How many times I myself had uttered such when on duty?

"We mean no harm." I had to moisten my lips twice with my tongue before I could shape those words. "Traveler's rights, herdsman. These we claim!"

Traveler's rights for a sandcat? To any there would be folly in such a suggestion.

"Saaaaaaaa!" Undoubtedly the voice was farther away. The watchman was true enough to his service to urge what beasts he could out of range.

My hand flailed upward, caught at the stone, and I had a firm enough grip to hold, to pull myself up on a flat surface. I got to one knee and then made it to my feet which were shaking a little as I forced myself away from the stone to look around.

Five yaksen, two of which were hardly more than calves, had moved away. I could see no more of them than blots which stirred uneasily.

"Traveler's greeting," I tried again. And to prove the rightness of my claim for such consideration I added:

"I am Hynkkel of the House of Klaverel. I am faring forth on my solo."

"You bear weapons." The voice was thin, wavery, almost as if it had been but little used lately.

"Only such—" I was beginning when I remembered the arms we had taken from the massacre camp, "only such as a man may need hereabouts."

"You company with that which brings death—" There was accusation in the voice which had now taken on something of a whine.

"I company with a friend," I returned firmly. "This one is blood brother to me. Murri," I called to the sandcat. "This is a friend—"

"A sandcat has no friends among smoothskins," he spat.

"Then what am I?" I countered. That this stranger so well hidden in the shadows could make anything of our exchange I did not know. But having reconstructed a course of life after such a near acceptance of death, I was not going to surrender.

"By the blood which unites us," I spoke only to Murri now, "swear that we come in truce, as is the way of the land."

There was only silence and my frustration grew strong. If Murri was ready to separate me from my own kind after this first smile of fortune—

"Murri, I wait!"

"And die?" there came the cat's answer.

"Death! There has been too much of death!" My voice rose ever louder.

Once more there skimmed by my head a weight of hand-thrown stone.

"I come in trust," growled Murri. "But this one surely could not understand cat talk."

There was silence, broken only by the click of yaksen hooves. The small herd was moving.

"Stay then." The words were now lost in a heavy coughing and I heard a scrambling sound as if he who had spoken was now gone. All the taut readiness went out of my body and I fell rather than seated myself on the rock surface, depending upon the few small sounds my ears could pick up to assure me that, for the moment, there was to be no other attack.

12

THE FIRST STREAKS of pre-dawn were washing out the stars. Twice I had called upon Murri but the cat had not answered. That he was on the hunt I could be sure and a yaksen was no easy prey, especially if more than one were to be found. Their thick fur gave them some protection, and the heavy horns with which they met any assault, head down, were danger, for they fought in head fashion, the males and barren females surrounding the calves and any nursing mothers. While Murri, as large as he seemed when one compared him to a kotti, was not nearly the size nor had the brutal strength of his sire and dam.

There had been no sound since that scrambling which had marked the retreat of whoever had challenged us, he and the beasts whose scent had so surely drawn Murri. Somewhere and not too far away was an algae pool, that I could smell, inferior as my senses were compared to Murri's. My body's need for what that offered grew so strong I could no longer withstand it.

It was my turn to thread a way among tall spikes of rock. As the light grew stronger I could see that many of these had been worked upon by chisel and hammer. More than half of them were fashioned into cat guardians, their faces turned towards the death plain from which I had come.

The first were roughly made, with very little skill to give them life, but, as I worked myself inward, that skill improved, as if the artist learned by his mistakes. Yet there was a sameness in position and raise of head which argued that the one carver had wrought them all.

Finally I was confronted by a line of such, fast-wedged into an opening before two towering walls. The guardian cats were not so well based here and it was apparent that some had been fashioned elsewhere and brought to this place, packed into a wall one against the other.

I shed my pack, attaching one end of my rope to it, and set myself to a climb. The rough rock was scorching my skin, still not yet completely recovered from the torments of the journey. However, I doggedly fought my way to the head of the largest cat and looked down.

There was an algae pond right enough, but an ill-tended one. Here had been no careful pruning to discourage growth which forced out that more edible kind which was meat and drink for my species. While in other places the nourishing kinds had been too close-cropped, as if a herd had not been properly moved.

There were yaksen here and, in the morning light growing ever stronger, it was plain that they had been neglected for some time although they were not the smaller species which roamed free. Their heavy coats were matted and, with some animals, dragged on the ground, adding crushed algae and even small stones to a burden from which they could not clear themselves. Now and then one of the beasts would utter a small cry of complaint and strive to reach some weighty mat, biting fruitlessly at the foul caking of hair.

Of men there were no signs. Save on the opposite of the pool there was a hut of sorts—certainly no house such as any man of respect would claim, its walls a crazy patchwork of stones of all sizes, each fitting at rude angles into any space where it might be forced. On its crown was a reasonably smooth place and there was a patch of green-blue color, showing vividly against the red-yellow of the veined rocks.

Such a woven rug could have come only from Vapala, where, it was said, there were growing things not rooted in pools, which put forth tall stems to delight the eyes with new colors.

From Murri there was no signal which concerned me, but the yaksen were bunched together. Now and then a young bull would toss head and give voice to a bellow which was more an expression of uneasiness than any challenge.

By the door of that patch-upon-patch hut there was movement as a man came into the open, an algae-gathering basket in hand. His body was thin and old and I could see the most of it for he wore a kilt of fringed bits of rags, as if that garment was the last of a hard-used wardrobe.

His hair was an upstanding ragged mop, strands of which fell to his sharp-boned shoulders, giving him the look of those sand devils of childish tales. In one hand he held a staff much shorter than the one which served me, lacking metal tipping and edges. That he needed it for support was apparent as he tottered down to the pool.

"Ancient One—" His accent, in spite of the grating notes of his voice, had been that of the son of some House, no common trader. I did not know what title to give him. "Ancient One, I am no enemy of yours."

His head was chocked a little to one side as if so he could hear me the better.

"Not Vapalan then. Kahulawen to be sure. Traders? Have you wandered from those who now follow you? This is a forgotten place, you will find no succor here. There was—" He paused, frowning. His eyebrows were very bushy and beneath this overhang I could sight that one eye carried a fog-film. "There was a sandcat—"

"There is—my almost brother. It was his people who gave me aid when I needed it. They have accepted me as friend."

"Sooooo—" He drew the word out until it was near a hiss— such as Murri might give. "And I suppose now you will say that you are Emperor-to-be? If it is difficult to be a man, how much more difficult it must be to be a ruler. It has been a long time. The ancient ones—Karsawka—and by all rumors Zacan—should now also be waking. But there is nothing for you here, even though you carry the mask. Leave me in peace. I have nothing for the aiding of heroes, no matter how powerful they once were."

"You have what any can offer, Ancient One. I am no hero but I need food and drink—"

"If you are truly son of the Essence, that Karsawka who will be once more as testify the very ancient songs—" he frowned again and his expression was of one trying to remember, "then what man can deny you? Many songs have grown from your deed." Then he did what I never could imagine such an elder doing. He flung back his head and sang. There was no rusty coarseness in that singing— no break or difficulty. To close my eyes was to listen to some bard fit to eat at the Emperor's table.

> "From the sand draw the light.
> From the rocks learn the strength,
> In the storm wind walk without shelter.
> There is that in the land which enters in,
> And such holds two lives within it.

That which is gone, that which is to come.
Walk swiftly in the chosen way,
For the time of shadows is upon the kin,
Only he who shares life can live it."

I recognized the song, not in itself but for what it was—a puzzle.
The Vapalans, who consider themselves the only truly civilized
members of the five nations, have a taste for such, binding into
words some hidden meanings to which only few have a clue.
Some of the cliques and Houses among them have refined this
to the extent that only a handful out of their whole land may
understand—no one from outside their mesa country can hope to
know the meaning.

As his last word was echoed faintly back from some distance
the bard leaned forward on his staff, that feat of song seemingly
having weakened him. He was regarding me intently as if I
were enough a countryman of his to see to the heart of his
"tangle."

"Truly," I said and I meant it from the heart, "that is bard gift.
Never have I heard its like—"

"Never is perhaps right." There was a scoffing note in a voice
once more hoarse, perhaps even more so from the strain which had
just been forced upon it. "There are bards and bards, stranger. Of
them all the great ones are of Vapala." He continued to stare at
me under his bushy eyebrows as if striving to detect any protest
I might raise.

"Lord Bard, so will I agree. Also I would swear to you that I
mean you and yours no harm. I have no power to claim guest
right. However, this isle lies within the borders of my own land
and so is bound by the laws of my people—"

"Guest right." He mouthed the words as if he chewed upon
them. "Yet you travel with one of the killers of the desert. Does
he claim guest right also?"

"Murri—" I raised my own voice, giving it the particular twist
which was the closest my human lips and throat could come to
the speech of the Great Cats.

He came, seeming to rise out of the rocks themselves so close
in color was his coat to their surfaces. Padding to me, he turned,
as my hand rested on his head, to also face the bard. Then to my
surprise he opened his jaws and there poured forth a medley of
such sounds which I had heard uttered many times during the
festival of the cat people.

"Cloud—evil—not of night—" I fitted together the growls and snarls. The bard leaned still farther forward, an incredulous expression on his wrinkled face.

> "No blade can slay and still protect,
> Two battle as one—as it was—
> So shall it come again.
> Zacan rouses, stretched forth claw to rend.
> Where then is the LAW?"

The bard had been tapping out a rhythm on the length of his staff as he listened. Before the echoes of Murri's voice died he spoke:

"Old am I, cubling, and once I was known to many because I hunted forth the most ancient of songs and introduced them again. It was idle sport—and many held puzzles we could not solve. But it became a badge of proficiency among us to know, to try to understand. What—who was Zacan in truth? Lost." He shook his head and the long locks of his hair brushed back and forth across his shoulders. "But then they would tell us, these delvers into old stories, that nothing is lost—it may be hidden for a space and then brought once more, perhaps by chance, into the light—even through folly. It is enough that bard speak with bard, whether one wears a furred skin or goes bare-armed."

He took a step backward. "Into the land of the House of Kynrr enter freely, you who come from the desert." He pushed with the much worn butt of his spear, winding with it a floating mass of algae. This he then offered us, the host gift which would make us free for at least ten days on this holding.

However, in this bargaining he lost very little, for after accepting I made myself busy. Once more I worked at an algae bed, transplanting and encouraging new growth. I tended his yaksen also, grooming them, cutting out odorous mats of hair to free and cleanse them. The clipped hair I soaked and then combed it straight.

Kynrr's hut was the better for a cleanout, too, and that was what it got, perhaps the first in years. While its owner withdrew to a seat on a spire of rock and kept staring so intently in the direction from which I had come that I was led several times to turn and search that same direction—only to see nothing but rock and sand. He never gave me any explanation of what he so sought.

Murri went off by himself hunting. Through some delicacy he did not bring any game with him on return. He did inform me that this isle had its share of menaces, mainly at another algae pool which was attracting rats.

During my cleaning of the hut I found a Kifongg harp which in its day had certainly been a master's instrument. Kynrr watched me examine it with reverence and then signed me to bring it to him. He then began abruptly a series of lessons.

As all children, I had in my time been taught to use the Kifongg but I had never displayed any proficiency which led my father into having those lessons extended. Now I discovered that I had fallen into the company of a master musician and one who wanted not only a captive audience but a student.

The stiffness wore out of my fingers and I kept at the exercises set me. Mainly because Kynrr's eyes were ever upon me, I attained a measure of skill I never dreamed could be mine.

Perhaps because Kynrr had been so long alone to have company now was like someone opening the gate of a corral to allow an impatient herd beast down to the pool. While what my mentor talked of between bouts of music was the glories of Vapala of the Diamond Court, never did he tell me what had exiled him from all the luxury he had known and I knew better than to ask. However, it was plain that his position there had been a high one and he had been on familiar terms with the inner core of lords who dealt with great affairs.

He seemed to take pleasure after time in describing in detail court ceremonies, interrupting his accounts of such with scraps of gossip. It seemed more and more to me as I listened that the High Court was indeed a place of masks—that no one therein was, or wanted to be, himself, but behind their faces their thoughts moved in strange directions.

There were six premier Houses which had kept their position and identity through countless generations of time. There were other, newer ones, upon whom the six looked with emotions ranging from faint contempt to sneering intrigue designed to bring them down.

It was my belief that Kynrr had been caught in some such clearing of lesser Houses and had to flee Vapala for that reason.

On the surface the major occupation of the court appeared to be participation in endless and dull-sounding ceremonies which Kynrr related in detail. The dress, the action, even the sex of those in such interaction had a great deal to do with success. To humor him I became a sort of puppet acting out for him some bit of this purposeless play. Yet he took it with all seriousness and was so upset at my numerous errors of speech or action that I attempted to do his will to the best of my ability.

Murri found this dull. He would watch a bit from some perch among the rock and then disappear silently—rat hunting for the most part.

So days passed. I thought often of starting off again, but it was growing plainer all the time that the Kynrr's sight was failing more and more, that it was increasingly difficult for him to care for himself, let alone the dozen yaksen who were growing sleek and tractable under my ministrations.

It was one night when we sat together on a ridge, looking at the stars, rather I looking and Kynrr striving to point out guides he could not see any longer, that he spoke with some of the sharpness he used when trying to drive a bit of court etiquette into my thick head.

"Hynkkel, you are not made for a hermitage. Where will you go?"

I answered with the truth. "I have something of a gift with animals, Kynrr. It might be well to go to Vapala, as you have been urging on me, and there see if I can apprentice myself to a trainer of beasts."

"Trainer of beasts!" He cackled, then clapped his hands together as might a child delighted with some jest. "Yes, a trainer of beasts, and a rare one you shall be." He changed subject abruptly.

"The Emperor ails. Before your coming, there was a trading caravan off its course because of a storm. They had news—much news. With the Emperor dead—then there will be a choosing—"

It was my turn to laugh. "Ancient One, if you are suggesting that I set myself up for the trials, then indeed you have a poor opinion of my common sense. I was the least of my House, so poor a son to my father that he will show little sorrow at my non-return. I am no fighter, no doer of deeds which will make my name one for bards to remember. No, I am not of the stuff of which heroes are made. And that suits me very well."

I went off to check the herd, be sure that the rats were not a-prowl. But as I went I smiled as I thought of my brother's face if he looked upon the candidates for the Empire trial and saw me among them.

13

STILL I COULD NOT bring myself to desert the old man. Though I tried, even bluntly at times, to discover whether any of his House might be concerned with him, he evaded any answer, sometimes even getting up and walking away or shutting his eyes as if he had fallen into one of the sudden dozes which strike the elderly.

On all other subjects he was talkative enough and the longer we were together the more that he talked. At times his voice took on the tones of one lecturing students and he would spring questions without warning, keeping me alert to all which he said.

Murri, for the most part, kept out of sight. Though when the old man slept heavily he would come to me. The sandcat was growing impatient. Having been released by the custom of his kind from the isle of his birth, he was eager to be about his search for territory of his own to claim.

Though he might not be in sight, he sometimes lay in the shadows and I believed that he understood much of what Kynrr said. But it was the singing of the bard and his playing on the Kifongg which appeared to enchant the cat the most.

I certainly could never qualify for the place of bard before the high seat of any House but my playing was better than most I had heard, and that is not a boast. All of us of the Outer Regions have a liking for music—from the roll of the lookout drums which signify the coming of the storm to those small songs one sings to soothe a fretful child, we are surrounded with music from our birth. I had known to the last word some half hundred songs, both the genealogical chants which were the duty of each House child to be able to recall, to fragments of very old verse children used for counting-out games among themselves.

However, now I found that what I knew was nothing when compared to Kynrr's store and many of those I was able to keep

107

in mind. Though the riddle songs had no meaning and perhaps
had not held any for centuries out of time.

I experimented with the Kifongg when Kynrr passed it to me,
striving to fit chord to chord until I could mimic in part the singing
of the cats as I had heard them at their great meeting. Kynrr might
close his eyes during such efforts on my part but his hand kept
time, settling with little trouble on the underlying beat of what I
battled to bring into being.

"Soooooooo," he said one morning, "that is what lies behind the
Lament of Lasre. Here." He reached for the instrument and began
to pluck the strings, tentatively at first, then with more assurance,
so that even I could hear the thread of purposeful melody.

"What is the Lament of Lasre?" I asked when he was done and
sat with his hands lightly grasping the harp, staring past me at that
coloring of the rocks which faded subtly one into another.

"It is a tale." He sat up abruptly and started to wrap the
instrument in its silken covering. Kynrr might go in rags himself
but his beloved Kifongg fared much better.

"A tale," he repeated to himself as if he had a need for reassurance. "There are many tales from the old days, boy. Most of them
nonsense. It is said that there once was knowledge open to certain
of our people which is now long forgot. That there was a time
of darkness which was worse and thicker than any night across
our land. And then one Lasre went forth into the very heart of
the darkness and there he sang, and the Essence of all the land
and everything which dwelt upon it, within it, was gathered to
him so that he broke the cover of the dark. And at that time all
which lived were kin—even as you, boy, claim kinship with that
great beast of yours.

"And what will you do with him when you go on? For such
as he are hunted and slain wherever they may be found."

From time to time that same thought had troubled me. If I
picked up the caravan trail and made it into Vapala, certainly
Murri could not accompany me openly. He would be the target
of every frontier guard who sighted him.

If there was to be an answer to this it was not made plain
that day when Kynrr's yaksen returned from scrambling over the
rocks. They divided their grazing between the pool where Kynrr
had built his hut and that which lay at the side of a breakneck
ridge of rocks. This time answer did come when there was a calf
missing and his dam lingered behind, giving long, mourning cries,
pausing to look backward.

I was up on my feet, reaching for my bag of pebbles and sling, my staff already to hand. Though it was still early morning the heat was already arising from the rocks. I whistled to Murri and he appeared around a rock spur ready for action. Though it was difficult to track on the bare rock, there was only a narrow way the herd followed. I had not gone far along that before I found evidence of a rock slide, breaking off of the narrow ledge.

There was no sound from below. I crawled, belly down, as close to the edge of the depth as I dared. Having anchored my rope to one of the rock spurs, with the other end of that fastened about my middle, I swung cautiously over.

As I slid down the last portion of the rope, there came a wild squealing. The earth at the bottom of the crevice around the half-buried body of the calf was heaving. There broke through baby rats already jumping to fasten teeth in the long hair of the yaksen and pull it away from the flesh they longed for. I realized that what I had ventured into was a trap—some one of the females had established her nest underground nearby and her offspring ravenous from the moment of birth were seeking anything which they could devour.

From above I heard Murri howl a challenge and swiftly answered with my warning. There was no room in this narrow space, half choked as it was by the fall from above, for the sandcat to maneuver. We could only get in each other's way disastrously if he tried.

I backed against the nearer wall of the crevice and was using my staff. Luckily the lack of room was also a difficulty for the rats, and these were very young, though among them squirmed the body of the dam trying to head for me.

A well-placed swing of my staff bowled her over and instantly two of her own offspring were at her throat. It was then that I felt the tug of the rope against my body. But I dared not turn to face the cliff wall and so uncover my back to what was left of the ravening pack.

There came a shout and a rock sailed down from above, striking between me and the ratlings. A second rock more perilously aimed, for it nearly struck me, landed and I realized that what help from above which could be offered was on the way.

I made a last sweep with the staff, thrust that through my belt, and whirled about to face the wall. It was rough. There were plenty of finger- and toeholds, but how many of those were strong enough to take my weight? A fall might land me helpless in the midst of that pack of monsters below.

Another rock thundered by me. I forced myself to test my handholds and not be reckless in my choice. Then the rope about me grew taut and I knew that was being drawn up.

There was a blow against one of my boots, the sharp shooting pain of a tooth slash which had cut through the layers of hide as if they were the softest of skin. That was a spur which sent me reaching for a large knob of rock, giving me energy I would not have thought I would have had.

I was reaching to hook one hand over the edge of the cliff when I felt the pull of the life-saving rope loosen but I managed to make it on my own to sprawl forward.

Kynrr lay crumpled against a rock and beside him Murri was spitting out the rope. It was plain that they had united in getting me out of that trap. I crawled to Kynrr.

The old man was breathing in gusty gasps and I could see the fast rise and fall of his bare chest. Murri had moved out to meet me and was pulling at my cut boot, bringing the slashed hide away from the blood-spurting flesh beneath.

I managed to staunch that flow of blood and Murri lay licking at the wound while I saw to Kynrr. At first I believed that each of those difficult breaths was going to be the last for the old man. For a space we huddled together. Murri went back to patrol along the edge of the cliff. The loud squealing from below was silenced. It could be that the ratlings had turned on each other as they were well known to do and that we had no more to fear from them.

To get Kynrr back to his hut was a task which took far too long under the sunlight. Thin as the old man looked he was not a light weight, but somehow I managed to get his body over Murri's back. The cub was smaller than his sire but I was able to take a good portion of the weight and the bleeding on my leg had stopped. Perhaps there was indeed some virtue in licking the hurt the beast gave to a wound.

But we were both winded when we reached our goal. Luckily the algae bed was not too far away and it did not require any climbing for me to reach it. When I had recovered my strength somewhat I crept down and plastered my hurt, bringing back a supply for Kynrr in turn.

Towards nightfall the old man roused from the restless sleep which had held him throughout the day. I managed to get him to eat some of the algae, feeding him with my own hands as if he were a child. Twice, though he did not open his eyes, he carried on broken conversations with those who were with him from memory.

The longest of those dealt with Vapala, and he spoke as if his words were caresses offered to some enshrined lover. These broken pictures he so drew for me were indeed of a land far removed from the rock isles and ever-encroaching sands of my own country. He spoke of countryside covered with growing green which was not always rooted in pools, of scented woods and rich stretches of grass where yaksen and oryxen grazed in peace, where there was no hunger, no fear of storms or failures of the pools which supplied our only chance of life.

He began to sing and his voice was full. The melody he shaped brought with it a peace I had never known before.

Perhaps it was his own voice in song which brought him awake, for now his eyes opened and he focused his full sight on me.

"Of your heart kindness, desert born, let me see the coming of the stars once again." His desire to do that was very great as he levered himself up with more energy than I thought was left in his wasted body. So I hastened to help him to his favorite place on the roof of his hut and, because he always had it with him when he went so, I also brought his Kifongg to him.

He smoothed its arched sides back and forth with his hands. Then, with care, he tuned it, until he had tightened the last string and it lay across one bone-thin knee.

From his chosen place he could look out for limitless distance, if his clouded sight allowed. Now he began to point out the stars.

"There is Gurpan's Necklace—and it points to the Tree of Avor. Beyond lies the Gourd of Hinder— Mark them well." Some of the authority of the teacher returned to his voice.

"Follow the Sword, desert born—under it lies your fortune—" He hesitated and then actually cackled with a laugh which left him coughing. "Your fortune, yes. There lies Vapala. You have yet a space of the Waste to cross and that will be a testing—but not such a testing as you shall know later."

His eyes fell from the stars to me. It seemed that in the dusk they had a hint of glow, if only a hint, to be found in a sandcat.

"I do not seek Vapala." For at his words there awoke in me an uneasiness which threatened, but why or how I did not understand.

"Some men do not seek fate, that comes seeking them. Try as you will, desert son, you will discover that Vapala awaits you, twist and turn though you strive to do."

Once more he began to sing. Though the words could be understood one by one, their meaning was hidden when he fitted them together:

"Yellow bright, gold of the sun in glory,
Black as foul as the breath of death the rats serve their prey.
Mask of cat, jaw of rat—so shall it be.
One and two—a hosting of small powers, joined.
The path is set, the gate is passed—"

His voice grew weaker, was gone. Then he spoke:
"We can carry nothing with us when we return to the greatest Essence of all, save what we have made of the gifts, doubts, fears, weaknesses, and strengths with which we came. What we take lies here—and here—" He touched his forehead and then his breast.

Then he took up the Kifongg with both hands. It might have been a child of his blood, cherished and much beloved the way he held it. This he offered to me.

"Take it, desert son, return it whence it came. And say to her who waits, that the meddling is well begun and there is no turning back now."

I accepted the harp and then set it aside and took Kynrr into my arms, for he was coughing and from between his lips there dribbled a bead and then a flow of blood. As I eased him back his eyes once more sought the stars.

"There is a thought—Malquin said it once—that the stars mark other worlds. If that is true then on them men must live and die, be remembered, then forgot. Who was Kaland?" His voice grew stronger on that demand.

"I have not heard that name."

"I have not heard that name," he mimicked me. "Forgetting comes easily with the passing of seasons. Thus one who stood against the Great Dark has vanished from memory, as so *she* will, perhaps much faster, I lay this on you, desert son, by the Zancan and the Orb, by the Diamond and the Sword—"

I could not stop those words and I shivered for I did know what lay upon me now—a geas! And by the old tales the geas of a dying man was a burden no one would willingly receive.

"Get you to Vapala." His voice was fading again. "Tell—tell my lady that I have fulfilled my oath—let her see that she does likewise." His head settled back against my shoulder and there came from his lips a single clean, high note of a song which would never now be sung.

I was alone with the dead, and upon me lay the burden I could not forestall. Go to Vapala I must.

14

THERE WAS NO ESCAPING the sound throughout the city. The singing of the smaller mobiles was so much a part of our lives that we forgot they existed. But the beat and clash of the Emperor's seemed to rock the very walls about us. There was no sleep for us this night and Ravinga was putting the time when that usually held us into labor.

Around the chamber the curtain fell into place and I doubted that any of the smallest glimmer of lamplight could be sighted without. Yet there were six lamps, three set along each end of the table, and in the brilliance those gave us, not the smallest detail could be hid from notice.

Ravinga's fingers twisted and turned, handled needle, small soldering iron, tools so tiny that they were difficult to hold to their work. Beneath her hands the man doll took on shape and substance. As her last client had ordered she was busied with a mortuary doll—one of the Emperor himself.

To me she had given another task. I had never been set to work with those special chants to be spoken, those gestures to be used as I picked up one of the delicate tools or another. What I fashioned was not a man but a sandcat. The kottis of the household sat to one side watching with deep attention.

I had my guide unrolled on the table before me, each corner of that painted square held down by a carven weight. Those too were things of power. One was a replica of the Blue Leopard such as served always he who was Emperor, one was a yaksen herd cow, proud in the strength which made her guide and leader for her kind, then came a kotti carved of some very dense black stone, glassy smooth to the touch and unusually heavy for its size, the fourth a man doll, whose features were too well set to be aught but a portrait. And a likeness of one I knew—a trader about

115

whom they whispered behind their hands—that he was so lacking in manhood that his own family gave him no proper position—Hynkkel of Kahulawe.

I was twice as slow as Ravinga, for this was the first time she had set me such a task to be done by myself. It was hot in the shrouded chamber and I slipped out of my overblouse and ran the heel of my hand across my forehead as I concentrated on the miniature sandcat.

Ravinga fastened the last infinitesimal gem into the crown of the doll she worked upon. Then she turned it slowly and critically about.

Three times had I seen the Emperor close enough to mark well his features. Doll this might be, yet there was so much life caught up by Ravinga's skill that I would not have been surprised to see him slip down between her fingers and stand alive, his own master.

She stood him with care upon a block of black stone and then whirled that around with an impatient gesture so now he faced me.

"It is well?" and she meant that question to be truthfully answered. In all the years I had seen her as another pair of hands I had never before been asked my opinion of her work.

"By all I know, mistress," I replied quickly, "this is in truth an image of Haban-ji."

Now her one hand gestured but the other kept still a jealous guard between her and her masterwork.

I glanced down at what I myself had wrought. It, too, had a lifelike air to it. Almost I could feel this image looking at me measuringly as if it were indeed true one of the great menaces of our land.

"Call!" commanded my mistress.

I wet lips, desert dry, with my tongue tip, lowering my head so that my eyes were on a level with that of one image.

"Hynkkel," I named the name of the doll which stood to my right hand anchoring the cloth. "Desert warrior—"

The yellow eyes did not change. There was no sound of an answer—had I expected such? Using one of the small tools I still held as a pointer, I spoke again, quietly but not allowing myself to be denied.

"Enter!"

It was the desert cat, stretching as might one of the kottis—its front legs spread outward, its hind quarters stiff, again as a kotti before padding out on a nighttime prowl. It moved from the center of the cloth and there was something lightsome about its fur which matched a bit of the ancient markings on the skin it had rested upon as I worked.

Ravinga was not through with either it or me. Once more she turned the figure of the Emperor Haban-ji, now to face the beast I had wrought.

She had whipped up from behind her a length of fine silk embroidered with silver leopards and swung that swatch about the Emperor doll, hiding it from view. I had no more the feeling that the doll was what he seemed—that which had been life in him had departed.

The same was not so of the cat. Its head turned as it looked to the image of Hynkkel. One could believe that there passed between them some spark of communication. Ravinga reached forth across the table and caught up that miniature of the Kahulawen.

She put him down beside the cat and eyed the pair narrowly as if she was searching for one small error in craftsmanship.

Then again she gave her order in a single word:

"Speak!"

"Hynkkel," I obeyed. I was still and tense, disliking this thing that was not of my willing. She had taken me, I saw clearly over the years, to establish her will, overriding mine. This carried the bite of old anger. Yet she never appeared to sense that I was not one of her tools, to be discarded at will and reused again at a whim.

I saw the thin shadow of a smile about her lips. Whatever game she played Ravinga surely believed that she had it under her full control.

Long back during the years I had spent with Ravinga I had learned that there was time one did not ask questions. What she did in the privacy of the back of her shop was secret and often I never knew what it was. I studied her now with some of the same old unvoiced demand as she was turning on the doll Hynkkel and the sandcat I had wrought. The heat of the room was more oppressive. Still I did not believe that she felt it.

Then putting man image and beast one together in the middle of the table, she brought forward the wrapped replica of the Emperor.

Opening up the small box of minute gems, from which she could reproduce in miniature the heavy jewelry of state, she thrust the end of her most delicate tool into the massed bits of color and then lifted it out, a thread of chain dangling from it. Pendant from that was a tiny mate to that cat mask which she had given to the feckless young man at the trading square almost a quarter of a season back.

She dropped the circlet of that thread-thin chain over the manikin's head and sat him, so adorned, to face the Emperor whom she had unwrapped. Game—this was some game. Bits and pieces I had witnessed, words overheard here and there, they drew together in my mind.

The old puzzle was at the root of it. Who—what was Ravinga? She made no parade of any arts beyond what anyone might see, her use as a maker of dolls. Yet there was much more—very much more.

I had come to her not with any real hope drawing me to her household. For nightmare days and demon-ridden nights I had been hunted. And I knew just how much I was worth to any astute enough to break my disguise and spy me out.

When I was very small I had made a great discovery for myself. If I believed myself unseen, undetected, then it appeared that was the truth. First my nursemaid, and then old Vastar, my tutor in things suitable for a maiden of any House, could pass within touching distance and yet see me not.

Because I was a child in a household of adults, and ancient adults—the lady ruler being my grandmother twice over—I went much my own way.

Six Houses ruled Vapala and, through the Emperor and their support of him, they ruled our whole known world. Not outwardly, but in devious ways of their own. I was sure that the very deviousness of their dealings with each other gave them a cold yet intense pleasure.

Below the six, there were the twelve. More ambitious these, and more active outwardly, for they yearned to see their House standard set as near to the square before the palace of the rulers as possible. They had promise of gaining such heights. It had been done so far three times in our slow-moving history.

The twenty and five came next. And they were the doers, those who fought more openly for place. Among them it was not unusual for the Head of a House to challenge an equal, knowing that survivors in such a constant hidden war were the winners. These hunted for unusual powers and sought out knowledge long since forgotten.

There had been one such House lady under the banner of my line, and she had set herself up against the ruler of her own House, dooming it to extinction. I was nameless and clanless. No one in the whole of Vapala had so before brought to naught as old and mighty a House.

Ravinga bore a twisted scar across her shoulder which she ever concealed with a scarf. That brand I owed her recompense for.

From the first she gave me an established position in Vapala. For, having declared before the council that I was her chosen apprentice, I was removed from the wreckage of the House and even out of the ranks of the nobility, which did not bother me in the least.

My education was strict and I was put to learning things which a year or so earlier I would have argued did not exist. I discovered that, just as within the Houses there are intrigues, so did veiled action continue elsewhere, not only in Vapala but in all the queendoms. It was very much a matter of not accepting the surface but relying on one's knowledge of what lay below.

Now it would appear that my education was to be furthered. Ravinga planted her elbows together on the table and cupped her chin in the palms of her hands, her attention now on the two images, man and cat.

"Last season," she began abruptly, "there came one from Azhengir, a trader of salt, the one I told you afterward to keep well in mind."

I remembered clearly the woman she meant, hard as a lump of her own dusky wares, her skin dried and chapped, her eyes buried in protecting wrinkles raised against the shifting, smarting dust of her country. She had walked into Ravinga's shop with the sure tread of an expected visitor, though I had never seen her before.

Once inside she had done an unusual thing, dropping the heavy butt of her traveler's staff against the door so that it denied entrance to any following her.

She had shrugged off her pack, giving a wheezing cough as she set it down.

Then as if she had seen Ravinga only an hour before, she said:

"I've come—the waiting is done with." She had made a gesture before her breast as if tracing some symbol there. A twitch of the rope which fastened her backpack together followed and the hide cover, rimmed with crystals of salt, opened stiffly.

My hand had gone for my knife and then a moment later I
knew that no active defense was needed. The thing crouched
stiffly within her pack was truly dead.

Much of the body was gone, showing a lattice of bones, but the
head, frozen in a snarl, was still intact. I have many times seen
the bodies of sand rats, had even fought against them and had
drops of their dark, sour blood eat into my flesh. But this dead
creature was many times larger than the only ones of its kind I
had ever seen.

Also the skull was misshapen with a high dome of forehead as
if to give room to a man's bulk of brain.

"I see." Ravinga made no attempt to draw closer to the displayed creature. "This came from whence?"

"Our caravan was attacked just at the border of the Plain. And
there were four such as this which kept its fellows at battle to the
end. Since the Fire Dawn there have been no changes in men or
beast—though they tell us that before that time there were such
unchancy things. The winds blow, the storms strike, caravans are
lost, our kind dies for one reason or another. Why else were we
given wardenship of the Waste in the far times but that we watch
for such?"

Ravinga shook her head. She spread her hands wide as if she
would measure something invisible to us. "What do I know,
Bissa?"

The woman showed her crooked teeth. "Ask rather what you
do not, Voice. But the time grows short, I think. I have heard that
the Emperor fails."

Ravinga nodded.

"How long since we have had a Watchment for the ruling?
Perhaps we should ask that?"

"There is no way of influencing the choice."

"They tell us that the Emperor must be the Essence of our
countries if we would stand tall, unbroken. And the people have
some rights—"

Ravinga's eyes had narrowed then and she had spoken coldly.

"They need demand no answers from me. I am only a watcher—"

"See that you be more when the time comes," the other had
answered and began to rewrap her package.

Ravinga had spoken once more. "For the time there is no one
we can appeal to. Watcher, that I am, yes. And perhaps can be
more when the time comes." But the woman had picked up her

burden and gone quickly without glancing at the dollmaker again. Nor, to my knowledge, had she ever returned. And surely Ravinga had never mentioned her again.

"What would she have you do?" I asked, daring as I never had before.

Ravinga shrugged. "Perhaps she herself could not have said. One cannot fight mist and shadows with steel of knife or spear. However, the seasons have turned, Haban-ji is dead, and now we must look to another. He comes, oh, yes, he comes! There shall be changes in plenty." She picked up a strip of crimson silk and tore it in two with jerks, wrapping half about the man and the other half about the sandcat. I needed no spoken word of hers to dismiss me.

15

MURRI AND I made what preparations we could for continuing our journey. Though all my instincts were to cling to the land to which I was bound by birth, as is the molding of my kind, yet it became more and more apparent that perhaps Kynrr had been right, I would best cut free from a past which no longer held anything for me and begin such breaking of bonds by going to Vapala, which, like or agree with the belief or not, we of the outerlands accepted as the paramount center of our being.

At least I knew by Kynrr's drilling how to reach the nearest caravan trail and we would not be striking out too blindly. Though how long a journey we faced I could not reckon.

Kynrr's hut formed his burial place and I worked as carefully as I might to seal it past any entrance of rats or storms. I took nothing from it save two water bottles and the Kifongg which the bard had given me and which I would cherish, not only for the fineness of workmanship but also because it kept alive when I held it all the close companionship I had shared with its owner. Kynrr's stories were now sealed into my memory and, while my voice could not even echo the glory which had once been his, I had a number of ballads which he had taught me. Though coming out of nowhere, and with no patron to speak for me, I could not hope to be accepted as more than the humblest of tavern bards in Vapala.

I gave careful tending to the six yaksen that formed Kynrr's small herd. Made sure they were carefully groomed, their hooves inspected for any cracking and then well smeared with rat fat. The algae pool was a small one but its harvest would be entirely theirs after our going. Murri was making sure of that, systematically clearing out all the rats, and showing me new skills in such hunting. Their stringy meat went onto drying lines and their hides used to cobble together foot covering.

I had selected Bialle, the oldest of the cow yaksen, for our beast of burden. She was calfless, perhaps past the time of bearing, but her senses were still acute and she was well trained as a sentinel for the herd.

Also she must remember best the ways of the trail. Once so trained any beast that had been of the caravans would fall naturally again into the journey patterns. With her broad back for burdens we could hope to carry far more in the way of supplies.

I had lost measurement of time—my illness among the sandcats might have lasted a number of days' duration. However, the season of storms could not be too much longer delayed.

Along the marked trader trails there were shelters set up for the protection of travelers. Once pointed along one of those roads, what safety this land knew could be counted upon. Still I could find one reason or another each day to keep me there, away from the actual carrying out of the choice I had made.

I had baled up a good amount of dried algae cakes and gone over again all my equipment. That evening when I visited the yaksen for a final check, I stroked each animal, speaking to it, though its language I did not know. Mainly I did this for the comfort it gave to me to hear my own voice. Murri had been casting out from the isle on prowling of his own kind.

His impatience was growing and I knew that I would not be able to delay much longer. Thus we set forth from our refuge, Murri scouting ahead, I matching my speed more to the plodding of Bialle.

I watched the stars, steering the course Kynrr had sketched out for me earlier. His Kifongg rode in its own soft casing on top of Bialle's load. We crossed a short strip of sand in no time and found ourselves once more treading sharp pebbles. Bialle also wore boots to protect her hooves but I discovered that her greater weight made those wear out the quicker. At the end of the first night's travel when we set up camp, extending my very badly worn cloak with the quilted patchwork of rat hide, I checked all our footwear and discovered that I must indeed reshoe the yaksen.

This open land under the full light of the sun was a torment which grew every day. I had thought that we could be not far from the caravan route Kynrr had spoken of—yet, though I checked the stars, and Murri scouted a wide fan of countryside ahead, we came across no suggestion of a trail. Murri and I might have made better time together. I began to wonder uneasily if I had made a mistake in bringing Bialle, even though the amount of supplies she could carry was an advantage. Her hooves cut through the hide coverings now in half a period of travel and our own supplies for the gear we needed to keep from going lame were fast being used.

Sometimes I wondered if I were deceiving myself, if Murri also suffered from some evil in this land, which forced us to go in circles and that we had not in truth traveled any distance. Though the isle of Kynrr's exile was out of sight.

To push on was more and more of an effort. The flesh melted from us and sometimes the smallest of acts came as an almost unsurmountable burden.

It was on our sixth day after leaving Kynrr's isle, or so my stumbling thoughts counted, that misfortune struck, as hard as if we had lain between its paws from the start of our journey and now it tired of the game and would put an end to it.

Bialle no longer walked at her steady pace; rather she staggered from side to side, her heavy head but two palms' height from the rough ground. Now and then she uttered complaints which were like a man's sigh increased a hundredfold. She needed frequent rests and I would stand panting beside her. Murri I had not seen since that start of this night.

A yowling cry of fear aroused me. That it was Murri in difficulties I had no doubt. But where? By what could he be menaced to bring such a cry from him? For if he were prepared to give battle his voice would not have held that wild appeal.

Bialle bellowed, swung her heavy head, and moved forward at a stagger but I was in front of her, though the treacherous footing slowed me. Then we were on the edge of a slight hollow. Almost this had the general shape and size of one of the algae pools. Out in the depression Murri was struggling, more than half of his body gripped by one of the worst of the land's traps, a hidden sucking patch which gulped greedily anything unfortunate to come within its borders.

From where Murri flailed, trying to find some firm land, there came puffs of foul stench as if indeed it were the mouth of a living creature and not the ground itself which struggled to engulf him.

I shrugged off my small pack and loosened the coils of rope.

"Murri," I used the cat sounds as well as my human voice could utter them, "do not struggle—you break the crust all the more. Be ready, take up the rope when it reaches you."

I fastened the end hurriedly to Bialle and pointed her away from that hidden trap. Then, lying belly down, searching the ground for any mark which might guide me, I wriggled forward, my staff holding a loop made from the other end of the rope. My hands shook from the effort of keeping that above the grip of the sucker pot, and yet close enough to the surface to make sure Murri could reach it.

He had stopped his wild threshing about. However, his fear was as plain as the stench which set us to coughing. My eyes watered and stung from the fumes and I had to keep blinking out the tears which made my vision waver.

"Bialle—Var!" I shouted the herd cry which the yaksen were trained to obey. She gave a second bellow but she was moving, if only at a clumsy, tottering pace.

Now it would depend upon me. I had once seen this type of rescue when on the trail. There was so little time. The sandcat was submerged now nearly to his chin. I angled the staff and it shook back and forth in my hand though I summoned all my strength to hold it straight.

Murri made a sudden desperate twist of his head and a second later the rope snapped taut along the staff. I pulled that back and the rope, shaking free, was still tight and stiff.

Dropping the staff, I edged around so that the part of the rope in my hands was now across my shoulder. It was a struggle to get to my feet without losing grip on that but I made it, though the power of the sucking pulled me backward as if to join me in Murri's danger.

"Var! Var!" It was more of a breathless cry than a shout of encouragement. But the rope tightened yet more as the yaksen gave her strength so we pulled together.

Though Murri was little more than half grown he was certainly heavier than I. His compact body, even thinned as it was by privation, was still too much for me to draw free by my own. I could only hope that Bialle's ability to pull, developed as her breed had been used for generations to drag carts along the trails, would provide the extra power we must have.

I slipped to my knees once, skinning my legs on the sharp pebbles, but, by fortune, the shock did not make me lose that hold on the rope. There was no longer in me breath enough to call to the yaksen.

Back! I was being drawn back! I dared not waste time nor effort to look over my shoulder to see how near I now was to surface of which I could be sure.

"Var!" No shout this time but a dry-mouthed whisper. However, as if Bialle could hear that, she gave a sudden lurch ahead and I threw myself into aiding the pull.

For the space of several hard-drawn breaths we kept on. Then the rope was not so taut ahead. It was as if Bialle could no longer maintain the extra effort which had won us so far.

The fumes from the sucking pot were stronger and a racking cough reached my ears from behind. Although—if Murri held the rope in his fangs as I believed, that might endanger all our efforts. Yet the rope was still drawing against my shoulder, chafing through the clothing I wore to erode the skin below.

"Bialle—" I called that beseechingly. I knew that I was very close to the limit of my last surge of strength. The hard traveling of the past days had taken its toll of all of us.

Once more the rope ahead stiffened, there was a forceful pull, and I added to it as I stumbled on. There was a sudden sharp give from behind.

"Murri!" My cry was more a scream. The loosing of that bond had brought me once more to my knees. I must force myself to look back, to accept the fact that our best had not been enough, and all that strength, beauty and lightness of spirit which had been my companion was swallowed up in foulness.

Somehow I made myself make that turn to look.

There was a black blot against the faint glimmer on the ground. Part of it moved feebly from side to side, then eyes opened and were lamps to guide me.

"Murri!" I flung myself toward him, my rope-burned hands catching fur matted with the evil-smelling substance of the trap.

"Brother kin—" The words were only a rumble in his throat. He was still fighting to rise and I added my strength to his, getting him somehow to his feet. Then we wavered and weaved back well away from that place of death to collapse together.

Just as Murri's cry for help had urged me on before, now did a low beast moan pull me upright again. There was infinite pain in that—could this whole countryside have been hollowed by such traps and the yaksen now caught in turn? To free her would be impossible.

I crawled to the top of that rise which formed a rim around the sucking pit and saw a large bulk staggering ahead. Praise Essence, she was not caught in one of those fearsome pits.

No, she was not a prisoner. Still this treacherous land had dealt her a death blow. She was struggling to get to her feet as I reached

her, but that was impossible, for it was plain that she had broken
a foreleg, that some one of those punishing rolling stones had
brought her down.

She turned her head to look at me. Yaksen eyes by night did
not hold the gleam of those of the cats but I felt her pain and
knew her despair. That we could hope to heal her here was beyond
possibility.

"Bialle." I knelt beside her, my hand smoothing the heavy
mane fur about her ears, scratching and smoothing as I did
when grooming, actions which always relaxed the great creatures.
"Bialle, Great One, Strong One. For such as you there is pride.
Great One, open wide your heart, let in the essence of the land,
of the spirit, be one with the land and with all living things. Pain
shall go and that which is truly Bialle shall be free, even as is all
life when the time comes—"

As I spoke I loosed my knife. Might the spirit of all this land
be with me so that I did not falter but would strike true. Though
I could not see their glow I knew that her eyes were turned upon
me and that she knew what I would do and welcomed it as the
kindness of one who had never wished her anything but good.

In the past I had done this as herdsman and always was it like
a second blow struck deep into me.

"Bialle," I held my voice steady as I would when leading her
to a full pool and fresh growth within it, "go free!"

I struck the blow with all the strength I could summon, hoping
that it would need only one to loose this valiant friend. By fortune's favor it was enough.

But still I crouched beside her, drawing my fingers through her
sand-matted coat. Freedom from all the ills of life, yes, I must
look at it so. Her patience and her last life gift would ever set her
sharp in my memory.

There was a rattling of pebbles. I looked around. Murri was
belly down pulling himself along, by one paw outstretched and
then the other, to join me. When he reached the body he lifted
his head and gave forth a squalling cry.

16

I TRY TO SHUT OUT of memory that last gift which Bialle had for us. It followed the rigid custom of travelers and yet it was such that no one can lightly take, nor is it spoken of among us who have wandered far. We are assured that we are all linked, not only to the life about us, but to the very land on which we live. Therefore if one life or body may serve another, then that is the proper following of what may be demanded of us. Thus I put my knife to a second purpose, one so against my wish that I fought down revulsion even as I doggedly worked. Though I sensed it was not so to Murri.

Bialle had been one with us, yet he accepted, as was true of all his kind, that that which was the inner part of her had departed and what was left behind was no longer to be considered a trail comrade. That he would think my squeamishness to be a flaw I knew.

At least we need not fear that the scent of death and meat would draw rats down upon us. This land was too bitter and barren, not even the sandcats would range this far.

I sorted out our gear and made packs as large as we could carry, Murri, despite his loathing, having to again bear one.

So when the time came that we must stagger on, we bore with us that last food and moisture we could hope to find—unless I could discover the trail Kynrr pointed me to. I had not discarded his Kifongg though it was perhaps foolish of me to cling to such as part of my burden. Now I strove to keep off the demons of despair by humming and thinking of all the old bard had spread before me as a source of knowledge. If—when—I reached Vapala I would need his information to serve me until I did find some labor.

Still, how could I who had been but a servant, a herdsman, a family trader for a people considered by the mesa dwellers to be primitive barbarians, hope to find some outlet for my future? The traders' guilds would be closed to me as a single tradesman with no link to any House. If all the stories of Vapala were true, the inhabitants were more strictly allied to House clans than even my people, and there would be little welcome for outsiders.

I tasted dust and with it an ever-growing despair. Still there was not that in me which would allow me to sit in this dreary wilderness and wait for death to come. As long as I could move, I realized that I would place one stumbling foot before the other and shuffle along.

The stars I steered by were there but certainly I could not be sure, having periods of dizziness from time to time, that I was still on my course. The constant rustle of the shifting sands—

Rustle of the sands! But there was no sand! I came to a halt and looked about me, aroused from that haze of fatigue and self-pity which had near overcome me.

The harsh pebble footing was gone. We were back in the cushioning of true sand. I looked about me, fully alert now.

Thus I saw the light a little to the east. From there carried also the distant scream of an ill-tempered oryxen, an answer to that as sharp and warning. I turned a little and was able to plod faster, even though my bruised feet sank sometimes ankle deep in that very welcome sand. I could only be heading for a camp—

Traders? For that I could hope. That there were others who hung about the edges of the Waste was also true. However, if I had indeed found the trail, those would be wary about approaching a track which was constantly patrolled by the scouts of Kahulawe.

Murri dropped back, flanking me now instead of forging ahead, and I realized that, while I might be traveling towards safety and help, it was not so for a sandcat. Too long had our species been at enmity with one another. He growled and I knew that that same thought was shared by him.

First light and then sound! There were voices singing. I could not separate the words as yet but the tune I knew well. It was a traditional one much liked by the traders, and each party seemed to have their own version, for they added verses concerning their own ventures and any strange thing which they had noted or endured during that trip.

Then that sound was suddenly overlaid, drowned out—the beat of drums—storm? I threw myself forward, digging in with my staff to pull myself along at a faster gait, hoping to reach the trail safety offered by the camp ahead before wilderness struck at us. Then I realized the distant beat of that warn drum was different. What message could be of such importance that the drums only used for the greatest warning would be set to beating out this different pattern?

The singing in the camp had ended. Yet still the drum, distant, kept on. Now that rhythm was picked up by the order drum of the traders, transmitting the news, that it might be carried on through the night as was always done.

"Ssseeeeeeee!" the traditional hail of the traders came as the drum ended. Some sentry had sighted me.

Though my own travels had heretofore been limited to the short trails, I knew well the answer I must give. My throat and mouth were so dry that I found it hard to raise above a choked answer.

"Kkkaalawwa—" The recognition of my own people. I knew, however, that I would be under close observation until I reached the open light of the fire and that there would be those casting to be sure that I answered with a truthful sign.

Again that drum in the distance had taken up a steady beat. Not a storm warning, not even the former message, but a second I could not translate, warning against some uprising of outlaws?

The outermost limit of the fire touched me, by the way of torches upheld by two women, swords out and ready, but with their brands in the other hand. They were of my own people and one I knew.

"Kinsha-va-Guara!" I hailed her crack-voiced.

"Who out of the night bespeaks my name?" I saw that her grasp on sword hilt had tightened. She was peering at me and I realized what a strange and perhaps even frightening apparition I must be, in my rent clothes, my back bowed under my pack, the marks of my ordeals upon me. And there was also Murri—

"Klaverel-va-Hynkkel—and Murri—" I spoke the cat's name even as he was of us. "I have come from my solo—"

"Bringing death on four feet with you? That is a thing which has no meaning—" She relaxed none of her forbidding stance and her companion moved a little to her right so that if there was an attack she would be ready to give battle from another angle.

"I bring a comrade with whom I have faced death and to whom I owe my life. We are brothers by blood oath" (indeed the ceremony which Maraya had used was enough like a swordsbrother's life essence sharing to be termed that). "There is no death threat from us, trail mistress."

She stood staring at the two of us for a moment and then gestured us ahead with the torch, still holding her weapon in plain sight. I moved forward and Murri also, keeping close beside me. I was sure that the sandcat was not in any way afraid of any attack, being fully confident of his own strength. However, wariness was well bred into his kind.

"Off this!" he mouthed at me, giving a hard shake to his body to dislodge the pack he was wearing. That he hated the necessity of such service I well knew and appearing before strangers so beladen was highly hurtful to his pride. There was no reason why I should so humiliate him thus. I leaned down and cut the thongs so he was able to allow it to slip to the sands.

That second strange beating of the warn drum had died away, but its message was being echoed by the drum of the caravan. So we could exchange no more talk with that in our ears as we entered the heart of the camp.

There was an ingathering of the traders. As was often common among my people these were women. They have always been good at the task and early made it theirs. The color of their fringed tents was touched to brightness by fire globes, proving this party rich enough to transport such travel luxuries. While their own clothing might be the drab stuff worn by travelers, their profusion of gemmed belts, headbands, bracelets, necklets made them appear as wealthy as the Vapalans.

She who had questioned me motioned again to the center tent and there I saw the drummer, her hands flying as she struck with the flat of her palms. Behind her was an older woman, one who, by her wealth of jewelry, which she wore with pride and taste, must be the leader of this caravan, though it would be made up from several small groups, each commanded by the most experienced among them.

She I knew also. This was Elwene Karafa, truly a mistress of far trails who regularly made a full journey through the queendoms, gathering produce of each along the way and then heading for the great market of Vapala by the year's end.

I allowed my pack to slip from my bruised shoulders and thrust my staff deep into the sand, resting both hands on it. Murri swung his heavy head from side to side and, apparently deciding there was nothing to fear for the moment, flopped down beside me,

"Klaverel-va-Hynkkel," I announced myself. "Murri of the furred ones."

The drum sound had stopped and there was silence so that I could be easily heard and I added:

"To Elwene Karafa be all good fortune. May the trade be rich, the trail easy, and no storm of land or trouble strike her path."

I met her regard squarely. She looked from me to Murri, her eyes widening a little as she met his golden ones, and then her gaze shifted once more to me.

"What do you on the trails, not-warrior?"

Not-warrior. Instead of making me feel shame this time, I found myself able to hold my temper steady. It was the truth, was it not? I came from a warrior house but the sword was not mine for the taking. I knew well that the tittle-tattle of the feastings had dealt thoroughly with me who was counted a disgrace to his House.

"I have come from my solo, Lady."

She continued to study me and then she turned her head abruptly and spoke to the older of the two women who had brought me in.

"This one came out of the Waste?"

"That is so."

Now I suffered her regard again. "I think there is a tale in this. Trail welcome to you, Hynkkel, and also to this companion of yours. Yes, truly a tale lies behind this. A night of wonders to be sure. First we hear the death notes of the Emperor's passing, and long has he reigned. Then comes the summons for the testing. Yes, a night of wonders. Guest rights be yours, and later we must hear this tale."

Once they had accepted me, it was as if I had always traveled with this train. Food in quantities and of the best possible obtainable when marching was set before me, and a goodly supply of well-dried meat, not the rat flesh which had been his fare for so long, was given Murri. At first the traders were wary of approaching the sandcat and I fed him from the huge bowl they had placed before him before themselves withdrawing to some distance. When they could see that he communicated directly with me they drew closer, watching us both as if we were entertainers on our way to some feasting.

It was the caravan leader who showed no sign that this was more than any meeting which might happen along the trail, seating herself as my hostess within such reach as she could pass to me at the ending of the meal a bowl of the dried fruits which were such a rarity that the very offering of such established me in good standing in her sight.

I searched for some comment with which to begin a conversation, since, to plunge into the tale of my own adventures so baldly, without a second invitation, was beyond the bound of good manners.

"The Emperor dies—" I thought of Kynrr and what he had told me of the court at Vapala, of the bedazzling throngs who gathered there, always mindful of the least wish of the man, who, by his own endeavor, achieved the rulership. No one came to the Leopard Throne without undergoing such trials as would make even a warrior as seasoned as my father consider well. The struggle of one in solo was as nothing compared to that one who aspired to rule must face.

The late Emperor had been young when he had stood in the center of the Great Mobile and so triumphantly claimed his reward. He had reigned before I was born, and all I knew of his deeds were what had been repeated and repeated as news spreading out from Vapala.

He had been of the House of Vars, not one of the Great Houses of Vapala, but of the second rank. By custom he went without an official mate but stories had related his temporary arrangement with women from the Great Houses and even, when he was in the powers of mid-life, with the Ruby Queen. He had offspring, only the birthing charts knew how many, but Kynrr several times repeated in stories of the glittering past that most of his get had been daughters, only one son living to full manhood. That was Shank-ji. And Kynrr's tale of him was that, past all custom, he had several times openly said that he would try in the testing.

"The Emperor is dead," Elwene agreed. Taking up a pinch of sand between two fingers, she tossed it over her shoulder. "He was old, but in his time he did well enough."

Certainly faint praise for the ruler of the outer lands. Yet Kynrr, with all his detailed memories of the court, had never retailed any outstanding feat, save that Haban-ji had been able to keep down the eternal struggles for hidden power which had convulsed Vapala several times in the past. The Great Houses no longer reached for advancement by the way of sword and spear and the gathering of armed warriors. However, their many intrigues continued.

Though the trial for the Leopard Throne was open to all from every one of the queendoms, for several generations now the winner had been out of Vapala and it had become accepted by those of that nation they had first right to it.

I had listened to the talk of my brother's comrades, even to some of the discussions in my father's great room when he had guests of his generation. This matter of Vapala's supremacy was moving, through the years, from a small grievance to a major one. There would be champions from every nation and should Shank-ji triumph there might well be trouble among the restless, power-hunting young men.

We had so long been at such peace as to not need warriors, save for the patrolling of the trade routes, that men of martial tastes found little way of discharging their energy.

"It will be an interesting testing—" Elwene smoothed the stuff of her richly patterned cloak across her knee. "Some deem that the leopard has too often stood guard for a man of Vapala. I hear that this son of Haban-ji thinks to change the course of custom. We shall see. Now, brother of the trails, tell us your tale, which can be no common one—"

So I launched into my own story and perhaps some of the coaching of Kynrr came to the fore, for I found myself moving at times from the common speech into the rhythm of a bard—having indeed enough to deal with for the fashioning of any bard's song, even if it dealt only with the actions of one who was deemed a failure.

The dawn had well arrived when I finished the last of that story. They had all gathered to hear it. Only at times sentries to be relieved coming in and their comrades going out on station. But the newcomers settled down, eating as they listened.

Elwene nodded when I was finished at last. "Surely a venture unlike any other we have heard tell of. Perhaps, man of Kahulawe, you should be the one to stand for our land in the testing. It would seem that fortune has favored you many times over."

I shook my head. "Fortune favors no one for long. I have no desire to reach for any crown." At that moment I could not conceive of anything I wanted less. Though, a small inner amusement stirred, I was indeed at present a man without any work which was mine.

"At least if you plan to go to Vapala," Elwene said, "you are welcome to ride with us."

That offer I could accept and did so eagerly.

17

THERE WERE NEAR a hundred dolls laid out on the table before my mistress—each a replica of Emperor Haban-ji in his coronation robes—all ordered to be delivered as soon as possible. The Great Houses of Vapala would pay honor to their late ruler in the formal and proper manner—by placing one such in display in their gathering rooms. At the accession of each new Emperor such were prepared to await the call. These had waited for more years than I, myself, had to count. Haban-ji had reigned for a long time—

Ravinga inspected each minutely for any deterioration brought about by years of storage. I noted that she withdrew four, taking them into the workroom. Though she had pointed out to me no reason for repairs as she usually did, to increase my knowledge in such matter.

Now she brought them back and fitted them in their proper place in line. Within a chime time the stewards of each House would be calling to pick them up and transport them with due reverence to their proper niches in different halls.

As Ravinga laid them down she was frowning and once they were out of her hands, she stood, fingers pinching her lower lip, which signaled, for her, deep thought. Then she glanced at me side-eyed, and crooked a finger so I joined her on the other side of the table.

"Girl, are these in proper order? Need they any changes?"

I was a little agape at that question, for we had inspected them together last night when we had taken them out of storage and then to me they had seemed intact. I had not even caught the minute flaws which had led her to the morning's work. Obediently, I drew up a stool and seated myself. Taking up each doll in turn, I gave it the most searching inspection I could make. Then I paused and picked up a second doll, to hold it comparingly beside the one I had just taken, studying first one and then the other.

Haban-ji had not been portrayed in these as the man of many years that he had been when he died, rather as one in his full prime as he had been when he first ascended the Leopard Throne. He had been a noted hunter and patrol officer of native Vapala stock, the son of one of the middle-status Houses. Thus he was presented in the two dolls I now held. Yet there grew plainer and plainer to me that there was a subtle difference between the two.

The stance and the magnificent robes, the crown worn by both with a certain prideful arrogance—those were alike as far as I could determine to the last tiny jewel, the last stitch.

It was the facial expression, I decided. The one I had first taken had the impassive features of a doll, an image meant to depict a real personage and doing that faithfully. But the second doll's eyes—there was a spark deep in them! Also I could believe that they were observing me as intently as I was studying them!

The first doll I laid down but the other I kept to hand for comparison as I examined the others. At last I had lying to one hand those dolls which Ravinga had taken into her workroom and each had the same peculiarity, living eyes!

Pushing back a little from the table to look up at my mistress, I had questions but I did not know how to frame them. That what I had discovered had some important meaning I was very sure. Yet I schooled myself to wait, for I had learned long since that Ravinga parted with knowledge at her own time and by her own choice of methods.

When she did not speak I was driven by curiosity (had she not asked me to make this discovery?) to say:

"The eyes, mistress. They might be all-seeing—"

"Just so, just so. And for good reason!"

However, she did not seem inclined to add to that assertion. Instead she turned and reached down two other figures from a shelf behind. Both of these she held out, not as if I were to accept them, but rather for me to only look. And those I knew.

There was the sandcat and the youth from Kahulawe. The same two she had evoked during that ceremony days ago. They, too, appeared to have living eyes.

"Come, there is yet much to be done."

I got up and followed her into the workroom. There she settled in her high cushioned chair where she spent so many absorbed hours. Settling the two figures before her, she opened a small box which had been standing to one side. Many tools were stored in similar cases in the workshop and I knew well the use of all of them, had held most in my hands. However, these she brought out now were needle delicate, and were of some substance unlike those we used commonly. They were a milky white until she took them up, then from the place where her fingers touched there spread a threadlike streak of blood red, suffusing the whole of the handling rods until they glimmered as if lit from within.

Picking up the sandcat, she settled the figure in a small padded vise which would hold it immobile. With her blood-fused needle tool she probed into the head just above the nape of the neck. The tool was turning white again as if the color drained in some fashion into the head of the cat.

As she did so she uttered words I, too, had learned, though I had not been instructed in their meaning. Each craft has its own mysteries and there are certain patterns of action which each creator uses to seal her work. I had always thought it a matter of wishing good fortune on one's labors and that formality I was well attuned to believe.

When the tool Ravinga held was completely white again she freed the sandcat and set it to one side. Then she arose and motioned me to take her place, much to my surprise. As she leaned across my shoulder to set the likeness of Hynkkel into the vise she spoke:

"Matters will move fast. There is dire trouble ahead, Allitta. I am not an old woman grumbling at senile faces. Nor are you completely what you believe yourself to be. There is that in the Essence forming, the wholeness of our being which at times seeks out those who will best serve its purposes. You would have come into my household in any case, for I saw in you the skills needed. But there are other skills which can be sensed but must be more subtly studied and honed, as one polishes a weapon or a tool. Those you have also.

"Now comes close the time when those who hunt will sound the drums and those unprepared will be the hunted. We must prepare for such battles as our people have near forgotten. The musty intrigue between House and House, as vile and bitter as it often has been, is as nothing compared to that coming upon us.

"Here." She held out to me the same tool she had used on the sandcat doll. "Do you also to this one as you saw me do. Use the care you would with the setting of a small jewel—you have such dexterity in your hands and you have been well trained. Do as you saw me do!"

I knew that this was no time for questions. There was arising within me an excitement which was usually the result of my carrying out some very delicate piece of work, as if I and I only could do this properly.

Leaning forward I studied the doll. The hair was looped up in the usual knot of one who does not wear a ceremonial wig, and that neck, which I could easily have snapped with my fingers, fully exposed. I glanced at the tool: as it had in Ravinga's hold, so now it was red again. My fingers tingled. It was as if something of my own was feeding into that tube, that a kind of strength I had not known I possessed was being drawn upon.

I pressed the tip into the proper point on the back of that very small head. It slipped in easily for a fraction and I felt that strange drawing growing the stronger. Then I knew that whatever task I had to perform was done—the needle rod was clear and there was now a lifeless feel, as if it were only a tool and not linked in any way with me. So I took it forth.

Ravinga set free the doll and placed it together with the cat. I slid out of the seat and she retook her place there. She placed a fingertip on the head of each figure and closed her eyes for a long moment and then nodded.

"So far it moves as it should. We must prepare for visitors and for what those shall bring." Drawing a deep breath she leaned back in her chair. Her hands were now clasped under her chin and she looked straight ahead.

"It begins, at last it begins!" There was a note in her voice which I associated with a demand for deliberate action. It was as if she could fashion time itself to her pattern even as she did her dolls.

Well fed and with the warmth of acceptance of those who, if they were not kin, were yet of my own land, I settled in to sleep. There was yet the long trek into Vapala before us, though the excitement which gripped the caravan at the thought of the coming assembly at the capital had begun to flower in me also. Vapala had been for so many years a storied place that the chance to see this proudest and wealthiest of the queendoms was something to look forward to.

Yet it was not Vapala, or even the trail ahead of us, which twisted my dreaming that night. Once more I stood in a strange room, one different from any I had ever seen. The walls rose into a darkness so far overhead that I could not distinguish any ceiling in that gloom. They also stood far from the surface on which I stood. Around me were great boxes and coffers, some taller than I and many nearly as large as my small dwelling at home.

I was not alone. Murri stood by me, as still as if he listened for some faint sound which would release him eager for a hunt. What I saw above me were great twin orbs of a silver brightness, and these were set in a vast expanse—

A face! So great a face that for me the features could not easily be fitted together. It was as if some craftsman had turned the whole of an islet into a single giant head—not that of a boundary cat but of a human. The eyes moved, blinked.

That I was the object of their survey was very obvious. I strove to move. There was that in that regard which I found vaguely threatening. Yet I was as frozen in place as if I, too, were a fashioned thing and not of flesh, blood, and bone.

Then I strove to speak to Murri. But that power had been taken from me also. I was a mind, an awareness, locked into an image.

"You will come—" I had expected any voice from that vast overhang of face would roar like thunder—but this was no true voice. It was an order which flashed into my mind. "You will come—" There was a repeat of the same words and then an addition. "Ravinga waits—"

The face vanished, the walls, the very surface on which I stood was now gone; rather it was as if my own eyes had been detached from my imprisoned body and looked down from the sky on which could only be the sprawl of city buildings—but such a city as if my well-known Meloa had been enlarged a hundred or more times over.

It spread farther and farther, the details became ever cleared as I dropped nearer to it. Now I could see that, unlike Meloa, it had a wall about it and there was a wide gate. Warriors moved there. Their battle wigs were the clear white of mar-stones—their skins also paler. While those who came into the city (they were but shadows shown me in no detail) must stop by these warriors as if to assure the keepers of the gate that they had a rightful business there.

Starting from the gate, that which was the part of me was sent upon a strange journey swinging over a street, pausing above a building which had about it a very large space, in which sheltered

many oryxen and I thought that it might be an inn. My sight of
that lasted for only a second and then was pushed on, down a
short side way, keeping to more of such passages, away from
the main thoroughfares where there was a constant passing of
the shadow people, until I came so unto a dead-end court and
halted (or my sight did) before a building which showed marks
of age—in fact at one time it might have had another story, for
the top was ragged-looking.

The court was a narrow one, its room shared only by two other
buildings, one of which was definitely a ruin, its roof long gone
and only part of the outer shell still standing.

Here was no stir of the shadow people. Only it was made
clear to me that I should remember well this place and seek it
out.

Once more I was drawn back along the same way I had come
and I found that I could easily remember every turn or change of
small side way and alley which had brought me here.

I had returned to the inn when there was a loud sound, one
which shook the whole of the scene I looked upon, as if that was
a curtain stirred by a breeze which rent it.

There was no longer any city. Only darkness—

"Rise!" That I had certainly truly heard. I opened my eyes.

One of those I remembered from the night before—one of the
caravan guards—stood beside me. The sun was near down and
the whole of the encampment had come alive.

Yaksen were being harnessed between the shafts of wagons or
stood patiently waiting for their packs to be adjusted.

"We move out," she who had awakened me from that very
strange dream said impatiently. "There is food at the kettle fire
but that will soon be gone."

Remembering my bondage in that dream, I half feared that I
could not move now, or was this true reality? I rolled that extra
sleep cover I had been loaned and stuffed it into my package,
making very sure that the Kifongg, Kynrr's gift, was well shielded
from any chance breakage.

I was not the last to fill my bowl at the fire—the others being
sentries of the last watch. Murri had kept close beside me and
accepted from my hands a second bowl. I had feared that being
among the yaksen and the two or three oryxen which were the
mounts of the caravan leaders, he might cause trouble with the
animals who would very quickly pick up the scent of an old
enemy.

However, it would seem that there was some sort of a truce among them. He did not venture too near, and, though they turned heads and moved nervously as he passed, they did not stampede. For which I was devoutly thankful. If I had had to choose between Murri and this company as to which might be my only salvation, I feared I could not have faced that choice with any fortitude.

As it was we took up our position at the tail of the caravan. The sun was gone and the twilight welcomed travelers to the road. Somewhere along the strung-out line of riders, beasts of burden, carts, a voice started a song and the rhythm of that singing carried us at a steady pace as one after another picked up the refrain.

We halted at intervals to rest the beasts. Dried fruit chunks were passed from the forage cart. These were a treat which only the best of the caravans could afford, for fruit was a great delicacy. My own people never tasted it except at ceremonial feastings, and I found the gummy sweetness could be chewed for a long time, well satisfying any thirst or need for other food. Even Murri, meat-eating predator that he was, appeared to relish it.

There was much talk of the future, speculation as to the choice of Emperor. There would be one trial for each queendom, and only when those of that section of the land accepted the candidate as a success in his endeavor, could he pass on to try the next.

The dead Emperor had such a long reign. In fact so long that those of my father's generation had been children or quite young when he had taken the trials in triumph. He had displayed successful power of character from the first. It had been he who had put down the custom of duel wars between the Houses, and had not been greatly beloved among his own Vapalan country people for that slighting of what was their cherished belief in "honor."

However, though they might not still fight openly, there were still personal grudges and struggles in the dark between House and House, yet all would close ranks against outsiders. The oft-stated opinion of those I now traveled with was that it was time for the rulership to pass from Vapala, that a winner from one of the other nations would bring welcomed changes at court to be the benefit of the others. The Vapalans, with their noted arrogance regarding all other peoples, needed a taste of a few new changes.

Since this was a Kahulawen caravan, there was talk that it might be one of our nation who might achieve this. But no one name seemed to come to more than one or two at a time.

"It will be Vapalan once again," Lara Musa, one of the guard who shared paces with me, stated, "if Shank-ji has his way. They say he is a man of power. We may see changes which will not be good if he wins. It has never been our way that the reign should descend from father to son. So would one House, one land, easily gain power over all. Such a change of custom might be welcome in Vapala but I think that we of the outer lands would not greet it. It has always been that the tests, which are of the essence of each land, make sure that he who commands the Leopard Throne be above all House allegiances, free from such ties, that he may treat all equally."

"How long before these trials?" I asked. There would be many coming in from each of the queendoms to celebrate something which only happened once in a lifetime. I was sure that my own kin might well choose to be among those.

"The Emperor must be sealed," she answered, "and the Grand Chancellor and the Voices of the Essence make a deal of that. They must wait until the Queens are gathered before they may proceed. But even before the sealing there may be marshaling of those who will be committed to the testing." She nodded to the carts ahead.

"We have a good cargo and there will be a profit when we market it in a city full of visitors. Prices will go up." She nodded with satisfaction.

"Also," she added a moment later, "we shall be early in and our mistress can have a chance to arrange for a very favorable market site."

With this indrawing from all the queendoms, I thought, surely I would be able to find some employment, which, if only temporary, would keep me for a while. I shrugged my pack to relieve shoulder strain. There was the Kifongg. I was no trained bard, but then I would not be seeking employment at any lordly House. I might find myself singing in some inn or even in the marketplace and garner in enough to keep me and Murri while I waited for an opportunity to do better.

18

WE MADE GOOD TIME, keeping a steady pace between the necessary halts, and on the second day there loomed up, from what I thought earlier might be a bank of clouds, the bulk of the great tableland, well above the sands, which was the Diamond Queendom. I had often heard it described but that telling gave no good impression of the vast cliffs which supported Vapala.

Our slickrock islands varied in degree of shape and size, but this was something far removed from what now would seem a handful of rocks tossed idly to lie hither and thither on the Kahulawen sand waves.

As we drew closer (we now marched by day) that cliffside was daunting indeed. While we began to hear those crystal-noted chimes of the mobiles which kept ever in song on the surface of the mesa well above.

Also, for the first time in my life, I saw patches of vivid green. For Vapala was not dependent upon algae beds. There grew plants, even the fabled trees. It was a land rich in many things that we of the outer lands did not know.

There was a guard outpost below, flanking the beginning of that road which climbed slantwise up the cliff wall. Looking at that pathway, the mere fact of its being was overwhelming. How long had it taken the determined people from above to carve that way out of rock? Surely whole lifetimes had gone into its construction.

Yet the fact that it was the only entrance into Vapala made the Diamond Queendom a well-guarded fortress instead of just a country. Warriors would find defense of that roadway an easy thing. Only a few bowmen, stationed well above, could sweep the path of any invaders and keep it clear.

Before we came to the border station the caravan mistress

appeared on her mount from the fore of our outstrung line of travelers and spoke to me:

"That one," she pointed with her whip to Murri, "will not be welcome here. You had best free him—"

"Free him?" I interrupted her. "Murri is as free as I—he is a companion, not a serving beast. Do you speak of freeing kottis? There are a number of those with the train, are there not? Do you haul them along so by collar and lead rope?"

She considered Murri, who eyed her straightly back.

"To those of Vapala he is the prey they prize. Those of the Houses count hunting his kind as a sport, while others who have beasts look upon sandcats as a menace to their herds. There will be arrows in him as soon as he is sighted from the post."

She was right. Yet also I knew that there was that which linked the two of us, Murri and I, which would not be denied. I spoke to him now in the language of the Furred Folk and he nodded his head.

"True," he growled. "Yet not true. There is no sleekskin who can command one of the Free Folk. Tell her what she wishes to hear and—you will see what can be done."

"This is a well-guarded place ahead—safe only for such as I," I answered him. "It can well be that you would be attacked on sight."

He blinked his eyes. "On sight—maybe. If there is sight. Let me handle this, brother-by-the-tooth."

There was nothing I could do for the moment but answer:

"It shall be as you point out, but be of great care."

Then to Elwene I added, "We shall take your warning."

She nodded and rode on to her place at the head of our line, ready to answer the challenge of the guards. Murri watched her well away and then approached the last of the carts, one which carried our food supplies and was now riding light since those supplies were near exhausted. Two of the kottis rode in the back, peering out of the opening of the covers with the usual curiosity of their kind.

They centered their gaze on Murri and then drew apart, leaving a space between them. The sandcat, so many times their size, leaped up into the cart and disappeared, while the kottis drew together again. Their eyes swept coolly over me and it was as if Murri had never been.

Surely the guard would investigate the caravan wagons, all of them. I had traveled so long with Murri that I was hardly aware any longer of the slightly musky odor of his fur. Would the presence of the kottis be enough to conceal their larger kinsman? Luckily Murri was still far from his full growth, or there certainly would not have been any way of concealing him.

I chose to tramp beside that slow-moving vehicle. I had no idea what I might do if his presence was discovered. I only hoped that I could somehow distract any guard long enough for the fast-moving sandcat to get back into the dune waves.

The caravan came to a halt. Some of those ahead took the opportunity to sit as if they expected a wait of some time. Apparently there were formalities to be observed. From the heights above, the chimes of the wind-blown mobile makers of music sent their clear notes down. These mobiles were the pride of the Diamond people. But the greatest one of all—that was a symbol of the very land. It was only unhooked and freed to ring upon some great time of emergency— Though it was pent again now, it had chimed upon the death of Haban-ji.

Music it made, yes, but also it was death—a deadly and slashing death. Any who had committed certain crimes past all redemption were forced into the circle of the unevenly hung chimes, which were set with diamonds along their separate plaques so that they slashed cruelly as the chains which held the whole Great Mobile were kept whirling by guards well trained to the job.

Also—it was the last test for him who would set himself up to be Emperor. He must pass through the freed chimes successfully and without hurt to reach the crown set at their core. I wondered at the skill and courage of those who had tried it in the past— they must have possessed the agility of a master swordsman or of a great dancer in order to tread that path. One moment of faltering, one mistake in judging the swing of one plaque or another, and they would die painfully, as if they had been set up for targets for the practice of inept swordsmen.

There was a drum note from the head of our line—we were to be on the move again. What was the penalty, I wondered dourly, for one who tried to smuggle a sandcat into Vapala? Would he face the dance of the chimes? Yet I followed the cart at the steady pace set by those ahead.

To proceed was a test, almost as great as that endeavor wherein I had brought Murri out of the sand trap, as the tail end of the caravan passed between the rows of guards to start up that precipitous way to the land above.

I looked from right to left, taking the measure of these warriors.

They were brightly accoutered, their armlets, breastplates, belts bejeweled with more elaboration than even that worn by the Head of a House among my people.

Their hair was hidden under the massive wigs, those silver-white wigs which were surely sprinkled with diamond dust so did they glitter in the sunlight. Each was armed with a spear but also carried a bow unstrung at his back, and their prowess with both weapons was very well known across all the queendoms.

They stood in two squads, one on either side of the entrance of the upper road, and their officer, holding a tally in one hand, was a little to my right. It was apparent he was counting and checking both carts and people as we went. As I drew near he looked straight at me snapping his fingers, the gesture one used to summon a none too reliable servant. I bit my lip. Was it coming now? My staff and my knives were my only weapons and surely those were nothing against the metal a trained warrior could bring into service.

"You—what name?" He spoke with a strange clip to his words and certainly not as he would address an equal.

"Klaverel-va-Hynkkel, Sword Lord."

"She of the caravan has said you were solo lost."

"That is true."

"Your plans here, outlander?"

"To see Vapala of which we have heard so much in the out-lands," I returned. His voice and attitude were such as I had faced before—from the companions of my brother and the elders who visited with my father. How could he have faced some of the ventures which lay behind me now? For all his diamond dust, his war art, his place as keeper of the door to Vapala? For the first time I felt not the usual half-apologetic reaction I had done in the past. I did not wear a sword, but I had survived and in that much I was his equal. I rubbed the healed tooth mark wound on my wrist. No, I was even more!

This one might hunt sandcats, but I had seen their councils, shared in part their starlight dancing, was blood kin to them now. There was none in Vapala who could match that!

It was growing near twilight before the whole of the caravan finally reached the top of the mesa. That was a chancy path, one which was usually only taken by day. Late-comers camped by the guard post would have to await the next dawn. To my relief the guards had made no inspection of the last wagon. The kottis continued to sit together, lazy-eyed, covering the space they had made for Murri's entrance. I began to wonder what communication might exist between them and their much greater distant cousins.

The feral leopards, who had not joined the guard of the Emperor or those of the various Queens, were rumored to be enemies of Murri's people. Though of any actual case of one attacking the other I had never heard. There had always been a bond between the leopards and my people, though perhaps not as close and familiar as that the kottis granted a household or a single person.

I thought I knew what to expect when I reached the top of that climb, for the greenery natural there had been many times described. The ferocity of the few storms which hit all our lands from time to time (little to our aid, for any fallen rain was very quickly sucked up by the sand) might strike here but the water did not escape. Those of the Diamond people had studied such problems from time immemorial and had their way of funneling such downpours, not into sucking sand but into reservoirs in the foundation rock. From those they drew to irrigate symmetrical patches where they induced growth, even trees tall enough to reach above a man's head like some tall rock spur. These were a marvel in themselves. As we passed along the upper road on our way to the city, I could see rows of these well tended and heavy with fruit. Between their columns were shrubs—some which gave off the tang of those spices which brought such high prices in the outlands.

There were other wider spaces, fenced, in which were fine herds of yaksen, even once such an inkeeping where oryxen of plainly high breeding had gathered to watch our passing, several exchanging challenges with those being part of the caravan.

Though my own House was considered prosperous and we had a good herd of yaksen and several finely bred oryxen (in fact my father, though he was inclined to make little show, lived as well as a noble might), no one of such standing had such a show of land wealth as I saw here.

However, looking around at all this spread of growing things, I found them strange, and I longed for the rock isles and algae pools of my own land. We are a part of our homes and I think there will always be a feeling of loss and ache within when we cannot longer actively communicate with our own special places.

Now I was overwhelmed and began to think ever more strongly that I had taken a wrong path. For all the disappointment and heart loss I would have to face had I returned home, yet I was of Kahulawe. The Diamond Queendom could bedazzle with its richness and it did. At the same time the stranger here must be more of a stranger even than elsewhere. Those of Vapala might think the outer lands too harsh—for barbarians only. However, for untold time they had lived so until they could not conceive of any other way of life.

We were still a day's journey from the city, since it was situated more in the interior of the country. That night we tail-circled in a place prepared for caravans—and there camped. Elwene summoned all her staff (there was no need for sentries here) and began to lay out their program for setting up an impressive booth in the market—discussing prices and duties of those who would take care of the actual sales, and those who would continue to care for the beasts and the possessions of the caravan.

"Raffan is holding room at the Three Leopards," she said. "Vara brought us assurance of that. He is tight-fisted and it is needful to stand up against his overpricing, but he knows better than to try to take any high-nosed stand with me. What we put in his treasure pouch at the end of the marketing will be reasonable. As you know his beds are clean, he has a weekly immersion room, and the food, if it is plain, is well cooked."

Immersion room! Those two words struck me. Such was an often-told wonder of the Diamond Queendom. Many of the Great Houses in their palaces had private immersion rooms. For the most part we of the outer lands are a cleanly people, though we have not the washing use of our tongues, kotti fashion, to keep us so. But we do lave ourselves daily when possible with sponge mats of non-edible algae and even scrub before that with sand. To actually put the whole body into a large basin full of very soggy algae—that was a luxury I did long to try, having been so long without even a renewal of clothing.

Yet the thought of going to the inn was something I must consider. I could not let Murri show himself and an inn was a very public place. Also, though I carried some good lumps of turquoise which I had garnered along the way (also those gems which I had discovered in the destroyed caravan—though those were not mine to use), I could not exchange them for lodging without knowing their true worth here. Being the imperial capital, there would surely be workers in gems, though my own land was most noted for that. I must see about selling what I carried, and I knew enough of the value they had from my sister to ensure, I believe, that I would not be cheated in a bargain with a maker of gem-set wares. Also I was not a member of the caravan, and rightly I could not claim a share of the arrangements they had already made.

I had reached that point in my musing about the immediate future when there flashed into my head the map of streets and alleys which had come out of that vision dream. If I deemed it a vision and not just a dream, then I had my answer to the problem of where to seek guidance as to lodging and information in the city.

Knowing that, I faced my entrance to the city far more confidently. Luckily it was beginning to be dusky. Though the main thoroughfare down which we passed was lighted with globes which might have contained the brilliance of diamonds, so did each illumine its section of the way. The buildings were white, for the most part not higher than two stories, a precaution they followed from the far past against the worst of storms. The closer in we drew, the more we could see of larger and more ornate buildings. Statues of black leopards held some of the globes and there were traces of color, some mosaics of small gemstones, on the walls of the larger houses.

This splendor was indeed far from the homes of the isles and surely meant, in part, to overawe those who came as visitors. I had drawn near to the cart in which Murri still rode hidden. For him to emerge into this well-lighted place was to betray him quickly, for there was traffic which thickened as we came closer to the center point.

That morning I had given my thanks to the mistress and offered her her choice of the rough stones I carried as my payment. I had also given her note of the gems from the massacre, asking that she might perhaps discover their new owner. However, she had seemed doubtful that might ever be done. My stones she had refused in such a way as I could not feel as one given charity, saying that to aid any coming out of solo was the duty of all wayfarers, as of course it was. Thus I had now to make no farewells to those I had traveled with, only to reach the inn towards which we must be bound and then somehow get Murri to follow me into that maze so imprinted in my brain, using all his hunting skill as a skulker to do so.

When I started to convey this information to Murri, the kottis politely drawing to one side so I could approach as closely as possible the end of the wagon, I was interrupted with a swift answer.

"Know way, shall be ready."

Did Murri have visions also? If I accepted that which had been so offered us—what might be the pay asked in return? I was wary of the future—sometimes there came the feeling that I was being moved, not by my free will, but the power of some essence that I could not understand.

There were lights in the inn courtyard where the caravan drew up to sort out and empty carts, unpack the beasts, and see that they were escorted to the place set aside for them—the extra stable. I was watching the wagon, lingering in the shadow of the gate and keeping as inconspicuous as possible. Murri slipped over the tailgate, the kottis again standing aside, and was gone. I had already shouldered my pack to follow. The street outside was well lighted and there were both walkers and riders but somehow Murri had slid from one bit of shadow to the next while I crossed to the mouth of the narrower way which was the first part of the alley maze.

Once I was sure he had not been sighted we again crossed a wider way. At last I heard a cry and I took firmer hold of my staff and hurried along to act as rearguard if necessary.

It was then that I saw Murri take to an overhead path, making it to a higher way in two bounds from a single-story roof to a higher one.

We had not been followed after all. And this section of the town had fewer lights, and those of subdued radiance. There were signs of shabbiness about buildings here. No fine mosiac work was picked out on walls and the carving about doorways and windows was often broken. The narrow path into the last court was entirely in the shadows as night had closed in. There was a faint light only in one place, over the doorway of the house my vision had shown me.

Murri appeared suddenly and was waiting by that door even as I reached it. I raised my hand to knock. There was one of the musical mobiles hanging there and it swung and chimed to my gesture. As if I had been impatiently waited, the door was opened at once and Ravinga's girl apprentice looked at me.

"So you have come—" If it was intended as a welcome it was a cool one. But she opened wide the door for Murri and me to enter. The sandcat showed no signs of hanging back but went in as confidently as if he were entering some lair of his own people.

19

THE FOREROOM OF THE HOUSE was plainly a shop. Though there was a single light by the door, it did not reach very far towards the shelved walls. The girl held a lantern globe in her hand and the glimmer of that picked up from what stood or was seated on the shelves bright sparks of eyes, as if all those figures there were watching us as we passed by.

I felt wary as if I were now in a place where there were secrets. The dolls I had seen Ravinga sell at the market in my own land had been very good but always there had been one or two among them so perfect in face and form as to suggest that it had been modeled with great skill from a living person. Those had sold only for a very high price, usually to some collector of curios. For my people had a liking for trinkets as they could afford, and like my sister's fine jewelry the makers of such were esteemed and their craft stalls in the market were sought out by House lords and mistresses.

I paused now to get a straighter look at some pieces of which I caught a glimpse and would have liked to see the better. There was surely a sandcat on one shelf, sitting upright, both forepaws resting on a drum as if it would play for one of those air-floating dances of its kind.

However, my guide was already holding aside the curtain of the door which led beyond and Murri was heading in that direction. The curtain was of light hide and now we did move into a larger room which was plainly made for living and not for a shop, though there was another doorway displaying a light beyond and that curtain was looped away to show a work table well loaded with what must be the raw materials of Ravinga's craft.

The dollmaker herself appeared there a moment later and held out both hands palm up as she would greet a favored guest. To my astonishment Murri raised a forepaw, his wicked claws well sheathed, to lay against hers, his so large that it nearly spanned both her hands. Deep in his throat he made that sound which those of his own kind used in greeting.

Ravinga bowed her head in courtesy.

Then she made the same gesture to me and I hurried to touch palms. Though I knew that she must have been tending towards the later years of life, she remained the same as I had always seen her—from many seasons ago when I had first spied her work in the market and had stopped to admire a fully armed warrior figure which had all the pride of my father when he made his annual visit to court.

She had greeted me then not as a child who must be warned of meddling with fine things but had spoken with me almost as if I were a fellow craftsman, taking time to answer my questions concerning the warrior and his gear, which was slightly strange to me as being that of the Azhengir, those whose women also once rode to war.

Since that day I had always been glad to see her, though the last two seasons our meetings had been a little awkward, as, for the first time, she had brought her apprentice with her, and Allitta had made it very clear that she had not the friendship for strangers which her mistress showed. The girl had always made some excuse to busy herself with the merchandise, even to keep her back to me as she fussed about rearranging displays or sitting in the corner busy on small repairs of the figures people brought in to have their treasures returned to full value again.

Now she had already left this room, vanishing through the other door. I thought her churlish, though I had never sought out the company of aught but my sisters. It would have done me no good to attend any festival of first heat where choosing would be done. It was most plain that I had nothing to offer any mate-minded maiden. Now in my rags of soiled travel I must present an even less attractive appearance.

"Accept guest right, Hynkkel," Ravinga greeted me with words more warm than any I had ever heard from even kin.

"You are gracious to one such as me, mistress—I—"

"You were summoned and this is your place for now." She had the same authority in her speech that my father used. An authority which for the moment, daunted me from asking questions.

She asked nothing concerning my travels but led me on through that other door where Allitta had gone, and into a section which had a kitchen to one side—good smells coming from that making me feel at once the hollowness of my stomach. Murri was seated right within, watching the girl who moved between stove and table. His whiskers quivered as his mouth opened a trifle to let his long tongue sweep across his lips, plainly in anticipation.

Without pausing there my hostess showed me into one of the other small rooms, plainly private sleeping quarters. This was the type of lodging one would give an honored guest. The wall carvings were of sandcats in dance and those caught my eyes immediately, for only one who had witnessed the real ceremony could have wrought that. However, there were other luxuries waiting. A very large basin—perhaps not the baths of a House palace but well enough for anyone to wish for—stood to one side, and from my first sniff I knew that the sponge algae within it had been mixed of those kinds which were made to soothe as well as cleanse the most weary and long-journeyed of travelers.

In addition, laid across a cloth pole was a rust-yellow kilt, and a long coat of a blue-green, embroidered at throat and hem with a pattern of small crystal beads. While, heel and toe together, a pair of soft oryxen-hide boots waited. I stared at this display as my backpack thudded to the floor.

A night's lodging, food, yes, those were often guest-offered, but this city finery—why? Again that feeling that I was being moved by something I did not understand made me uncomfortable. Yet I could not reject what was so offered without giving offense, that was certain. Though such a welcome to one returning from solo was right—yet it should be in gifts from kin and not from one who had no blood tie.

I pulled off my rags of trail dress, bundling them together. For the most part they were past wearing. I must see to replenishing my wardrobe as soon as I could.

Then I stood on the wash mat and sponged myself down with the algae. It was warm and my abraded, scarred, and dried skin soaked up the moisture. I could feel my body relax. I no longer even wondered as to why I was received with such a welcome, I simply sank into a kind of yielding bemusement.

The clothing fitted me. Which was another surprise—unless Ravinga was so versed in the making of clothing for her figures she could reckon in her mind my size—even though she had not seen me for a season. The boots were a little large, but no matter for that, at least they did not abrade the skin as did those many-times-mended ones I just discarded.

When I was done I stood and viewed myself in a mirror. It did not show the whole of me, but I thought for a moment that by some device I was looking at one of Ravinga's dolls raised to man height. My face was thin and darker, my hair had grown longer so that even when I pressed the keeping ring about it the ends switched my shoulders behind. My sister's parting gift was bright on my arm, and on impulse I added the cat pendant which I had kept concealed for most of the time during my trail walking. That glinted now against my chest between the open edges of the coat and certainly was such an ornament, even by the famed wealth of Vapala, as could not be easily equaled.

Feeling very much as if somehow I had come into that room one person and was going out another, I went in search of my hostess.

Murri was already occupied with the contents of a large basin when I entered the eating place. Facing him in a solemn row were three black kottis, their attention full upon him, cleaned plates before each of them.

Ravinga waved me to a well-padded seating mat beside her own and there were polished knee tables before us. A third was set at a right angle to Ravinga's and there Allitta seated herself in turn, having placed the last of a series of covered dishes before us.

To one who had been living off the very rough fare of the country for so long this was in truth such as would be provided at only a Great House ceremonial feast. I tasted food which was common here, grown in the fields of Vapala, but unknown, since it could not be transported by any lengthy trailing, in my own land. There was also fresh fruit to end the meal, as well as a drink made from subtly flavored stuff which brought a warmth not only into my middle but into my mind. This night was taking on the quality of a dream.

My hostess did not make conversation, and following good manners I addressed myself also to the emptying of my bowls, twice over—which perhaps was true greediness. Allitta arose twice to bring on further supplies.

Murri had polished his basin clean and used a ready paw to clean whiskered face. Trailed still by the kottis, he had crossed the room and now was stretched full length behind me, though his bulk was not well fitted into the limited space. I could hear his purr, kept to a faint rumble.

When the meal was at last done I ventured to break the silence.

"Lady, your House may rest in pride. Such bounty to a stranger is beyond reckoning. Now—" I hesitated trying to find the proper words, not the blunt ones which were already on my tongue.

She pushed the knee table a little from her and sat with her hands clasped lightly in her lap. Allitta made a quick matter of clearing away the remains of the feast, leaving only three cups of fine design and a flagon of the soothing drink there.

"Now," Ravinga said when the girl had at last returned to her own place, two of the kottis immediately pushing each other to establish favored positions in her lap, "now you have questions, as who would not." She paused again, not looking at me but at the opposite wall as if she saw there something of intent meaning.

"We are a people who have forgotten much, and some of that I believe was induced—as a punishment, a warning, an escape— who knows which? The most ancient of the bard songs hold hints. Hints that predate the wars before the uniting of the outer queendoms. Most of our lands are harsh ones and the lives we have made for ourselves here have demanded that we become what we are now.

"The unification has done away with war between nation and nation and that paves the way for something more. If we have fallen from some former estate, perhaps we are now very slowly climbing back, as ones who would find a way up a slickrock island new to them. But at present we are more like travelers trapped in some sand pit, and hiding our eyes against what is before us—or must be before us in the future.

"We have grown complacent. Oh, some of our customs we have held to—the solo to toughen our young for example." Now she did glance at me. "Is it not true, Hynkkel, that you are different now?"

"I believe so—" My hand sought the cat pendant and I saw the scars on my wrist. Different, yes, a whole new dimension of life had been opened to me. I had danced with those who were the fabled enemies of my kind, I had listened to Kynrr's tales, I had come away from my roots and at the moment I realized that I had indeed broken out of the shell which had once held me.

"My House," she seemed to change the subject sharply, "is a strange one. I have only two of blood kin left—and one is not truly of my nature." Suddenly she stretched forth her own wrist and pushed up a wide bracelet circling that. I saw on her slightly puckered skin scars similar to those Maraya's teeth had left on me.

"For many seasons there has been trouble, trouble which was so faint that even the Great Essence could only dimly convey—and then only to some born sensitive to such nuances. Now this trouble is rising faster. The Plain of Desolation has a lord power."

I think I was staring at her gape-jawed. Trying to make sense of such a wild statement. For there could be no life in the Great Desolation—no House for any lord power to use.

Behind me I heard a sudden growl, felt Murri stir.

"Listen—" his throat speech carried. "This is the speech of wisdom."

Even the kottis, those on Allitta's lap and the one which had settled down beside her, opened wide their eyes to regard Ravinga's with that unblinking stare of their kind.

"There are the great rats—" Suddenly I thought of those we had slain and how they were different from their fellows. And I had heard tales of how such large ones have come out of the Desolation—though how they could abide there—

"Yes, the rats—a testing—to see how alert and ready we may be." She reached within to a pocket of her robe and brought out in the hollow of her hand a round ball of a dead-black substance, a black so intense that it appeared to draw light to it for the quenching and the room became darker as she set it down on the table before her.

I leaned forward to take a better look but her hand curved over it instantly, shielding it from my sight. "Not so! I do not know the full power of this. You have one shield—" she pointed to my pendant, "but you have had no training. We do not risk you now—"

"Risk me?"

"From the day that you were able to find the cursing on my beast I knew that you had that within you which might answer." Again she changed the subject. "The kottis, the beasts, they sensed it in you, for in many ways their measurements are more accurate than ours.

"Allitta," she nodded to her apprentice, "is also one who has inner sight. She has learned a little in her way, you have in yours. We shall need those who can stand up to dangers far different from any that our peoples have known for generations."

"I am no warrior!" I protested. Had not all the trouble in my life sprung from the seed that I was not by nature such?

"There are many kinds of struggle, and a sword, lance, or other weapon in one's hand may not be the answer to such. We need others than warriors, though it may well follow, and probably will, that we shall see lances readied against what comes.

"We need more now those who can walk other ways, who are ready to be attuned to the most subtle warnings of the Great Essence. Firstly we are in need of a new Emperor. Vapala has supplied the last two Emperors. There is a candidate very ready here now who would change the source of custom—for it has always been forbidden that the rule should rest in the hands of any one House.

"Though we now dwell in peace as to nation, there are dark workings between House and House." Her hand went out and touched that of Allitta which now lay on the table. There was a harsh stiffening of her apprentice's whole body, an odd sharpening of feature which could be evil memory possessing her for an instant or two. "Yes, there are many darknesses under the surface of our apparent safety. Thus we need no scheming of House against House to add to future danger. Our Emperor must this time have no tie with Vapala."

She spoke as if she were issuing an order and now she turned her head and looked straight at me as might a commander look at his troop.

"No!" the denial burst from me. "I am no Emperor, nor can I be! Nor will I try—"

The girl leaned forward and her sharpness of feature was matched by her voice as she said:

"One does what is demanded of one—or one is—nothing!" She smacked her hand, palm down, on her own small table so the cup there nearly toppled to its side. Her eyes were as cold as those my father had often turned on me and there was certainly a measure of disgust in the curl of her lips.

"I am no Emperor," I repeated firmly. The thought that these two women could see me a candidate made me suddenly suspicious of all the vague warnings Ravinga had been mouthing. That I should offer myself for such a trial—there would rightfully be mocking laughter and I would be ranked one bereft of wit.

But Ravinga now did not seem disturbed. Her hand that was over that black ball raised and under her touch the ball rolled towards me.

"Let us see," she said.

As when her mistress had given me the cat mask long ago, Allitta made a disputing gesture with her own right hand but said nothing.

The ball rolled across Ravinga's table, passed on to mine. I could not understand how it had crossed the short space between the two tops. Then it was before me. Though Ravinga did not order me—she did not this time refuse my study of the object.

It had nothing of a crystal about it. There was no gleam or glitter. The sphere repelled the eye as might a ball of some noxious dried algae. I had no desire to touch it. But it was changing before my eyes. The ball outline writhed, it became different shapes. For an instant only I was looking down at the head of a cat—not a kotti, nor of Murri's lineage, but the sleek one of a leopard—the same leopard which, when blue, was the symbol of rulership.

Leopard it was, but it went on changing and then I saw a rat—the representation of one of those strange and direful larger beasts.

Leopard for ruler, that symbolism flashed into my mind—and rat—rat for the end of all good.

20

FOR ONE used to the relative silences of the outer lands Vapala was a place of clamor—though I could not say that my ears were assaulted by raucous sounds. Those musical mobiles which were a part of the inner city were always a-chime from dawn, when they were released to any wind which might be blowing, to dusk. The streets teemed with life, and during the next few days when more and more travelers and trading caravans came crowding in, one had to push one's way through throngs such as an outer dweller certainly never saw gathered together even for a major feasting.

I had hoped for more enlightenment from Ravinga, yet at the same time I did not want to become involved in any argument over the preposterous idea that I would put myself forward for the Leopard Throne. She had somewhat ensorceled me by all the hints she had made on the first night I was under her roof. But in the morning she did not take up the subject again, nor was I minded to do so either.

It was a busy time within the shop. Emperor dolls were in demand—even when they were only clay images of the cheapest sort bought for a couple of fruits, or a small bundle of firewood by those too poor to have anything in a purse. To display one of these over one's doorway, even the doorway of a dilapidated hut, was considered necessary by custom. I saw that Ravinga and Allitta even gave these away to those who looked longingly but had not anything to trade. The Emperor might have been absorbed in the Greater Essence, but it remained that something of his strength might still abide with those who so honored him.

For the time being there was little trade in her other products and I was able to survey them at my leisure. Men, women, and children from all the queendoms, of every rank from the Queens and their courtiers and guards, to the lowest of servants or slaves, were represented in the collection.

Whole companies of desert scouts were assembled with their mounts, their equipment complete to even the deadly boot knives which were now worn mostly for show and no longer settled death duels. There was one entire trader's caravan which marched along a top shelf. The salt gatherers of Azhengir with their crystal-lined branches were there, the guides of the dune sail riders with their light craft from Twahihic. Nor were the miners of Thnossis nor my own people lacking. And in the fore were the lords and ladies, the people of Vapala itself, from the lowest street cleaner to the Queen and her court.

If Ravinga had fashioned examples of all the two-footed inhabitants of the queendoms, she had done as well for the four-footed. There were kottis engaged in all manner of play and hunt, there were oryxen, their fierce horns not trimmed, patient yaksen, with and without carts, and, in a corner to themselves, sandcats.

In this land where such were considered menaces and the best of prey I was surprised at the detail and lifelike appearance of Ravinga's collection. Here were free sandcats engaged in their own lives as I had seen Myrourr and those who had gathered for the "sing." These had surely never been fashioned by one who had only seen them from a distance, or stood above dead bodies after a hunt.

I thought often of the scars on my hostess's wrist, hidden always by her bracelet. She had not mentioned those, only was sure I had seen them. When had Ravinga entered that other world and why? I had made the point of watching Allitta and she certainly bore no such markings.

From childhood I had been schooled to patience but sometimes now I wanted to confront Ravinga and demand answers, clear-cut answers. Since the night that she had shown me that black ball and taken it again out of my hand while I still goggled over what I had seen and what might be the meaning of it, she had spent very little time with on me, being occupied with the shop—and her work table.

I made myself useful on the second day—the first I had gone to the market to inspect the dealers in stones and jewel work. Twice I had seen pieces which undoubtedly were from my sister's fashioning being resold and at prices which I think would have truly astounded Kura. I began to plan how that her work might be brought directly to Vapala so that not only might her fine creations be appreciated by collectors but that she would have the pick of stones and other raw material, the like of which never appeared in our own trading fairs.

Ravinga not only sold from her shop, she had also a leased market slip and it was there that during this time her servant Mancol took the less of her wares. I helped him transport and set up the stall before I wandered about on my own.

The turquoise I had brought out of the outlands I was able to sell for some silver shavings which seemed a goodly bargain to me, though I am sure, had I known better the ways of this market, I could have made an even better trade. But there was too much to see and listen to, so much which was distracting.

Processions wound up and down the streets. There were constant cries from harsh-voiced running servants to clear the way for those of one Great House or another. Youths in their finest were arriving—perhaps not to make the trials—but to mingle and gamble, race their mounts outside the city, drink the wines known nowhere else, generally show their arrogant persons that at times were boorish beyond belief.

Once I saw Shank-ji with a crowd of followers. He was fair-skinned as any Vapalan—but he did not wear the bush wig of a warrior, though he was armed well enough with superbly forged weapons, gem-hilted. His own white hair was knotted back in as simple a fashion as my own, though the clasp which held it so blazed with diamonds.

His face was narrow, clean of any hair on cheek or chin, though most of his companions sported narrow threads of mustache or jawline of beard. There was something oddly masklike about his countenance—no expression showed. Heavy lids appeared to hide, by chance or design, most of his eyes. There was certainly that about him which drew the attention—perhaps a certain tension throughout as if he held himself in tight rein against flaming action for which he longed.

He was young, though there again one could not say he was like the other youths. Rather there was about him some of the authority which my father has always worn as a daunting cloak. Still, Emperor's son though he might be, he had by custom held no open power in Vapala and ranked lower even than any House lord.

People made way for his party. I observed that some in the crowd looked at him oddly in question as he rode by. Once I saw a woman's fingers move quickly in a sign which in my land was used to ward off ill fortune. On the other hand there were a portion of those who called out his name, though he did not look at who so hailed him or make an answering gesture.

During my prowling of the market Murri had withdrawn to the ruined house in the small court where Ravinga's shop stood. When I questioned his safety Allitta said, with that stiff impatience she always used for me, that the ruin also belonged to the dollmaker and there would be no one to visit it untimely.

My desert-born comrade was bored. Had it not been that at night he could come back to Ravinga's own roof and that the kottis appeared to trot back and forth regularly to his place of refuge, I think he might even have climbed to the housetops again and gone exploring on his own. I took to describing to him in the evening what I had seen. How much human affairs meant to Murri when they did not actively affect his own life I could not tell, but he listened, and once in a while asked a question which surprised me.

He seemed particularly interested in my sight of Shank-ji, though he growled several times and at last stated flatly:

"That one kills—kills not to eat—but to—" He seemed to be searching for some way of expressing a thought important to him in the limited vocabulary we could share. "He kills—to wear teeth—to take skin—for the seeing of others."

A killer for red sport. Certainly that could be true of more than half those I had watched riding so proudly through the streets. Yet Shank-ji, if he shared that with most, had more. Kynrr had been hostile and forbidding at our first meeting, yet there had been that in him which I could understand. Even my brother I could read after a fashion. However, this would-be Emperor— no, he rode alone.

"Not one—" Murri broke in upon that thought, "two—"

"Two what?" I asked.

The sandcat blinked. Again it seemed he struggled to make clear some thought. Then he answered:

"Here stands that one." He placed a paw flat on the floor close to my knee. Then he moved his other foot to position several finger lengths behind the first. "Here—other—"

"Other man?"

Again Murri blinked. "Other—" I thought I could sense puzzlement as if he could not truly give a clear answer.

Someone behind Shank-ji? That suggested that the Vapalan's bid for the throne of his father might indeed have covert support.

I had heard enough sidewise comments from time to time since I had reached the city which suggested that there was an unrest under the surface, that all was not as it had once been in the Diamond city, bound by custom into a narrow trail.

That I could get any more out of my desert-born companion was impossible now. I only hoped that what he might know or learn in the future he would share with me.

Night's shadows lay on the city. The shop was closed, and, though the music of the mobiles was still in chime, this pocket of a court which held us was relatively quiet. For the first time since I had entered Vapala I brought out Kynrr's treasured Kilongg and tuned it, glad to see that the hard trek had not affected it in any way.

The bowl was worn indeed, polished very smooth by long handling, so polished that only the faintest of designs remained— an intricate twisting of lines of which I had never been able to make anything. They could have once been a running script such as those of Vapala used for their "high" writing of music and sound.

I moved my fingers back and forth in an exercise to limber them, then dared to strike the chords of one of those songs Kynrr had taught me. Allitta had gone elsewhere in this sprawl of building which I had never fully explored, keeping strictly to the section Ravinga had made free for me. The dollmaker herself came to settle on a pile of mats, sighing as she relaxed, rubbing her back with one hand as if hours spent above her work table had left her aching.

One of Kynrr's songs came easier as I reached the proper strings. I kept my voice low. Murri loosed a rumble of purr and the three kottis gathered in about Ravinga, watching me as they rubbed lovingly about the dollmaker. They were as one in their black coloring and always they went together as if invisibly linked. They had paid me the courtesy of notice now and then, but it was plain that in this house only Ravinga and the girl rated their whole attention and devotion.

I sang the song which Kynrr had himself fashioned in exile, one which spoke of the stars he loved to watch, the softness of the nights, the harshness which came with the day, and above all the loneliness that ate into one apart.

Why that one of all the songs of his own making he had given to me came now I did not know. It was as if this was proper and rightful for this day and twilight time.

"Where learned you that?" The last notes dropped from the strings even as Allitta was upon me. There was not the scornful withdrawal which always seemed to possess her when she looked at me. She was inwardly aflame, almost I could see her hand tense as if to aim a blow.

"From its maker. He who called himself Kynrr—"

"A dead man does not sing!" she hissed as might one of the kottis.

"True. Yet when he taught me this he was not dead. Though the Great Essence took him later."

She raised that fisted hand and bit at the knuckles. Across those she looked at me as if she would reach into my mind and pull forth the stuff of memory.

"But that is not— There was no known Kynrr's song in this tune!"

"I knew such." Swiftly I spoke of the hermit and of his place of exile. Of how he had spoken of Vapala and of how he had died, having given his strength to my rescue.

She listened. Then I saw that her eyes in the lamplight glistened.

"Kynrr," she repeated the name when I had done. "It was indeed Master Kynrr whose blood that one bore. I believed him dead in the night's slaughter. That he won free—" She shook her head slowly. "The last of the sworn ones, and so that was his ending."

She might be speaking to herself as she dropped down upon the cushions opposite me. Some strength could have, for the moment, gone out of her. There was desolation in both her eyes and her voice. Now she reached forward and touched the Kilongg I had put down, touched it as if she might so put finger on a great treasure.

"True enough—this was of Kynrr—and Kiticar treasured it. Had any saved it, it would have been him. Many times I have heard him play—he was one of the great ones, even as was Kynrr long ago, though ever said he was not the master as that one was."

She grasped the Kilongg fully now and drew it into her lap. Her fingers found the strings. What came forth was not the lament which had been born by my playing, but rather small gem notes which spoke of growing things, of the dancing of feasters, of the quicking of hearts. Never had I heard such from the man who had called himself Kynrr, yet somehow I knew that this song was also of his fashioning in another and happier time.

I leaned back a little against the bulk of Murri, who, as usual, had settled behind me to listen in delight. There was something which came to lighten the heart, assure the hearer that beyond all cares lay happiness and beauty.

It was not to last. Sharply came other notes, crystal clear but with nothing gentle in them. They rang through the walls. Allitta's fingers ceased to move, she was again stern of face, shaken out of that which had possessed her. Ravinga straightened in her place.

"Haban-ji goes to his sealing." she said. "A time ends, new begins."

I wondered what mysteries now were in progress in the Vapalan House of the Past. How long would this new resident there be remembered? Oh, yes, any child could recite the toll of Emperors going back for generations. The sing-song of that roll came even now to the fore of my mind. But how many of them had set any lasting mark upon that roll, save for their names?

"Tomorrow," Ravinga had to raise her voice to compete with the chimes of departing, "they will choose."

I moved, shifted. Must I now again face her belief that I was one who would make that choice? If she expected some answer from me she did not get it. After a moment she arose to go into her own quarters. Allitta slid the Kilongg from her knee to the floor and abruptly departed also without a word, leaving me to seek my own bed. However, this night I did not go alone, for Murri paced beside me as he had in that trial by travel through which we both had come.

The chimes sounded once more in the morning, all of them in a clamor which was ear-splitting to one who came from the relative silence of the desert. Still I was drawn with Ravinga, and Allitta, and seemingly all those of the households of Vapala who could crowd into the square before the Hall of the Past.

There was a bright splash of color on the high flight of stairs leading up to the wide portal of that hall. The Queens were a-glitter with gems, their foremost courtiers made a back tapestry. Before them were the Herald and the Head of the foremost House of Vapala. Between those a sleepy beast wore a netting of diamonds about its ears—the Blue Leopard, always companion guard to the Emperor, in himself the symbol of power.

For a last time the chimes of the Great Mobile, shining rainbow patterns in the sky above us, sounded and then were silent as the

Herald came forward. He had the reaching voice of his office and it carried over the throng massed below.

"The Great Haban-ji is now of the Final Essence. There must be one to follow him. These are the tasks, O men of courage and skill. Listen well and then take oath you shall reach for the triumph of the crown." He pointed to the Great Crown set in the heart of the mobile.

"From ancient times it has been that he who would rule must prove himself to each of the queendoms, that he may well understand the life of those whom he shall rule.

"First: in Thnossis he must venture close enough to the ever-flowing lava river to bring back one of the ruby cats of Qurr from that temple which the river now threatens to engulf.

"In Azhengir he must join in the harvest of salt crystals, proving to those who labor there his fitness to be considered their equal in skill.

"In Twahihic he must harvest from the haunted garden.

"In Kahulawe he must discover and challenge the Leopard Keeper of lasting knowledge that he may touch the talisman and so be given the high power of judgment both good and evil, himself being judged thereby.

"On his return here, he must claim the crown from its place aloft.

"He who can return a victor in all—Emperor shall he be!"

More likely, I thought, he will have passed to the Essence. What mortal man could survive that? Each of the trials was long known to be well nigh impossible. Yet I also knew that there would be no shirking, that it must and would be done even as the Herald had outlined. Among those massed here below was a man who would stand there at last with the crown in his hands, no matter how many lives would be gone to gain that.

21

MASSED BEFORE THE STEPS on which the dignitaries stood were those who offered themselves for trial. I knew that many of them had started from their homes before the actual death of Haban-ji, when the first rumors of his decline had been spread. Now they were gathered, each in a group of the land of their birth—clad in their best finery, armed, and already on show to their fellows.

To me, well back in the throng, they were one mass of warrior wigs, to be sighted now and then when there was some ripple of movement in the crowd. I heard around me some names mentioned, but none of those except that of Shank-ji were known to me.

The leopard stirred and of a sudden the hum of the gathered people ceased. Though the chimes of the lesser mobiles continued, those of the great would not be heard now until the final test.

Down the steps flowed that sleek animal. The sunlight made an azure glow of his fur, his eyes were fierce gems of a milky grey. He came to the candidates. The crowd about me pressed backward until I was near the opening of one of those streets which fed into this plaza. I could no longer see what was happening, but I knew well the leopard was a-hunt.

There was a rising sound. Those who had come from Thnossis opened their tight group and from that a single one of their number stepped to the second stair to face his Queen, who greeted him as her champion, gave into his eager hands the emblem of this search. From that moment forward he would be free of all other demands upon him, set only to the task ahead.

So was he joined by the select ones from Azhengir and Twahihic. Then Shank-ji, who could not be taken for any ordinary contestant. Again there was a murmur arising. There had been no candidate as yet to walk forward from those representing my own land—yet I

169

had earlier marked the number of volunteers from Kahulawe.

The crowd behind the groups of chosen were in movement and again I was pressed back. I had already lost touch with Ravinga and Allitta. Those about me were Vapalan townspeople of the middle classes, exchanging comments in their own clipped speech. I gathered from what I heard, the information spreading, that the leopard had passed by all the men of Kahulawe as if they did not exist and was now entering into the massed throng.

I could see the rippling which must mark the coming of the beast, those drawing from side to side away from that embodiment of imperial power. That ripple spread to where I stood.

Men and women drew away to afford clear passage as the beast came striding as might the Emperor himself. He halted— before me!

Moon-silver eyes regarded me, sweeping from head to boots. Then the gaze centered on that pendant which I had dared to wear this day. Leopard and sandcat were no brothers in blood bond. Leopards had hunted sandcats with the men of Vapala for generations. I saw the lips of this one curl back to show the fangs which seemed to shine in threat. Still the beast paused only for a moment before it came directly to me and then yowled as one which had fastened upon the prey it sought. Though it had not cried out so when it had made its other selections.

There was a quick surge away from me so that now I stood alone with only the leopard. It looked once more into my eyes, and, much as I wanted to slip into the street behind me and be away from it and what its interest in me meant, I knew that escape was now past my ability. Between me and those steps on which stood the four already selected was a clear aisle and the leopard turned to tread it. Without hope of outwitting fortune I followed behind.

Around me there was a clamor of speech in accents of all the queendoms. I wondered if this had ever happened before—and resented that it had happened to me. I was not any young blood, steeled by desert patrolling, safe in the esteem of House or clan. Those with whom I must vie were certainly as different from me as the burning sun from the cool of the night.

I came to those from Kahulawe and, though some made a path for me, there was another who made a firm barrier of his own body. He had turned to face me as I came and I knew that this, my brother, carried not contempt for me now but something approaching hate. I saw his hands as they hung by his sides open and then clench as if upon the hilt of a weapon. His eyes were narrow, and hard, barriers to veil his innermost being. We could have been enemies from years of struggle instead of two who shared the same blood.

The leopard had passed him to return to its statue pose on the steps. However, Kalikku did not move to let me by. It was plain he was daring me to join those others selected by fate—or the whim of a beast.

"This one is a servant!" His voice arose and those about him gave ear, their silence spreading. "This one is no more than a herder of beasts, a carrier of burdens. He is not fit—"

Now he swung around and spoke directly to our Queen, who had descended a step or two drawn by the strangeness of this selection.

"Great Lady, this one is a shame to those of Kahulawe. It is wrong he should be chosen to disgrace our nation. Surely such a selection cannot stand!"

The Herald was now beside Queen Alompra Eakanna. It was he who answered:

"Be silent! It is not for any of us to say this one or that should try for the crown." His hand went out to almost touch the head of the leopard. "From the beginning it was given to this one and his kind to bring forward those who are on trial. Do you dare to question the one who is the servant of the Great Essence? If even a slave of Azhengir is so designated as a candidate then he must be given his full chance."

My brother might have been rendered unable for any more protest, but his eyes told me of the fury that gripped him. One of his companions caught his shoulder and jerked him back, leaving me at last a free path. I longed to cry out myself at that moment, that much of what Kalikku said of me was the truth. I was one ignorant of warrior ways, one who had been a servant even in his father's house. Yet I knew that that would avail me nothing. My fate had been settled when the leopard had looked me eye to eye.

Thus it was under escort of Queen Alompra's own guard that I returned to Ravinga's home to take up my pack again. Of Murri there was no sign and I hoped that he was well hidden. That the dollmaker would somehow get him out of Vapala I was sure.

She had ready for me the pack I had brought out of the desert, but its outer wrappings had been renewed with a fine new blanket and she had also prepared for me the clothes of a traveler, the heavy boots, the short coat, the thick leggings—all of outstanding quality. When I had changed and left the finery she had given me earlier, I picked up the Kifongg. This fine instrument should be left here in safety. Allitta stood in the shop and I held it out to her. "Maiden of the House, this is best in your hands now."

"If you wish." She was cool, but then she added, "The Essence be with you, seeker of thrones."

The Queen's guard had a led oryxen for my riding. And that resented my pack until I calmed it with that skill I had learned among my father's herds.

I had no time to really speak with Ravinga. But I sensed that she wished me well. As I swung into the saddle I saw her fingers move in a small, nearly hidden gesture which was one to summon the good will of the Great Essence. But what was more strange was that Allitta, now in the shadows behind her, made the sign in addition to her spoken good wishes.

It was the custom that each contestant begin his trials in the country of his birth, and to the border of Kahulawe we moved at a goodly pace. The first night out, as we camped, I found myself very much alone. None of the warriors of this company spoke to me in a friendly fashion, rather only with the aloof speech of the court. I was left to myself largely, though I realized that every move I made was noted and perhaps commented on.

My brother had served his allotted time in the guard. Did his opinion of me hold with these men? That could well be. They had offered me my choice of weapons and though no one sneered openly I took only those with which I was familiar—a wayfarer's staff (though one much better than any I had before seen, as this one had longer blades of fine metal set in the length) and a knife. I was not offered a sling. Doubtless that was considered so far beneath the proper equipment that they did not even possess them, but my own was fastened in my belt loop.

It took us three days of fast riding, changing mounts along the way at the camp points on the traders' trail. Then we were across the border and once more the essence of my own place enveloped me with more comfort than any cloak or blanket no matter how well woven.

Once in Kahulawe I realized that we had a follower, Murri, though I could never catch sight of him, nor could any who rode with me do so. The relief of learning that lightened my mind. There was an ordeal before me which was none of my making but one I could not escape. Twice I dreamed that I sat once more at that table in Ravinga's house and looked down upon the stone of dull black which was first the head of a leopard and then that of a rat.

Rats were a matter of conversation about the campfire at night. There had been a steady flow of information open to the guard concerning packs of the creatures, larger and apparently more intelligent than any we had ever known. They were said to have near completely overwhelmed one of the crystal-enclosed cities of Twahihic coming up through earth tunnels and slaying more than ten times ten hands of people—such a disaster which none of us had heard of before.

Morning brought the arrival of the Chancellor of Kahulawe and she came to me directly. There was no sign of favor in her manner.

"You go thus—" She turned a fraction and pointed westward. "The rest of this journey is yours alone, Klaverel-va-Hynkkel." Her lips folded tightly together.

It was plain that in her eyes I was no fit representative for my country. Her scorn did not strike me less strong as such had done in the past, for I might not be a warrior, but I had—my one hand clasped and caressed the scars on my other wrist—danced with the sandcats and out there waiting for me now was one whom none of these would face without drawn steel.

I bowed my head with courtesy as I answered:

"Great One, I accept this path."

Once more her lips twisted as if she tasted a sour and bitter mouthful. "May the Essence possess you in this—" The tone of her conventional words left much to be desired.

I laid out my pack to discard all which might make an extra weight, slowing me down. Somewhere ahead was an island of legend. What I was to confront there I was not sure. I could only hope that in this test, which was of my own land, I would not fail.

At twilight I set out and they watched me out of camp. There were no cheering words and about me their disbelief was like a smothering cloak. Only that was a spur to action and not a deterrent.

I had pushed well away from the torchlight of the camp when there was a darker spot against the night gleam of the sands and Murri came to me. He rubbed his head against my thigh and I went on one knee to stroke the thick fur of his head and neck, scratch behind his ears. Our meeting was heartening. Under just such rising stars as these had I seen his kin in their dancing and, even as that memory crossed my mind, the sandcat whirled about like a kotti playing tail-I-must-catch, giving voice to a singing purr of excitement.

Hardly knowing what I did, my own steps became not those of one patiently slogging through the sand, but rather I, too, advanced in the formal steps and then short leaps I had used at the feast meeting of his clan.

For some moments it was so with us and then that which I must do broke through the small snatch of freedom. Murri ceased his own bounds to come to me.

"What waits—?" he asked.

I shook my head. "Truly I do not know, save that I must search out the heart of Kahulawe and there face that which guards it—and they say the path lies ahead."

We traveled on in the direction the Chancellor had set for me. There arose out of the sand two of the stone guardian cats, set on a line, with a space between them.

Unlike the other such guide posts of the land, these each held up a paw as if in warning, and the gem glow of their eyes was the orange red of those gripped by the heat of anger, ready to attack all who might dare the road between them. Still they did not stir as I walked between.

Against and rising from the gleaming sands was an isle, dark, very dark in the night. Murri slipped ahead of me, to stand waiting at the foot of what seemed to be a cliff. When I reached him I near gagged at a stench which seemed to be exuded from the very rock.

That stench I knew well. Somewhere, not too far away, was a befouled algae pool. Befouled—by the rats?

My staff I must sling across my shoulders if I would climb. My knife? I loosened it a little in the sheath. Then Murri rumbled:

"Evil ones have been here—"

His natural senses were all much keener than mine. At this moment he must be my guide.

"They are still?"

"Who can tell?" His answer held little satisfaction for me.

Already the cat was clawing his way up the cliff. I dropped my small pack, lashed a rope end to it and the other end to my belt. Then with my staff securely bound to my back I began the climb. It was not to be easily done—the handholds and toeholds (for I had also left my boots within my pack) were not easily found. Had I not been faced by similar demands during my days as herdsman I might have found it even more exhausting than a night's march.

However, at length, I won to the top and found that so I was on the rim of a hollow, almost as perfect in contour as the inside of a ceremonial cup. From that rose an overpowering stink. Under the sun, I thought, that it might well overcome any who dared draw near its source.

So rough were the edges of that cup that, after drawing up my pack, I needed to use both hands and feet in a kind of crawl to make my way around towards that part of the island beyond, which appeared to be again higher.

I had gone only a short distance when Murri, still proceeding me, stopped short to look down into the pool of noisome stench. My staff was in my hands and I squirmed around until a spur of rock was at my back so I was best ready to face attack.

"What you seek is there—" Murri jerked his head forward and then coughed as if the stench had eaten at his lungs. I looked down into the hollow.

The walls appeared even more precipitous than had those of the outer cliff. To venture down into that stench—I had heard of herdsmen and hunters who had been overcome by the reek of spoiled algae. If I was to try that descent and should become light-headed—

Murri was still looking down. One half of the cup lay in full dark, the wall holding it in shadow. The other side was revealed somewhat by the glimmer of the rocks under the starred sky. On that side there was carving again.

A giant cat, fashioned as if it were emerging from the wall, sat upright there. Between the forelegs showed a dark opening into what must be inner ways.

Murri's head swung towards me and his eyes were lamp globes in the dark.

"I not go here. Be place for smoothskin only."

I stared down into the bowl-like valley below. The overpowering stench of the rotting algae was sickening. Could I dare such a descent?

My pack lay at my feet and I stooped to open that and rummage within. There was a mass of soggy algae in a container—the medicinal scent of which reached me even through the overpowering odor about. With my knife I worried a strip of cloth from the edge of my cloak and rolled that mass within to tie it over my nose and mouth. It limited my full breathing to be sure, but still it kept me from the threat of reek of this place.

Fastening my staff firmly to my back, and looping a rope end around a spur, I pushed over the rim, leaving Murri behind.

The descent was not as difficult as the climb up the outer cliff had been. My boots thudded to the ground in the shadow thrown by the rise behind me, but the cat-guarded entrance I could see very well.

I must pick a careful way to that doorway. The poisoned algae spattered by my boots might well touch skin to raise dangerous blisters. However, it was not algae alone which made a stinkhole of this place. The carcasses of rats were scattered about. None of them bore long fang tears so it would seem that they had not been brought down by their fellows as was the custom when part of a pack turned upon the weaker members for food.

As I approached that dark doorway in the wall, so overshadowed by the pillar-like forelegs of the cat, I found more and more of the dead beasts and they looked as if they had tried to make some advance in that direction and been mowed down.

There were among these at least three of those larger rats, and one had reached a point nearly between the cat's feet.

I circled by the body and, with staff in hand and ready, lest the darkness ahead could hold some of the pack more lucky, I entered that portal of darkness.

22

I WAS IN UTTER DARKNESS, so thick that I swung my staff before me, sounding walls and flooring lest I be swallowed up by some crevice. The dark gave me such a feeling of being smothered that I pulled down the mask I had assumed against the stench. Luckily here I found that the odor was much less and continued to disappear the farther I advanced.

As I went I listened for any sound which might be that of a rat that had managed to reach that point, but only my own breathing, the muffled thud of my boots against rock, and the swish of my staff were all which reached my ears.

I have no idea of how long that shaftway into the rocky heart of the isle was, though I tried to count strides. To me, in the present case, it seemed to reach forever.

Then, as suddenly as I had come into this thick and stifling dark, so did light break upon and about me.

Here was a circular room but its rock walls were utterly unlike anything I had seen before. They were veined with glittering riverlets of gold, silver, copper. And those riverlets were on the move, twisting and turning, sometimes slowly, sometimes racing, always giving off a light as vivid as a score of lamps.

In the exact center of the chamber was a pedestal, as wide as Ravinga's work table, and on that rested a great ball—clear as glass.

Within it floated, or raced in their turn, motes of vivid color. Those, as light as air, were ever in motion, to form colonies for an instant and then break apart again into separate strings and whirls. Once seen, it held one's eyes, kept one's full attention.

Until something behind it moved. There arose to overshadow that globe and its dancing motes a leopard—not the blue of that

177

imperial symbol—but rather as black of fur as that passage which
had brought me here. And it was larger than any leopard I had
ever seen, even larger than a sandcat.

One giant paw, claws extended in warning, arose to flatten on
the top of the globe. The ears tightened against the skull and the
lips a-snarl showed fangs which glistened of their own accord as
if coated with diamond dust.

"Thief!"

Even as I could understand the sandcats, so did that throat
rumble make sense for me.

"Not so," I struggled as always to produce the proper sounds
with my ill-fashioned human lips and throat.

I laid my staff on the rock floor and did as I would with a
stranger of my own species—holding out my hands, palms up
and empty, in a sign of peace. My sleeve had been rucked back
and the scars of my blooding among the sandcats showed.

The leopard eyed me from head to foot and back again.

"Smoothskin—what you—what you do?"

"I seek the rulership—to lead my kin—"

"You are not of the blood—yet you speak—" His ears went
up, but his giant paw still embraced the globe.

I reached within my clothing and pulled out that which I had
worn secretly while with those who brought me to this shrine—
the cat mask pendant. Like the vivid color lines in the walls, that
flashed brightly.

The great eyes of the leopard turned upon that.

"I dance with the furred ones," I said slowly. "I wear this, and
this." I held forth my wrist still farther that the tooth-carved band
might be seen. "I go not armed against the kin." It was difficult
to shape throat speech, and how well the guard beast understood
I could not tell.

He watched me still, but I thought no longer as he might possible prey. Then he drew back, lifting his paw from the globe. I
had been given no instruction as to what I must do in this hidden
place to prove my "worthiness" but it seemed that the Essence
had its ways of guidance.

I stepped over my staff, moved forward to the pedestal. Reaching out with my hands, though I did not will that gesture myself,
I put them palm down against the sides of the globe.

Those spots of color within were set in frantic motion. Patches
collected to form the shape of my hands within as if they were
inner shadows. The cool surface of the globe began to warm.

The more that the colored patches thickened, the more that heat increased.

Now it was as if I had laid my hands against sun-warmed rock at mid-day, then as if skin and bone were thrust into a fire. The skin itself became transparent and I could see the bones through it.

Fire, I was afire and still I could not loose my grasp of the globe. Nor was I aware of anything about me now, nor saw anything but my two transparent hands with the shifting colors in the globe.

This was like the torment which had been forced upon me when Maraya had given me the wound to make me free of her kinship. What would be the consequence of *this*?

I thought that I could summon no more strength within me to counter that pain which ate through my body. Yet somehow I held fast.

It was some time before I realized that that pain was growing less, receding. No longer could I see my bones through the skin. The motes within were breaking up their concentrations, whirling back into a dance—forming lines and blots which looked almost like the words of some very ancient records. I had a feeling that if I could only make a fraction more effort, I could understand what was to be read there.

However, the last of the energy had been leached from me by pain. I dropped to my knees, my hands slid loosely down the globe sides to hang limp. My breath came hard as might that of a man who had made a mighty run or pulled himself up a high cliff.

The play of lights in the globe still held my eyes, though there was a flickering now which might even mean that they knew exhaustion, too. What was the meaning of this test I did not know. Nor could I even be sure of how well I had acquitted myself.

With an effort I broke eye connection with the globe to look for its guardian. There was no leopard there. A little wildly I turned my head from side to side seeking the beast. His black form was nowhere in that chamber. He might have been a dream save that I was very sure he was not.

I settled back and lifted my hands. By the rights of what I had endured they should have been charred and useless stumps. However, what I saw were normal. Then I turned them palm up. In the shallow cup of flesh at mid-point there was a dark spot. My head still was unsteadied by pain and I had a hard time focusing my sight on those spots.

The skin was not truly charred—as the color of those spots indicated. Rather I now bore on both hands a branding—the head of a leopard to resemble the guardian of this place.

Gingerly I touched the brand on my right hand with the fingers of my left. There was no pain; rather the flesh there felt hard as if I had a thick callus won through demanding labor.

Within the globe the motes had formed a single line, coiling from the base to the top. They moved no more, resting frozen in that loose pattern.

I got to my feet. It seemed to me that the lines upon the chamber walls were dimming. The belief grew in me that whatever I had come for in that testing was now a part of me—a part which I would always wear.

When I stooped for my staff I felt as tired as if I had ventured a whole night's journey on foot, and that at a goodly pace.

With my mask once more in place I again entered the thick dark of that corridor to the outer world. In spite of my weariness I felt something else, a small spark of confidence, almost a flare of pride. I had faced the testing of my own land and I was alive and free. One of the trials was behind me.

There were the first heralds of the sunrise in the sky when I came out between the legs of the cat. In this better light the horror of devastation was more fully revealed. I wanted nothing but to be out of the stink, away from the threat of poison.

My weariness, however, was with me still. Even by the aid of the rope it was difficult to gain the heights above the befouled pool. One of the rocks uncoiled proving to be Murri, his fur so much the color of the land about us that he was hidden until he moved. He came to me in a bound and licked the hands I held out to him, the rasp of his tongue moving over those imprinted palms which I was now sure I would wear until I was absorbed by the Last Essence.

"Good—" he told me. "Kin brother—great fighter?"

"Not yet—" I sat down beside my pack. "There will be more—"

"Kin brother do, do as easily as oryxen kill," he assured me.

I was too tired to protest. My exultation had faded. All I wanted was rest and I pulled back into the shadows of a rock spur which was nearly wide enough to be a cave and there fell almost instantly asleep.

I dreamed—but this was a dream which had no problems—nor did I see Ravinga. Rather I roamed the land freely, with no burden of duty laid upon me. Murri bounded at my side and there was a sense that this world was ours together and always would be. The feeling of well-being which that gave me carried over into waking.

The sun rays were already in the west. There was an ache in my middle which I recognized, after an eye blink or two, as hunger. The dried cakes of algae in my pack had little taste, but I chewed them slowly, dividing that Murri might have his share. I did not want to return to the camp of my escort, yet once more the pattern of duty held me fast.

I found them waiting—Murri had disappeared discreetly before the sentry challenged. When I came into the direct firelight, the Chancellor of Kahulawe stood waiting me. There was no lighting of countenance in greeting, and once more the old soreness of being one not counted as profit to House or clan haunted me.

Not speaking, I rammed my staff point down into the earth and held out my hands so that she and those hard-faced guards behind her could see the signs I now bore.

"So be it." No congratulation in her voice, only a murmur from those gathered there. I wondered, first dully and then with growing anger, if they had been willing for me to fail and that my success was only to be recognized grudgingly.

So be it, my mind answered that thought. Now there was born a determination in me—I would no longer be swept into this by custom, an unwilling participant in this time of trials—rather there *would* come a day when I would reach for the crown and my hands would close upon it! These who still looked upon me as nothing— they would learn!

We were five nights of travel away from the border of the land where my next ordeal waited. But only one day were we in open camp. Instead we were given hospitality by various House-clans, and the last night we approached the isle owned by one of my out-kin—the sister of my father.

She was older than he and even in my childhood I had counted her ancient and kept away from her. For her sharp remarks and piercing looks always weighed and discarded me, or so I thought. But as we came to her guesting house at sunrise, one of her serving maids waited with the message that I was to come to her.

Though I had no robe of presence to wear, being less well clad than her servants, still I was enough in awe of her to answer that summons after I had done no more than clean the sand dust of travel from my face and hands.

The woman I had remembered as majestic as our Queen in her person sat now in a pillowed chair. At her feet was a grey-furred kotti—its color the same as that of my hostess, for not only had her hair dulled to the color of fas-sand but her skin had paled. Still there was the same vibrant life in the eyes she turned upon me.

"So, Hynkkel, you come as a stranger—after all these years. Also you come as one who attempts much."

Those were statements which needed no answers. I had only murmured the conventional greeting before she had spoken. Now she leaned forward a little among her cushions. Out of the dusk behind her quickly moved a maid with a cup she held ready for her mistress. The clawlike fingers of my aunt curled about that and to my deep astonishment she held it forward in a gesture which meant I must accept it.

Never had I been offered the guesting cup which was the greeting between equals. That she should do this now—

Part of me wanted to put my hands behind me and refuse to accept what had never been so offered before. Another and stronger part took the offered goblet.

"To the House, the clan, to she who rules here, may all good fortune come. May the Essence of all be hers—" I said.

As I took the ceremonial sip and returned the cup to her, she accepted it with one hand, but her other shot forward. Those claw fingers braceleted my wrist, turned up my hand so that the marks the globe had set upon me could be clearly seen.

"To he who comes with the favor of the Essence." Still holding my hand in that grip, she drank from the cup which the maid then took from her. Now she peered up at me.

"Judgment may be made too quickly at times," she observed. "You are far more than you have ever been thought to be, brother's son. May you prosper in days to come."

Her eyes fell from my face to the mark on my palm and then she ran her fingers over the scar which I wore as a bracelet.

For a very long moment she stared at that. The kotti at her feet suddenly reared as if some morsel of food was dangled just out of its reach. I saw that her tongue tip ran across her lips.

"You have danced, you have sung." There was a note of awe in her voice. "So it has not been with any for ten generations, and never with one of our House. Truly you have a strange path to follow."

I asked then:

"Have others known the Great Cats?"

She nodded. "There are tales. But who can sift the truth in such ancient matters? Go you, brother's son, to your destiny, and may it be that of the Old Ones long before you."

She sank back again in her nest of cushions and her maid came forward hurriedly, raising a hand as imperious as her mistress's to wave me out.

However, I was left a new thought to chew upon. So one of my own blood knew of the sandcats, and said that in the past others had also danced under the stars and watched the great beasts actually take to the air, and heard them raise their voices in song. Yet never in all my life had I ever heard of such a thing until it happened to me. Ravinga's half revelations, which had certainly never gone far enough, returned to my mind. Her belief that I was part of a pattern— What I truly wanted was the freedom I had dreamed of.

I was ready to go on the next night, impatient to do so. For it seemed to me that the farther I traveled into this maze before me, the quicker I might learn of why it was so.

When we came to the border we met with another company. There rode the guards of Thnossis and with them one of the candidates, he whose homeland it was. We had no speech with one another but the very fact that we had met was assurance that he had completed his task and was eager for the next.

Thnossis was a land of raw violence, or so it seemed to me after the quiet of our own sand desert and rock islets. There were rocks here also but they were tortured into grotesque shapes, uplands showing against the sky before us where trails of smoke twisted from the tips of certain heights. This was where there was no peace. The inner fires of our world were still alive and now and then broke forth to send waves of sluggish streams of molten rock wending down their sides. The sky was overcast and the sun was overveiled in haze. While the air one breathed carried with it the stuff of chemicals which led to fierce coughing.

The people of Thnossis had long ago mastered both the use of these sullen undying fires and the metals found in the mountains wherein the earth fires lay. Their work was such as no other race could equal. My own staff with its skillfully planted deadly edges had been cast here. And those ingots of gold, silver, and copper upon which Kura depended for her fine work with gems had been mined and melded within the hills ahead.

Truly it was a harsh land and those who lived there were a rough-and-ready people, far more aggressive than my own kin.

There was far less ceremony practiced among them and I knew that a man was judged here for strength and courage above all else.

We were three days reaching the foothills of the mountains. I found it difficult to slip outside the camp with food for Murri and it seemed to me that the cat was growing gaunt and finding this trail a hard one. We had come to rocks underfoot and these chafed my boots. How much worse were they for Murri's pads? Yet when I suggested that he stay behind he violently refused—as if he, too, were being put to some test he must face.

At length we camped in the upper foothills below one of the mountains which coughed forth smoke. There awaited us the Chancellor of this realm and his private guard. He was harsh of feature and there was little in him to suggest that he in any way wished me well.

The mountain before me was my path forward and near its summit was all which remained of a very ancient shrine to the fire essence. Twice had flows of lava near overwhelmed it and the way to it was now menaced by fire holes and crevices from which came gusts of the stifling fumes.

I was allowed, however, the equipment of their own miner-explorers—the prospectors for new source of ores and gems. So I changed into far more sturdy boots, and into outer clothing, a hood lying over the shoulders ready to be drawn into place as a guard against inhaling the worst of the exudations of the country. One of their master miners instructed me briefly in the proper way to cross the more menacing sections of the trail. And I knew what I was to do—the threatened shrine held a series of cat figures, each carved from a single great ruby—one such I was to pry loose and bring back.

Though I was equipped as well as any who dared the climb could be, the same was not true of Murri and when he joined me after I had put a ridge between me and the camp, I pointed out that this climb was not for him.

"Not so," he rumbled in return. "Kin have come into Thnossis. There are fire lizards—good eating—" His tongue whipped across his whiskers.

Older and more traveled sandcats might well have dared to hunt here but Murri had no experience and I was worried, though I was sure there was nothing I could do which would turn him from his chosen course.

So we started up the trail which had been shown to me. The rock was not only sharp-edged but in places brittle. I was near to death once when a great puff of yellow smoke burst upward from a crevice near to. I jerked the hood over my head just in time.

Murri! I peered through the eyeholes in the hood sure that I must see him overcome. But he was well ahead. He had lengthened stride to bounds, nearly as high and as lengthy as those I had seen in the dance. And he appeared to have an almost uncanny ability to avoid all the dangerous crevices and the fire holes.

Twice I had to make detours around those. The heat gathered inside the clothing I wore; it was almost as if I were traveling now under the full sun of mid-day. At times I had to stand still for a breath or two to fight giddiness. I felt sick also and wondered if the fumes had somehow found their way inside my protections.

I marveled that these of Thnossis accepted such venturing as an everyday way of life. At last I came to a place where the paths appeared to be wiped out by an emergence of wide crevice from which curled the deadly fumes. However, those did not hide the form of Murri as he was airborne in a great leap which carried him forward through that deadly haze. Though my protective clothing was heavy upon me I could see that I must follow the sandcat's lead.

Edging back, my attention all for the spot where Murri had taken off, I then ran forward once more and jumped, not daring to think at the moment of what lay below. I sprawled on solid rock, sliding along as if my suit was a slick blob of algae.

Murri turned his head to look at me and I saw what nature had given my companion in the way of defense in this land of ever-churning flames. Those great eyes were narrowed into slits, and there appeared to be skin flaps masking the nostrils in his wide muzzle. It would seem that Murri and his kind *were* equipped to hunt here.

He was already on his way upward again. I chose to follow his path with care. There were no more leaps over runnels and at last I saw, through a haze of throat-rasping cloud, what must be our goal.

It was a squat building, one end of which teetered on the very edge of a drop into a much wider river of slow-moving lava. Sooner or later it must be engulfed by that but there was still part of a doorway showing.

A doorway—rather a hole meant for one of the lizards Murri had mentioned. To enter there a man must go on hands and knees and there was no other sign of door—I thought of being caught within if the whole would sink into the rock flow.

Murri crouched flat and inched forward toward that portal as if he were a-hunt. I went down on all fours reluctantly, knowing I could do no less.

So I squeezed into a room. It was dark, for none of the mountain fire penetrated these walls. I felt the nudge of Murri's shoulder and reached out a hand which struck painfully against the wall.

Then that small point of light which was a fixture of my hood was triggered and I could see a little. Underfoot was a mass of stone and what appeared to be shattered glass but which glittered brighter than I believed glass could.

23

THIS BROKEN MASS was a barrier between me and a shelf along one wall. On this sat three figures of cats. There had been more as the jaggered remains showed but some catastrophe (or perhaps malice) had struck. Of the three remaining all were at the far side of the room. They must be over that portion of the structure which hung above the river of lava.

The shards on the floor were a threat to even the stout mining boots which had been supplied to me. Murri had edged back by the door. It was plain that here he dared not risk his pads to such a menace.

In the very limited light I tried to pick a way which offered the least threat. But the stuff crunched underfoot and splintered ends scored my boots. I won to the shelf. Now I had to venture to the left along it to lay hands on the first of the figures.

The cat was about the length of my forearm in height and when I tried to lift it I discovered that it was firmly affixed to the rock under it, almost as if it were an extension of that. Since it would not come free from its upright position I attempted to turn it around as one might unscrew it. But it remained adamantly in place.

I carried no tools with me which I could use as a lever. So I crouched lower to search among the debris on the floor for something I could employ so. Now I thought I could understand the shattered fragments. They must be results of other battles in this place.

Murri moved and I glanced quickly to him.

"Wait—" Even through the wrappings of my hood I caught that word.

His head went down, he had extended his claws and was worrying away with his teeth at one of them. I had often seen the kottis

187

do so, shedding the outer covering of a too-long claw to give that new growing more room. So did it happen with Murri. He spat forth a curved length of old claw perhaps as long as my hand.

My fingers in the protecting gloves were too clumsy. I shook off a glove and picked up that claw. This, too, if it were like those discarded by the kottis, would be brittle. I was not sure of what use it would be but I could try.

I edged back to the shelf and examined with desperate care the base of the figure. It met the stone so tightly I could not see even the mark of a crack—though I was sure it was *not* an outgrowth of the shelf itself. I remembered that there had already been one successful candidate here—I had seen him at the border of my own land. Thus what I attempted could be done.

With the point of the claw I drew a line completely around the figure, making sure it met the juncture of rock and gem. There did not show even a scratch to mark my efforts. Then, drawing a deep breath, I dared to force the claw between one of the foot paws and the shelf.

There was movement? I exerted more pressure, this time at the other paw. Finally I had gone completely around the base of the figure. With the care my sister would have shown in the intricate setting of a gem, I grasped the ruby cat with both hands and slowly turned it—there was no result as I tried it to the right, now I reversed and tried it to the left.

It gave grudgingly, as I did it only a fraction at a time. Yet it moved. Still, though it would turn on the base I could not raise it. I was panting now, my breath coming in gasps. This end of the room was hot— The cumbersome suit which was my protection weighed on me, and my shoulders ached with the effort of trying in so delicate a fashion to achieve my ends.

One felt the desire to jerk, perhaps so to destroy utterly the figure. Impatience had to be contained, subdued.

Again I inserted the claw and held it in place while I turned the figure slowly. It was tipping when it met that obstruction. Suddenly opposition gave and I nearly lost my balance, staggering backward, crunching over the debris, but with the red cat in my hands.

When I turned I saw that Murri was gone, and I knew a thrust of fear. Had this venture proven too much for the sandcat, even though he had boasted that his people came to hunt here?

Cradling the figure against me I got out of the door, crawling at the best speed I knew until I was able to stand. There was a fountaining of fire not too far away. The noxious haze was thick and I realized that I could not mark the path by which I had come. I had relied too much on Murri's leadership and had not memorized any portion which might now prove a landmark.

To my right, I could see only in small wisps of time as the smoke and haze eddied, the land appeared to slant downward. I had climbed to reach this place, so it was only reasonable that I must now descend.

In spite of the fumes and heat, I dared to unfasten my miner's garment and place inside the cat for the best safe-keeping I could devise. Then I began to edge downward.

It required constant alert inspection of the way ahead to avoid dangerously ridged rock which might trip even the most careful, or the flame- and smoke-emitting potholes. My legs trembled, not only from the strain of the climb and this descent but from my inner fear of taking the wrong step. Also I looked for Murri—

Had the Great Cat been overcome? If so how might I carry him down? Though he was far from being as large as his sire, yet he was a burden I was sure I could not bear.

I dared to halt, to raise the edge of my hood, and I cried aloud:

"Murri?"

There was movement through the haze which was not a fountain of fire. I turned in that direction. My furred companion stood there, his head dropping forward, his huge body trembling visibly. I reached his side and laced my fingers in the stiff ruff of fur at his neck. His head came up a fraction, turned. I saw that his great eyes were fully shut.

"No see—"

There was panic in those two words and that panic fueled true fear in me. Had the fumes blinded Murri? How would we find our way down? That I would part company with him now was impossible.

I pulled at his ruff and he came with me step by staggering step. Meanwhile I tried steadily to tell him what lay before us. It was not until we got to the chasm which he had leaped before that I faced the fact there might be that I could not do for Murri.

"Go—call—many times call—"

Such a hope was impossible. He nudged me with his head.

"Go—call—" Then he coughed heavily.

"You cannot—"

"Go—call!" This time he showed his fangs at me and his words ended in a snarl.

In the end I went, thinking that perhaps this was the only chance for both of us.

I found what seemed to be the best place for a takeoff—the opposite side I could see now and then through the haze which was less heavy here. So I leaped and was flung forward on the rock at the other side though I had wrapped both arms about the treasure that I bore, lest it be crushed. By some miracle it was not. Then I moved back a fraction from where I had landed and I loosed my hood again and called and kept on calling "Murri!"

He came, though he did not land well, his hind legs slipping over the edge of the crevice. I grabbed frantically for his ruff, twisting both hands in that and jerking him towards me.

That was the last major barrier that it was needful for us to transverse. I could pick a way around the other traps and bring Murri with me. Then we reached the last of the downslopes. Between us and the camp there was still the ridge. Murri—I could not leave him so and yet those encamped beyond would meet him with steel.

The time had come that Murri must be accepted as my companion. Surely my own position as candidate would give weight to my demand that he be tended. That I had been selected by the Blue Leopard for this round of journeying and life risk must have made some impression on my escort, little as those who formed it appeared to esteem me.

Murri offered no objection as I led him on by my grip upon his ruff. In me the fear that he was blind for all time hardened. To such as the sandcats this would be far worse than any death. Yet it was our custom—as I had done for Bialle—to release to the Greater Essence those who suffered past hope.

Though I had never been called upon to grant such escape to any of my own kind, I knew that that was also done upon occasion, and in this instance, were I as Murri, I would have welcomed the mercy knife quickly.

Still there was a chance. No one would venture into this land of fire and poisonous vapors without some manner of relief for burns and the like. I held to the hope that those who had brought me hither knew of such.

We ascended the ridge and paused there for a moment. I had thrown back that hood which had curtailed my full sight and now I looked carefully at Murri. His eyes were still closed and there appeared to be a yellow crust forming along the edges of the lids.

"You hurt—brother?" I asked.

"No pain—now." He held his head high as if he could see and I noted that those nostril flaps had folded away and that he was sniffing the air.

"They wait—" he rumbled.

That I could well see. Those I had left in camp were drawing in to the foot of the ridge. Two of them held bows with arrows nocked. And they were eyeing Murri.

I tightened my grip on the sandcat's ruff and moved so that any taking aim would find a target in me instead.

"This one is not for the killing!" I raised my voice in a shout to carry above the rumble of the tormented mountain behind me. "This one is under my protection."

Did that statement mean anything? I could not be sure. However, he who led the company of warriors made a gesture and the bowmen lowered their weapons.

We went together down the slope. Lucky here the footing was smooth enough and Murri, though he could not see, confidently set paws in places which kept him steady. Then we were on as level ground as this place offered.

I halted only a sword's distance from those staring at me. Thrusting my hand inside the protective suit, I brought out the ruby cat and, when the Chancellor made no attempt to take it from me, I set it on the ground.

"You have aids for wounds," I said. "Give me such. I have fulfilled your task, therefore you of Thnossis have no more power over me."

The Chancellor gestured, and one of his guard picked up the ruby cat, yet there was bared steel still before us and they looked to Murri as if they expected an instant charge.

I held forth my wrist, pulling back the sleeve to display the ring of the tooth scar. "This one is blood brother, after the rules which all warriors know. I bear the mark of it. Give me that which I can use now for my brother's easement."

There were two points I held fast in mind—first, that the persons of the candidates were to be guarded between their times of testing and what they asked for in the way of aid during their travels must be given them. Second—blood brothership through the exchange of vital fluid was not uncommon among warriors. And, while I could not be counted such in their eyes, certainly no one could deny that Murri was of noted fighting stock.

Now I acted as if this was only the proper thing to be done. Moving forward, my hand still to guide Murri, they did give way before me without question. Though the Chancellor and several of the guard looked bleak enough.

However, I brought the sandcat into the camp and I was supplied with a bag borne by him who was delegated to be the healer, though he only laid his supplies on the ground and stepped back, giving me no assistance. I could only act for Murri as I had many times in the past for herd beasts and kottis. There was a tightly closed jar which held some paste and that I recognized, by its odor, to be a prime remedy for wounds. Whether it would react on the sandcat's eyes I could not tell, I could only try.

Scooping out a finger end full of the paste, I spread it across each of those yellow-crusted eyelids. Then I caught up one of the squares of soft woven stuff from a neighboring packet and began, with the lightest touch I could hold my fingers to, to work at the edges of that encrustation. The stuff came off in small flakes which must be carefully cleared away lest they work into the eyes themselves and it was not an easy business. But, at last, I had rid Murri's eyelids of the last bit.

The sandcat did not open his eyes as yet. I scrabbled among the contents of the medical packet until I had found a package which was squashy to the touch and from which I could pinch out bits of water-soaked algae. With these I washed the lids twice over and then sat back on my heels, a fear still in me. Could Murri see? If my ministrations had done nothing—!

"Brother," I worked with lips and tongue to form my command, "look!"

Those eyes opened. To my sight they were as ever, round yellow gems, with only the thread of darkness in their centermost point to suggest that they were not the stone they resembled.

Twice Murri blinked. He raised one paw as if to wash his face, but did not quite touch his muzzle.

"See—little—"

Since I could not look through those threatened eyes I had no idea of limitation or whether that would be permanent. I squeezed out more of the wet paste and smeared it on another length of cloth, this longer, plainly meant to be a bandage. Murri had already closed his eyes again and I tied that as firmly as I could so that the soothing stuff was in place.

It was then that I took off the suit which had been given me. Glad to see the last of it. I wore only the breeches of my trail garb, while on my chest swung the cat mask pendant.

There was a stir behind me. One of the Chancellor's servants had brought my other clothing, but he laid it down some distance away and I saw that the company who had come with me ringed me around, watching. The archers had set aside their bows, and swords had been sheathed, but I could feel their watchful eyes, sense strongly their unease not only for Murri within their camp, handicapped as he was, but also for me since I had claimed blood kinship with their ancient enemy.

When I had pulled on the rest of my clothing I looked to the Chancellor.

"I have done what I was set to do, Ruler's Voice," I spoke formally. "Is this agreed?"

"It is agreed." His answer was short and he turned away, his leaving breaking that ring of spectators about me. Though I noticed that two of the sword bearers did not leave, though they kept their distance.

There was food and I divided my share with Murri before I guided him to the small tent which was my private quarters.

That night we slept together. For in Thnossis travel was mainly by day, much of the terrain being too treacherous to try to cross except under the brightest of sunlight, punishing as that might be.

Sleep did not come easily. I could not share my doubts with Murri. He had curled up, bandaged head on forepaws, and was already asleep. If in the morning his sight was still gone—

I must be on my way to Azhengir, that perilous waste of desolate salt pans, perhaps to all save those who lived there the cruelest of countries. No sandcat could venture there. No beast could, except the ever-present rats. I dared not take Murri, for I was sure I could not trust those with me to help the cat were I to fail. Nor could I leave him blind and helpless here. It would all depend on how well the remedies would work.

My own body was aching from exertion, and sleep came upon me in spite of the thoughts teeming in my mind, the worries which besieged me.

There was light, not the hard striking rays of the sun. Lamplight—soft and glowing, somehow soothing after my ordeal with the fires of the mountain. I stood on a floor of polished wood nor could I move. Then hands came from overhead, reaching plainly into the beams of the lamp, hands large enough to grasp my whole body.

They held an object which had the golden fluff of fur as they set beside me Murri. There was no bandage across his eyes, they were alive with the glow I had always seen. Yet when he was placed there he did not move. He might have been a figure such as the ruby cat I had worried out of its setting upmountain.

The hands now rested on the flooring a little before me and I studied them. Each finger bore a ring which was wide enough around to serve me as a belt. And each of those rings was of a different design. They had been fashioned to resemble heads, a man with a warrior's wig, a woman with an ornate crown, an oryxen with wicked horns which gleamed silver bright, a yaksen, a kotti curled at ease, its supple body forming much of the band of the ring. Those were on one hand. On the other there was clearly wrought a setting akin to the cat mask I wore, beside that a second crowned woman, then something which was not a head or face but an intricately entwined symbol, next a dagger fashioned so that it extended up and down the finger beyond the bounds of the ring band, and, last of all, what could only be the representation of a rolled scroll of high learning, the kind which each family guarded in their archives.

For a space those hands lay at rest and then they arose a little and the fingers moved, not joining together but as if each were fastened to a strand which must be woven back and forth. Then darkness enfolded me and beyond that light, the sounds of the camp awakening, drumbeats still troubling the air.

Murri sat at the entrance of our small tent. His bandage was in place. But he turned his head a little.

"This one would see—"

If you only can, I thought, but did not speak that aloud. Instead I tugged at the fastening and the strip of cloth fell away. To me his eyes looked normal once again but that he could actually see—

Murri held one of those lengthy stares which were of his kind and then a sound like a great sigh came from him.

"This one sees!"

I threw my arms about his shoulders and for a moment buried my face in his ruff. Far greater than any bringing back of ruby cats out of places besieged by fire was this!

"This one goes. Here is no welcome—" Murri arose to his feet and stretched as any of his species arising from sleep.

What he spoke was the truth. But how complete was the cure? Was it only temporary and he would go forth from this camp to be again stricken where there would be no aid? I had no time to voice any protest, he spoke again:

"This one—no go—salt place."

"If you—your eyes—"

"We meet again—after salt place."

He was already out of the tent. People were stirring within the camp but he took two great leaps which brought him to the outer limits. My last sight of him was his flying in the air—or so it would seem to those who do not know his kind—out and away. From his direct line of flight I knew that he could see and I must hold the hope in my mind that that was permanent.

For six days we crossed this world of unstable land and fire-breathing mountains. As usual my guards exchanged few words, and only those of necessity, with me. However, to my surprise on that first morning after the withdrawal of Murri, the Chancellor reined in his oryxen to match the pace of mine and addressed me:

"Blood kin to cats," he began abruptly. "And how did you win such a distinction?"

There was little formality in his speech. The words were more an order, though I felt resentment and I schooled myself not to show it. After all he who advised the Queen of Thnossis perhaps had reason to so weigh me as less.

I told my story in as few words as possible and it came curtly enough. He listened, I saw, with the same care he might give to some report of importance.

At the end I turned my wrist for him again to view that scar which was my key to the councils of those who had been so long the enemy.

He was frowning a little when I had finished. "That might be a bard tale," he commented, "save that you have shown us what you can do. Strange indeed, for between our kind and the Great Cats there has always been war."

"Always?" I was remembering then the half legends Ravinga had spoken of—of a time when man and sandcat had been fellow warriors against some great but now forgotten ill.

His frown grew deeper. "You speak of things which are not for all ears." He sent his oryxen forward, leaving me once more to speculate upon what seemed to be an unseen web which had somehow gripped me fast.

Nor did he speak to me again. On the fifth day we came to the border of Azhengir and saw there the guard and Chancellor of that land waiting. But this time there was no lucky candidate in their midst and I could guess at a failure, how disastrous a one I did not yet know.

24

We are all deeply akin to the lands of our birth. The essence of that enters into us so that no other place can mean so much. I had faced the threats of the fire-ridden Thnossis yet that in its way had not seemed as fearsome as did Azhengir, into which I now passed.

There were no insects in the slickrock country, nor had I suffered from the attentions of such in either Vapala or Thnossis. But here the salt pans sent up winds of them against all comers. They bit, they crawled across any exposed skin, they sought out the corners of eyes and mouth until their assaults were maddening.

Also, in some way the very Essence here was repelling. I felt that, following each stage of our journey into Azhengir, there grew stronger the feeling that I was an intruder to be routed, that the desolate world about me would spew me forth.

Yet to the guard who had met me at the border this land was a way of life, barren and hard as that might be.

The salt pans were in themselves traps. Azhengir's one export was salt but that could not easily be dredged from the pans, as its collection was a thing of peril. There were thermal pools within the pans and those grew no algae, or if a few plants made rooting there they were not of any use—either for eating or the soothing of any body hurt.

However, those of Azhengir planted in these scattered pools branched rods which resembled those of the trees of Vapala. Upon those branches there gathered in the course of time clear crystals of salt. These were the harvest which brought the trade to supply those who gathered such crops with the bare necessities of life.

However, to plant those bushes and then reclaim them with their fruit was a perilous undertaking. The harvesters were equipped with long rods of their own to sound out a path ahead, as the scumlike

197

surface hid sucker ponds which could draw into a speedy death any who broke their crust.

Nor could they depend upon landmarks to set a clear trail to any pond no matter how many times they made that journey. For the undercrust traps moved and changed in thickness. Thus each trip to the harvest was a test of skill in judgment, as well as a matter of sheer fortune.

On the fourth day after we had crossed the border we entered one of the small villages which were anchored firmly by the same rock ridge which formed the only road.

It was a squalid place, the buildings hardly more than huts, and, as far as I could see, no attempt had ever been made to ornament any of them. No guardian cat statues stood beside doorways, not even that of the largest hovel in which the chief of this village sheltered. No color relieved the dirty grey of the walls, no banner, save a large pole encrystaled with salt deposit, stood before that place of rulership.

The people turned out to greet us. Though I fought off insect clouds, those of the salt lands did not seem to mind when such crawled over them, raising a hand only now and then to drive away some more persistent attacker. The natives were dark of skin but it was not a ruddy darkness such as I myself show, or that possessed by the miners and metal workers of Thnossis. Rather this appeared to have an overshadowing of grey which was as repelling as their homes and echoed the lank locks of hair which hung about their gaunt faces. No one tied back those straying strands with any band, nor did their women wear the bright metal combs and catches I was used to. In fact there was very little metal in sight.

They watched us without expression and, as I slid out of the saddle, I knew that they were mainly eyeing me. Then he, as gaunt and colorless as all the rest, who stood before the chief hut, beckoned, making no move to step forward. It was as if in this place even the courtesy of guesting were unknown.

So I was led into the presence of Dar-For-It, Voice for the village. He was very old, a veritable skeleton figure crouched on a stool within the hut. One of his eyes was filmed as grey-white as his straggle of hair.

Behind him was a gathering of what must be his personal guard, though the only weapons they carried (if weapons those were) were long rods, the tips of which reached well above their unkempt heads. There were both men and women there, the Heads of various Houses, I judged. Yet none were better arrayed than the crowd of commoners without.

In the center of the chamber was a fire which was hardly more than a ruddy handful of coals. Over that, supported on a tripod of legs, was a bowl of discolored metal from which a lazy curl of smoke arose.

"You have come a long way to die." The greeting certainly was not in any way one to encourage. "He who was first here was of our kind and yet he is now gone."

There did not seem to be any answer to that.

The old man stared up at me through his fringe of hair. "It is only right that he who would wear the Great Crown must first share life with those to be governed, say you not also?"

"Yes," I made short answer. All knew the purpose of these tests—that the Emperor-to-be must know the life of others.

The chief nodded. Then he lifted a hand. Those who had stood behind him spread out, some of them circling behind me. I did not like the feeling which came with that encirclement. Again the chief signaled.

One of the others, a woman who looked as old as he and wore the first ornament (if you could call it such) that I had seen— a necklace of what could only be rat teeth threaded together with beads of salt—knelt by that slowly simmering basin and dipped into it a misshapen cup which, brimming with a sickly greenish liquid when she brought it forth, I saw to be an oversized rat skull.

"If you would be one of us—a harvester," the chief said, "then you will prepare even as we do to try the ever-changing trail. Drink, outlander!" The last two words were uttered as a firm order—one against which no argument could be raised.

The stuff gave off a vile odor and I guessed it would have an even worse taste. However, I had no choice. Somehow I choked it down and then had to fight against nausea. To spew it up again— I was sure that was what they expected. I would not please them so much.

The nausea remained and with it came gnawing pain in my middle. Poison? No, I was sure that they would not dare to dispose of any candidate of the trial. The cup I had put down was taken up by the women, refilled twice, and given so to two of the others.

That answered in part my question. It must be a required ritual for those setting out into the pans.

Somehow I got out of the hut, fighting the revulsion which gripped my body. A rod was pressed into my hand and I summoned strength to grasp it.

With at least half the village as an escort we made our way down from the firmness of the ridge to the edge of the pan. The chief did not accompany us, but the seeress was very much to the fore and I saw her eyeing me with a grin of anticipation.

Those two men who had shared the potion with me were already moving out on the crust, their poles swung before them, testing the way ahead. They were well away from the edge when they stopped and looked back, giving voice to a queer cry. The seeress was at my side now.

"Go, outlander. Our men have shown you the art of pan walking, it is now yours to do it also—there is a salt pool straight ahead, and the crystals there are well ripe for the gathering. We have kept it so for the testing. But to gain it you must watch where you tread."

My stomach still twisted with the drink. However, using the pole for sounding my path, I made a cautious way out on the crust. I could not take either path those other two had followed for they stood firmly in the way. I must prospect for my own trail.

I strove to center all my attention on my footing. Though the pain twisting in me, the clouds of insects which buzzed about, were hard to set aside. Twice my pole struck through the crust and I must stand on one spot of safety and cast on either side for secure footing.

At length I crept past where both of the others had halted and before me was only open pan. Neither of the experienced harvesters moved to accompany me. A cold bite of realization came: they would make no effort to rescue me if I chose wrong. From now on I had no one to depend upon but myself.

I did not look back. My attention was all for what was under-foot, or rather before foot. My shoulders began to ache at the constant swing of the pole in a short sweep from right to left before me. Once more the tip cut into a treacherous thin crust and this time I nearly overbalanced to follow. That I kept my feet was a sign of fortune I dared not hope might be mine again. I forced myself to a slower pace, tried with insect-attacked eyes to make sure that the next step was solid.

Before me at last opened the salt pool. From its surface pro-jected the ends of those branched rods which were the collectors. I was heartened by so much and gained another step.

Now the swing of my pole proved that the way before me was a trap. I moved to one side at that first testing, thinking to approach from a different angle. Again the pole proved that could not be done. So I struggled on, trying to find a way in. There must be such, or how could the villagers reach their crop? Which now appeared a carefully guarded secret, one which was not to be shared with me. I leaned on the pole and studied the pool.

Those branches were planted around its edge. Apparently there was no way of working them out into the middle of that pond. The nearest? I might be able to touch it with the end of my pole if I exerted my strength and extended it so that my grasp was barely on the end. However, the smoothness of the pole was no use in snagging a branch which I was sure had been firmly planted.

My clothing was that of a wayfarer. And I had no rope such as I had taken with me on my solo. I did wear a belt, though that was heavy with ornamental metal medallions. Now I unlatched that strip of hide and began to pry loose those rounds of copper and gold so that it would not be weighted down. At length, my fingers sore and gashed from the effort, I had a length of oryxen hide which was more supple without its decoration.

What I faced now was the need for skill. Could I put into service some of the ability which I used with a sling?

I attached the belt in a loop to the end of my pole, bending two of the gold medallions which had decorated it about the ends, testing what I had done with vigorous jerks.

Then I cast for the nearest of those branches in the pond. Four times I made that throw, pausing between each to rest my shoulder, trying to control the shaking of my arms.

This could not continue forever. At the same time I must not allow need to push me into a frantic struggle which would not serve any purpose save to use strength I needed so badly.

I stood, panting, looking at that branch. It inclined the least fraction in my direction. Once my improvised noose had struck against it, but not encircled it.

Now I measured distances again and upended the pole, thudding it to my right once again. To my relief it struck a firm surface and I stepped sidewise. It seemed to me that I was indeed closer to that branch. I reversed the pole and made my cast.

The belt struck against the branch, encircled it, slid down as I dropped the pole little by little. Delicately I moved the staff in a circular direction, twisting, or trying to twist, the belt which had nearly sunk from sight in those side branches which were spaced along these salt catchers.

Drawing a deep breath, I dared to exert strength to a pull.

To my joy there was resistance! The belt was securely entangled. Now it remained to be seen whether that hold was enough to withstand a strong enough jerk to loosen the branch.

I pulled, there was no answer, But at least my belt did not lose hold. There was only one thing left. I had no idea how the salt gatherers plucked these out of the ponds, but they could not be set so deep that they did not come loose easily, for there was too much danger of overbalancing and perhaps ending in one of the crust-closed traps.

Putting both hands to the pole I dared all in a single sharp jerk.

I slipped backward as the branch yielded suddenly. One foot went off the safe spot on which I stood. I fell to my knees, striving to throw my weight forward. With the crystal-beaded branch swinging over my head, I drove the other end of my support rod as deeply as I could into the secure footing and fought to draw myself towards that one hope of safe support.

For a moment I was afraid that I could never exert strength enough to draw myself to complete safety. Then I huddled at the foot of that planted rod, while over me swung the branch. For the first time I became aware that the day was near done.

Could I make my way back to the ridge land in twilight? I struggled to my feet, still holding on to the anchorage of my rod. Then I untangled the branch and, with my belt for a sling, slipped it onto my back. I edged around to face the direction from which I had come.

Those two salt gatherers who had flanked me when I had entered this morass were gone, but I could make out figures on the ridge. My legs trembled, not only with the reaction to the peril I had just escaped, but also from the strain I had known since I entered this place.

However, the coming night might leave me marooned here and that I could not allow. I would be no more ready to face return then, perhaps even less.

My rod swung out, prospecting for the next foothold, and I forced myself to the task of moving. Twice I again nearly lost my balance when the crust appeared to hold the rod and then it went through. My whole body ached with the effort I expended. The only small relief was that with the growth of twilight those ever-attacking insects were gone.

I kept my attention all for the next step, not for anything ahead, and then at last, when I was sure I could not travel farther, my rod thudded home hard enough to jar my whole body. I could not really believe that I had made it back until one of the salt gatherers confronted me and for the first time I saw a trace of emotion on his face.

He offered me a hand but I drew myself up and did not accept support. Rather I staggered up the rise to the main part of the ridge and there confronted the woman who wore the necklace of teeth and salt. It would appear that here she stood as judge. Swinging off my branch, I dropped it at her feet.

25

I WAS NOT the only outsider to shelter in the salt-gathering village that night. There was a merchant who had come through the land which I was to transverse the next day. His complaints sounded loudly from the chief's hut. He had been boldly attacked by rats, two of his yaksens had been brought down, and he had been forced to retreat leaving behind the packs of goods they carried. One of his men was under treatment, having had one arm mauled to the point that he might never recover from the wound.

However, the merchant had brought with him one of the attackers, dead of a skillful spear cast, in order to prove his point that this was no ordinary foe. Like those I had seen dead after our encounters in the rock isles, this limp carcass which had been dragged along after the merchant's oryxen was large—in fact larger even than those others I had examined. It could have equaled Murri in size, or even been a fraction the greater.

The villagers gathered around to inspect that trophy and it was very plain that they were shaken out of that impassivity which had welcomed me and my guard. I heard mutters which told me that the like of this creature had been sighted before and that one had slain an experienced salt gatherer, seeming able to follow the man across the salt pans by some uncanny knowledge of its own.

"There are enough of these vermin out there," the merchant declaimed as he came forth from the hut, still loud in his complaints. "But these—they are such as could take a whole trade party if they pushed attack. And what if they do?" He turned slowly as if he would catch the eyes of all those ringing him in. "Can any traveler stand up to such a pack? Can your village stand against them? I tell you that there is trouble brewing and you had best be prepared for more of this at your doors." He kicked at the carcass before he strode off.

However, at that moment I was more intent upon crawling into the center of my sleeping mat. My stomach still pained me and I had no desire to take my place by the cookfire of my escort. There was only this much in my mind—I had completed three of the five tests—and I realized that inwardly I had never thought that I could do so.

I was able to eat some breakfast the next morning. There was no explanation for the potion I had been forced to swallow—I could only believe that it had been done deliberately to make my task the more difficult and I felt far from kindly towards the village, very glad to see the last of it.

The guard rode at alert, a scout sent ahead. They were prepared for some such attack as the merchant had suffered. Still we made the six-day journey across this dreary and forbidding land without having to face any enemy. Twice we stayed in villages and I heard the officer who commanded my escort question the inhabitants closely about such attacks. The news he received was not encouraging.

That merchant who had brought proof of the nature of the enemy was not the first trader along the route who had been attacked. But the other had been far from lucky. A pair of villagers traveling along the ridge way had come across the remains of a small caravan where the stripped bones of both traders and their beasts were all which could be found. Even their packs had been gnawed open and the contents dispersed and befouled or missing.

It was the latter point which puzzled both villagers and guards the most. For it was plain that, while the rats had feasted on all food stuffs they had managed to find, why would they drag off trade goods? The accepted answer seemed to be that the scene of that battle must have been later visited by outlaws, who had made the most of their discovery. Though that any outlaw would be willing to linger in this land was more than I could understand. The villages certainly had little worth stealing. While their inhabitants, I was sure, had their own deadly methods of defense. Even I, who had little liking for them as a people, could agree to that.

As we approached the border of Twahihic a scout, sent ahead, reported that an escort was already waiting there and with a successful candidate in their care. We passed into that territory just at nightfall and for once the two parties camped together.

The attitude of the other escort towards their charge was far different from that I had met. And seeing him I believed I could understand the difference. This was Shank-ji. Instead of wearing drab trail garb he was decked out in the finery of a warrior in full dress. While he laughed and talked animately with those who had ridden with him.

I wondered how he would survive the treacherous paths of the salt pans, the fiery roads of the mountain, and last of all how he would confront the leopard whose mark I would always bear.

Custom kept us apart. Perhaps it was thought that one might advise the other on the trials ahead. Though I believe the rivalry which was strong among candidates would not have led to that. However, we did view each other from a distance. His contempt was plain to read, yet there was a shadow there of something else—perhaps a very angry surprise that such as I had lasted so long.

He might believe himself favored. For the trial offered in Vapala was last, only to be made when all the survivors had assembled within the city. I knew that one other at least had been successful in several of the trials, and that another had failed and was probably dead. Which left three of us to be accounted for.

The guard feasted that night and Shank-ji was very much a part of the festivities. Several of those who had accompanied him were wagering he would be triumphant and they found no takers against him. I watched from a distance and finally sought my sleeping mat to lie looking up at the stars.

That I had no well-wisher suddenly seemed to me to be a hard thing. I had ridden from one land to the next with the guard sent by each Queen in turn, yet none of them had shown any friendship, nor given me any wish for fortune, or applause when I had accomplished my task. While Shank-ji, who had faced so far but one of the trials, acted as if he were already victor and also appeared to be accepted as such by his fellows.

I faced this self-pity, tried to open my mind to the Essence that it might wipe clear this feeling which was weakening. Then I discovered that it was true what I had always heard of Twahihic. As the camp quieted down the haunting silence of the land closed in.

There was no whisper of sand—yet ahead were those mountainous dunes which the inhabitants had put to such good use. For the only purpose of this arid waste before me was to provide a play place for those of the other lands who were drawn here for sand-skimming races and the like. There were cities, each cupped within a bowl of green glass, cultivating within some the fruits which were only known elsewhere in Vapala. Each of the cities had its speciality in what it had to offer the visitor. There were contests of musicians, trained troupes of dancers, those who acted out some of the old legends of each land, as well as inns which specialized in fine foods, held gambling sessions in their top rooms. Here were women and men prepared to offer any entertainment which might be dreamed by those who came. Young people who vied with each other in the dangerous sport of dune skimming had their other desires catered to within the domed settlements.

However, now what I felt was a barrenness of spirit. Were there any here who sought out their private places and opened their minds and hearts to the Essence, waiting to be filled with that blessing which can be obtained only by long and diligent search? I felt nothing—it was as if a door had shut firmly between me and that sure knowledge of being one with the land, with all the life upon it.

We traveled on from that camp. Those of the escort who had been so cordial with Shank-ji kept aloof from me. We exchanged only the formalities necessary for everyday tasks. While, as I rode, the emptiness I had felt on the first night within the border here continued, wearing on my spirit in spite of all my battles against it.

I longed for Murri—had he indeed survived his ordeal on the mountain of fire? Was he again on the trail of our party? I began striving to somehow touch him, picturing him firmly in mind and then making the struggle to project my call.

On the second night I was answered!

"Brother-one—" It came very faint as if from afar.

"Murri!" There is a strength in names, perhaps that call of his would bring us closer.

"I—here—" his reply seemed to form in my mind. But where was "here"? I could not believe he might survive in this barren land of towering dunes, any more than he could have survived among the salt pans.

"I wait—"

Though I tried to reach him again there was no more. Wait—where—for what? Nor did I sleep well that night.

We pushed on until a four-day journey was behind us. Once we halted in one of the bubble villages. I dined as might the Emperor, slept soft, but still I was walled from all about me. Again I speculated whether this was not done with a purpose, that communication with any who might aid me in my set task was forbidden.

It was the second day after we left that luxurious stop that we were joined by the Chancellor of this queendom. She straightway summoned me, looking me up and down as if I were an oryxen of dubious value being offered her for sale and then she spoke sharply:

"Beyond those dunes," she indicated the towering mountains of sand to the left, "lies your task, man of Kahulawe. There is a village in which no one dwells, for an unseen evil lies within, and near all who attempt entrance disappear. Yet in its gardens grow malons.

"The nature of these fruits is that they must be watched with care for they ripen very suddenly. And they must be plucked when ripe. For otherwise, if left on the vine too long, they are as quickly taken by rot.

"He who would be judged by our land must enter into that shunned place, find two malons, and bring them forth untouched by any rot. Nor can anyone tell what other fate awaits there, but it is dire."

I could believe that she was striving to overawe me. Yet I knew that the peril of death *did* cling to each of the trials and there was undoubtedly some evil connected with the place.

She made no more move to direct me to the site of my testing. Nor did my escort. I strove to pass around the side of the dune in the direction she had pointed, wondering if these so feared what might lie within the shunned dome that they did not wish even to come into sight of it. Yet others—at least Shank-ji and the candidate who was of this queendom—had done this thing, and Shank-ji had plainly been successful.

I twirled my staff and watched the sun glitter on the blades which issued from its sides. Shank-ji might have gone in with better arms, but of what good was a sword to me who had so early proved that I was unhandy with such a weapon?

Slipping and skidding I won my way to the other side of the dune. There, as the Chancellor had promised, arose the green bubble of a dome. It was of lesser size than I expected. Perhaps its original population had been no more than what my people would reckon a single clan or House. The green glass was opaque, though I knew from my visit to the city that that did not prevent the entrance of sunlight, only screened it somewhat so that the heat and light of the outer world were tamed.

"Brother—" Out of the sand which was so close a shade to his own fur Murri arose, shaking himself.

The golden eyes turned to me were indeed unclouded as far as I could determine. Yes, he was as he had always been, save that he seemed to grow the larger each time we were parted. I dropped my staff, throwing out my arms as he approached, burying them in his ruff, while his harsh tongue rasped against my cheek. All the inner emptiness which had gripped me since I had entered this too-silent land vanished. What need had I for any comrade save the one I was welcoming now?

He raised a giant paw as he could to one of his own kind and rolled me over on my back, with a mock growl which I endeavored to echo as well as I could. At that moment I longed for the ability to take to the air in one of the great springs which marked the cat dances to prove how light my heart was.

Murri at last settled back to look at me inquiringly.

"Where go?"

I pointed to the green dome. "There." I explained as best I could in my limited grasp of his own tongue what I must do there.

"Not hard—" he commented.

"It must be," I continued, "or they would not have sent me here to do this thing."

"It gets no less, waiting—" I untangled that much from his complicated series of sounds. And he spoke the truth.

I picked up my staff again. Feeling able to face anything which might lie ahead as Murri paced beside me, I approached the dome.

The big entrance which had allowed access to the city was absent here. There was a portal no wider than would admit two walking side by side or a single beast with rider or driver. Across it was set in place so wide a metal bar as to suggest that what lay in wait within possessed more than human strength.

The bar was hard to shift. It had settled well into its hold-hooks and certainly had not been much moved for a space. Perhaps only by those candidates who had been before me here. I allowed it to thud into the sand which had drifted high about the surface of the door and pulled that forward, discovering that I had to exert some strength to open a space wide enough for Murri and then me to slip by.

The first thing I noted was a tangle of growth which had near buried the few buildings I could see. Loops of vines reached near as high as the upper curve of the dome in places. There was a strong smell, not of the algae to which I was accustomed, but rather like that I had met when I crossed the fields of Vapala.

In that other Twahihican village had been a wealth of scents, perfumes, spices, all those which proclaimed enticement for visitors. Here was only one. After a moment or so I found it rank and unpleasant.

There was no sign of any of the malons here. But there were marks, almost effaced by growth as if that which rooted here had been very swift to veil the damage done, a path forward which had been slashed and cut through this net. At least those I followed on this quest had accomplished that much for me.

Murri swiped at a tangle of growth with one paw, his talons cutting branches and leaves. That opened up even more the entrance to the passage which had been recently cleared and I began to use my staff, its blades extended to their foremost, to beat and slice my way.

Murri paused, his head turned to the left, and I saw the swell of his large nostrils as he tested the air. Then he swung out with a paw and slashed at the growth, jerking a wide swath of it out of whatever rootage it had found. I saw what it had hidden—a tumble of bones, among them a skull which leered up at me hollow-eyed. Undoubtedly the remains of one of my own kind.

Though there were no signs of clothing nor any weapon, I had the feeling that death had not come too long ago, clean-stripped as those bones appeared. One of my fellow candidates who had fallen to such evil as was hidden here?

Murri was still sniffing. He might have been seeking a trail. Only what he said was:

"Bad—danger—"

"What kind?" I demanded. That alertness I had learned as a herdsman was what I called upon now, searching for any clue as to the nature of the peril encompassed here, from which direction it might spring without warning.

There was no sign of any malon among these vines matted to encircle us, save for the path we had torn. It would seem that we must venture farther in.

Murri had not answered my question and I gathered that he was also at a loss as to what danger might lie in wait. Yet it would seem he had no intention of turning back; rather he attacked the tangle before him vigorously.

We had passed the first of the buildings, so embowered now that one could see only small patches of wall, but no windows nor doorways. Suddenly Murri gave a cry, not only of startlement but also fear. The paw he had just put forth to claw his way forward had been noosed by a thick greyish rope of sorts and a second one had snaked out across his body as he strove to use his teeth on that first binding.

I moved in with my knife-staff swinging. The blades rebounded at first from the ties which were fast netting Murri but a second slashing at the cut left by the first severed that which was tightening around his body. It uncoiled, fell to earth, and straightway twitched and writhed, a thick yellowish stuff pouring from the cut to release a foul odor.

This was no creature as I knew, rather a tendril of the growth about us. Across Murri's back, where it had tightened, the fur was wet and slimy and patches of hair missing.

He spat out that which he held in his mouth, and pawed at his jaws from which the spittle ran yellow. I feared that there had been poison in that thing he had chewed apart, for he behaved as a kotti who had swallowed a fur ball, vomiting a watery substance.

This I saw only with half an eye, as it were, for I was alert for another of the vine nooses. They appeared to spring out of the piece of ground we had cleared and were certainly vines, for the ends, still rooted, were putting out small leaves, of the same sickly yellow, veined in red.

I chopped, swung, chopped again and again. Then the ends which came wriggling up to the surface from the dank soil vanished. We at last had a space in which to breathe. I nursed skin across which one of those flesh-stripping horrors had passed, leaving welling blood behind it. The sting of that contact was worse than all the torment I had suffered from the insects in the salt land.

There was still no sign of any malons. Yet to venture deeper into this mass was an invitation to the lurking horror beneath the surface of the ground. I wondered if it was the vibration of our footfalls which had alerted it or if it had some other method of sensing prey. Perhaps even some of the leaves which walled us in acted as eyes, ears, or similar organs for what lay beneath the surface.

Still someone had managed to get farther on, as the signs, fast being swallowed up by fresh growth, showed. And I knew that Shank-ji, at least, had won his prize from this haunted place.

Our exertions had carried us past the first of the now netted buildings and now we were offered safety for a bit, for we came out of the massed stuff unto a circle of the clean sand such as covered the land beyond the bubble.

I examined Murri's back but the suckers of the vine had not injured him beyond loosening the fur in patches. And he had stopped his heaving. My own wound was small enough and I could not see that it was poisoned in any way—or so I hoped.

"Brother—" I laid my hand on Murri's head.

"I live—but bad here—"

With that I could heartily agree. Now I set out making the round of that place of sand where apparently none of the growth could find rootage. To the right of the place we had entered, there were again signs of another's passage. To make certain this was the way, there was a nauseating odor on the air. I had been told that spoiled or rotted malon produced such. Thus the "garden" which we sought must lie in that direction.

But for this moment we were content to sit in our pool of safety and only look towards what might be the second stage of a battle, and perhaps an even more difficult one.

26

THE SIDE OF THE BUILDING around which we had come to find this island of safety was bare of vine. Just as the other was so tightly coated with it. There had been a pattern incised there as I had seen in the city we had visited, though this had no bright color, rather stains as if vines had once clutched there but had been broken away.

I slung my staff across my shoulder and went to run my hands over that pattern. What I had suspected at first sighting was true, there were finger- and toeholds here for the climber. Slipping off my boots I began that ascent hoping so to view what might lie ahead. The top of the house had been rounded and over part of it crawled the vines. I edged around these so that I was still in the clear.

Ahead there was a bank of the tough growth, but beyond that again another stretch of sand. Through a hole in the growth I could see a line of malon vines, each trained over a trellis. On them the rounded globes of fruit, some already the deep purple of fully ripe.

I shared what I had learned with Murri. He was washing his face over and over, trying to rid himself of the last signs of that vine attack. With a growl which fully expressed his opinion of the whole business, he got ready to plunge into the struggle toward the garden I had sighted.

Though we went with care, we did not see any sign of those root tops wriggling out of the dank soil. And when we came to the clearing of the malons, the sand stretch there was divided into squares, every other one being earth in which one of the vines was planted.

There was a strong stench of rotted fruit. While the ground around each looped-up vine was a mush of fallen malons. Of those still on the vines the ones which had turned the full color of ripeness were useless to me, for the picking must be done at almost the very moment the purple streaked the bronze fruit, entirely encircling the globes.

On the nearest of the vines I noted three such which looked promising. How long I must wait until they were ready I did not know. Even as I stood there two others fell from their stems to squash on the piles already there.

We moved out on the sand, but kept away from the mess of stinking fruit. Murri lay down, his nose covered by his paws. I wished I could do likewise, for the odor of this place, even as the haze on the fire mountains, was dense enough to sicken one.

I had my eye on a fruit well at the end of one vine which I thought I could pull down within reach with my staff and moved near as I could get to that without venturing into the mess on the ground.

It was then that I saw a shaking and quiver of the spoiled fruit. Three of the last fallen tumbled away, shaken from below, and there showed for an instant the pointed end of one of the threatening suckers. This then must be their usual food. But I was warned by the sight of them feeding.

It was the nature of the malon that the last stage of ripening came so quickly that one could actually see the spread of the darker color. I was ready, my staff out, and I angled one of its edges as a hook about the branch, pulling it down. Freed by this movement the malon took to the air and I caught it, having dropped my staff into the mush on the ground.

With my prize safe to hand I cleaned my staff in the sand and tried again with the same success. Together we turned to find our way out of this place of hidden menace.

We made it to the circle of sand by the building. The path down which we had cut our way was already being closed by a lacing of smaller vines. However, we had learned our lesson and we cut our way past those sorry remains of the one who failed, gaining the outer door and the safety of the sand dunes beyond, the malons in the fore of my jacket.

If I expected congratulations for my feat I would have been disappointed. The commander of my escort turned the malons I delivered around and around in his hands as if seeking some flaw in the offering. However, the major stroke against me was that I came accompanied by Murri and this time I demanded what little

The Mark of the Cat

The Mark of the Cat 217

rights a contestant had that from hereon he would be my traveling companion.

There was a great deal of muttering and side-looking at me over this. Only tradition held fast. The person of the candidate between his trials was sacred and he could not be opposed unless he had failed.

Perhaps if I had been Shank-ji I would have been afforded a banquet in Twahihic's major city, presentation to the Queen, and a general flood of good wishes for my last trial to come. But I was as well pleased to take the trail back to Vapala as soon as possible.

When days later the guard which had been waiting for me at the border took over escort, I again spoke for Murri. This time the sandcat entered the Diamond Queendom openly and not by stealth.

I learned that I was the first to return and that news had arrived that two of the contestants had already been lost. That Shank-ji was not one of them was cheering to those around me and they openly spoke of his gaining the crown.

From the comments I heard as we traveled on towards the city, the younger members of the guard all favored the Emperor's son. Only those of some of the old and most conservative of Houses were opposed to such a break with tradition. I also gathered that he was a man of ambition and with a certain power of person which afforded that ambition a firm base. That he was one of their own countrymen made him doubly welcome, whereas the coming of an outer "barbarian" would be quickly resented.

We reached Vapala City itself shortly after mid-day, Murri trotting beside my oryxen. Oddly enough that beast accepted the sandcat, though otherwise they were natural hunter and prey. And he was still with me as we threaded our way through crowded streets, where the reaction of the crowd was such one might have thought I was an enemy of the state instead of the possible ruler.

The chiming of the unlatched wind chimes was near overpowering to one who had come from the quiet of the desert lands. When we entered the wide space before the palace, the resounding clamor of the great chimes overhead was almost deafening. I looked up and saw the whirl of the gem-set crown in the midst of those large plaques which the rope-tugging of a number of servants set striking one against the other.

This would be my last testing. I must thread between those swinging plaques, all of which were knife-edged, to claim the crown. Though I had survived so far, I watched the random clashing of the pieces and thought—this is impossible. There could be no possible way one could venture between such and not be slashed—cut literally to bits! Yet it had been done in the past and it was expected that it would be done now.

Shank-ji would be most familiar with the chimes, the only one who might know the way to approach them and reach the trophy within. Yet I was committed and this lay before me. Without being truly conscious that I sought some reassurance, my hand fell on Murri's head, and, from that touch, there flooded into me a strength which at least held me outwardly strong.

The final trial would not be separate as the others. We must wait until the rest who survived returned. They would have ushered me into quarters in the palace itself but once more I stood on my right of choice. I would go to the only place in this city where I might hope to find at least a suggestion of friendship. Since the candidates were allowed to claim shelter from kin or friends, I asked for Ravinga, though I did not know whether the dollmaker would receive me.

The crowd shrank back, giving Murri and me an open passage which did not have to be enforced by the guard, though those rode with me. At the end of the alley which gave upon the court of the dollmaker, I dismounted, turning my oryxen over to the officer. Then I went to the door which I hoped would open hospitably for me.

Ravinga had sat for many hours by her work table. But all the materials lying before her had long ago been pushed aside. She had stationed two lamps so that they gave light to a square of the age-polished and scarred board before her and her attention had been on that board. With the coming of dawn she blew out the lamps, but still she watched—what I did not know, even though as her apprentice she had granted me access to some of her secrets.

I had brought food, only to have it grow cold and left untouched, though she drank twice from the flagon of malon juice I had placed conspicuously close to one of the lamps. However, even during that taking of refreshment her eyes did not leave that stretch of wood. This was new to her, for since my coming into her household I had never seen her do so before.

It was shortly after dawn that her hand moved again, not reaching this time for the cup, but rather in blind groping among the scattered materials, for still she did not look away from that portion of wood. She dug into a tray and brought forward first a casting of gold. The form was still rough yet there was that which suggested the figure of a sandcat.

This she placed in the middle of that stretch of table top. For the first time she spoke:

"Bring the jewel casket." Her order was abrupt and suddenly there was a feeling which seemed to spread from her to me that there was a need of hurry for some task.

Goaded by that, I went swiftly to the far end of the room and there worked the name lock of the wall cupboard behind which such valuables as we had were stored. The jewel casket was heavy, being made of the stone of the fire mountains, polished and patterned. And that pattern clearly was of sandcats.

As I set it on the table before Ravinga, Wa, Wiu, and Wyna, the kottis of the household, appeared out of nowhere, jumped to the table top which was and always had been forbidden territory to them. I would have warned them off but Ravinga, without speaking, shook her head and I took that as an order to allow them to stay.

They sat in a line, statue still, the tips of their tails curled over their forepaws, their unblinking gaze upon what Ravinga was doing.

She had chosen from her tools a slender knife and was working at the soft pure gold of the figure she had selected. Hair-thin shavings of the metal fell away from her tool. At length she had finished a perfect figure. Then she turned to the small cabinet on the table. Once more there was a finger lock to be mastered and this she did for herself, for that particular piece of her equipment had never been opened to me.

From small shelves within she took a small flask of metal and dipped one of her delicate brushes into the narrow mouth of that vessel. So she painted the golden figure with great care. The liquid she used was colorless but she gave three coatings to the sandcat she had created.

Now she opened the jewel case. On a square of dark cloth which she brought out first she began to lay out stones. The rich yellow of the finest citrines shone and she matched and rematched these with care until she had two which were perfect twins. These she set into the figure for eyes.

Having finished this job, she searched again among her materials and produced a plate of dingy metal, so blackened I could not have said what it was. Directly in the middle of this she put her sandcat and around it she poured, from another flagon out of the cupboard, a stream of dust-fine crystals, heaping these up until the mound covered the whole of the figure.

"The taper—" Another order.

I used the spark snap and lighted the taper on the table. Grasping this firmly she touched the fire to that powder. There was a glow spread from that point of contact. The kottis moved back. For the first time they gave voice—a murmur which was between a mew and a purr—almost as if they sang. While there was a flare from the plate and an outward puff of smoke.

Ravinga leaned back with a sigh, her hands falling limply into her lap. Her face was haggard and I caught at her shoulder.

"You must rest—"

She smiled slowly. "We have a guest, two guests on the way, girl. Yes, I must rest for there will be much to be done."

The haze on the plate spiraled away into wisps of smoke. All the dust had vanished, only the sandcat sat there. The kottis' song died away. One after another they stretched their necks out, audibly sniffing at the figure head, and uttered a cry such as I had never heard before. Ravinga nodded. "So it is well done, is it? Let it be what is best needed in the days to come."

She put her hands to the board and levered herself up from her so-long-held chair as if the strength had been leached out of her.

"That," and she pointed to the golden cat. "Put it away carefully for it is now a thing to be guarded."

She staggered and I would have gone to aid her but she fended me off with one arm. "I but need rest, Allitta. Rest before our guests arrive."

Our guests came with such an escort as this quarter of the city seldom sees, unless there is some dire trouble between Houses and some assassin has chosen to flee hither. For it was a detachment of the Queen's own guard which brought Hynkkel back to our doors. Beside him openly paced Murri, the sandcat, whose life I would have thought would have been forfeit the moment he appeared within range of any of our proud hunters.

The warriors did not follow Hynkkel into our small court. I very much disliked the idea that they had come even to the end of the short way which opened into it.

I am free of many of Ravinga's secrets, if not all, and some of those are such one would not want to be discovered by any in authority. That she was engaged in some great plan which had many parts and reached far up into certain Houses as well as down into the company of those who seldom slunk forth in the bright light of day—that I was well aware of and had been for many seasons now. That I was part of her plan was also clear to me and I did not resent it.

There has always been a thirst in me for learning and while Ravinga was a figure of awe, she was also a ready teacher. If with her one craft overlaid another, then I was all the richer for being admitted, even if only into the fringes of her planning.

I sighted Hynkkel's arrival from our own private lookout and hurried down to open the shop door before he had a chance to knock. Mancol sat on his stool behind the counter unmoving. I wondered, as I had many times, what the old man knew, what he guessed. However, that he was devotedly loyal to Ravinga I had known from the start of my own introduction to this place.

Hynkkel entered, behind him Murri. There was a rustling past my skirt as our three kottis pushed forward. I raised hand in greeting to the man, they went to touch noses with the beast.

In the light I saw the black blot which near covered the palm of the hand he had raised in answer to me. Something had been branded there into his flesh. In other ways he was changed. There were new lines in his narrow face, a strange sense of power learned and used clung to him. I knew its like from my life with Ravinga. This one had gone in strange places and had wrought well there.

"To the House be welcome. To the hearth fire come safely. Under this roof know all are friends." I repeated the formal greeting mechanically.

He smiled and that erased from his face some of that power sign.

"To the House be all honor. I accept what is given with a heart of cheer." That return, in its last words, appeared to be more than just formal. There was a warmth in it which suggested that indeed he found comfort here.

The door was safely closed now against all prying eyes—though why that thought crossed my mind at that moment I could not have said. That we were not overlooked by any of the guard, as blandly innocent as our meeting was, seemed to be a thing to be desired.

Once more I brought him into the room prepared for him. As he laid aside his staff I saw the better that new brand on his palm—

the head of a leopard. I did not know its meaning—save perhaps it signified that so far he had overcome and survived in triumph the tasks set him.

His Kifongg sat against the wall and now he stooped to take it in hand, sweeping his fingers across the strings.

"Well and skillfully tuned." He glanced at me with another smile. "I thank you for this courtesy, Allitta—"

I shrugged. As always I felt stiff and even suspicious with this man and I almost distrusted that Ravinga had woven him so tightly into her web. He was comely enough, if slight of body, certainly no match for any of the young warriors of Great Houses. But what did he matter to me? I had had my fill of those standing higher in the world, more resplendent than he—and I had found them very hollow beneath all their fine showing.

"A good instrument needs attention," I said with all the indifference I could summon. "My lady will be with us later, she labored late."

He nodded as I stepped back from the doorway to let Murri past and then I went to the kitchen, intent on preparing such a meal as would tempt Ravinga after her ordeal, as well as satisfy these guests whose purpose in our lives I could not puzzle out.

27

THE LAMPLIGHT lay across the table and I found it oddly welcoming. This was a room in which I felt at home—in spite of the fact that the girl by the fireplace showed me always so cold a face. But by the rest, I was cheered, experiencing a warmth which came, not from the outside, but from within.

If Allitta gave no welcome, I received it from Ravinga, and it was mainly to her I told the story of my ordeals. On the bench at the other end of the table sat the three black kottis and it was as if they listened too and understood each word I said, or perhaps they gained their knowledge in some manner through Murri, who lay at ease on the floor in that complete relaxation of his own kind.

The Kifongg rested on my knees. Now and then my fingertips brought a note or two from it. Then I realized that I was following the actions of a bard delivering a message.

The story took us well past nightfall. I had eaten of the wholesome fare the dollmaker had provided and still had a tankard of fex juice by my hand to wet down my throat as I talked. Then I became aware that Allitta had left her place by the fire and had come to the bench which she shared with the kottis.

"Thus have I won so far," I concluded.

"So far," Ravinga echoed. "There remains—the gaining of the crown."

I had tried to put that out of mind for a space, for I knew very well that this end test was indeed the trickiest and most demanding. How a man might ever gain the height to free the crown with those swinging, knife-edge plaques hung all at different lengths was something I could not understand. Now I felt chilled in spite of the welcome warmth of the room.

Each of the trials had threatened death. I thought that I had faced that fact. Now I discovered that fear still was my shadow.

I placed the harp on the table and looked down at the hands on which the guardian had set his mark. Then, as if pulled by a power beyond my conscious understanding, I reached two hands for the mask pendant at my breast.

Ravinga had arisen and without a word left me sitting there to face what I had striven for the whole evening to push away from me, that weakening fear. Shank-ji and any of the others who had survived had not yet returned. There was a stretch of time then which I must wait out, and to be companioned by fear during that time—

The dollmaker returned out of the shadows beyond the lamplight. She laid down on the table a staff but one which bore no relation to that which had accompanied me during my journeying. This was no herdsman's weapon and companion. Now it was a symbol of power, power—

The rod length was golden and set in a curling pattern for most of its length of small jewels. The rubies of Thnossis, the topazes of Azhengir, the sapphires of my own people, the other gems which were the badges of the five nations fashioned in those whirls and spirals. At the top was the figure of a seated sandcat, also golden, with gem eyes which outflashed the other jewels below. It was fit for an Emperor as a rod of office—for an Emperor!

I gazed at it dazzled. This was of workmanship as fine as that from my sister's hands—heretofore I had believed that no one could surpass her craft. I put forth a hand and yet I dared not touch it—this was not meant for me.

Ravinga might have read my mind.

"It is yours in truth, Klaverel-va-Hynkkel. Or will be soon."

"Why?" I suddenly knew that chill of fear close about me a hundredfold. "Who am I to be Emperor? I am not even a warrior—but rather a herdsman and servant in my father's household." I did not want to look ahead. I dared not build upon that which I now believed would not come true.

To those of Vapala I was a barbarian. Among my own people I had been weighed and found wanting. I was—

"You are," her words carried with them something of a command, "what you believe yourself to be!

"Have you not gained brothership with the desert lords?" Her eyes flitted from me to Murri and back again. "What other man for generations out of time can claim that?"

It was as if my eyes turned inward and I saw not this room and that blazing rod of office, but rather the rocks of the isle and the dancing cats. Faintly I could even hear the strange sound of their singing. Once again I witnessed their unbelievable leaps and bounds, the fact that they could even coast afloat, their fine fur fluffed, the air they swallowed holding them aloft.

At the time it had been a sight of wonder, to me now it was even more of a mystery and even delight. Those graceful forms absorbed in their own release of feeling. I remembered my own attempts to match them and take part in the joyful expression of their love of life.

"Yes," Ravinga's voice cut through that half dream jerking me back to the here and now, "remember that, brother to the furred ones. As to why you," she paused as if she might be hunting the proper words—as an adult who must explain something obtuse to a child, "do not expect me to answer that, Hynkkel. I only know that for many seasons it was set upon me to seek out a certain man. When you laid hands on that trophy of the devil knotted into the mane of my yaksen I knew that I had found he whom I had sought."

Now I arose to my feet and leaned a little across the table, my eyes striving to hold hers fast.

"Who are you, Ravinga? What purpose made you seek so?"

She hesitated and then she slipped down onto the stool where she had sat earlier and, with the gesture, ordered me back into my own place.

"I am Ravinga, a maker of dolls—" Again she paused and I interrupted her:

"And of other things. An Emperor perhaps, dollmaker? But men are not such as can be made—save through their own actions."

"We are all of the essence of our homelands, and also of the Great Essence. There stirs now that which once before strove to break the tie between people and their world. There is a Will which holds itself greater than the whole. I am one of a few who might be called Watchers, Guardians." She stretched her wrist now into the full light so I could see the scars there, so like to the ones I also bore. "I have danced with the furred ones in my time, for they have a part to play in what will come, even as they did long ago.

"I do not know when the Shadow will advance upon us—now it flits—it tests. There must be an Emperor who is of such nature that he can, in the time of need, draw upon the Essence—not only of his own country, but that of all the outlands, men, women, beasts, the land itself."

"And you believe that I can do this?"

Now she fingered the staff lying on the table. "Would this have been wrought, did I not?"

"I—I am not what you seek!" All the years behind me arose to argue that.

"You shall be what you make yourself, Hynkkel. Chew upon that thought. Get you to your rest, for the morning comes far too soon."

So abruptly she dismissed me. There was a wanness on her face as if her explanation to me had drawn out much strength. I might have been for her just such an ordeal as I had faced already. I picked up the harp and murmured a good-night, leaving her there now gazing down at the staff of power.

Chew upon her planted thought I did and sleep did not come easy that night. This time Murri did not slink away to hide but rather shared my chamber.

"Brother—" I drew my fingertips across the strings of the Kifongg, but kept the chords which arose soft, "what lies before us now?"

He had been licking a forepaw and now he raised his head to look at me.

"Much," he made short answer.

At that moment I wished with all my will that I were back in that small hut which had been my own before this whole venture had begun. I was who I was—how could such as I aspire to Emperor? I had never wanted power, to herd the beasts, harvest the algae, make a trading venture into town—that was all the life I had known and I was not fitted for more.

"Not so—" Murri rumbled.

My hand had fallen on my knee and I looked down at the brand there. Memory arose strong, vivid. I heard through the walls of the room, saw beyond the house, the city—

The sandcats in their grace and full beauty danced beneath the night sky. They sang their own purring, growling chants. There was such freedom, such a uniting with the Essence. Muscles twitched in that moment. I wanted to fling myself out again, to be one with them, with their world.

Then again I faced the black leopard and his jealously guarded sphere. I rubbed one hand against the other and looked again at the brands set there. There was the mountain of fire, the treacherous plain of salt pan, the tangle of vines—

I wished so much for my own old place on the dome of my

house where I could look upon the stars, open mind and heart to the essences into which I had been born. By touching such I would know who I truly was.

All the stories which Kynrr had related in detail about Vapala— the court—the under struggles of one House against another so that the country was rife with intrigues. How was I to face that?

However, I could not be sure that I would be called upon to do so. I remembered Shank-ji and the fact that this land was his and so would answer first to him.

I set aside Kynrr's instrument and sought the bed mats where Murri had already settled himself. Perhaps it was the purring of my companion which brought me sleep for it speedily came, even though I had enough twisting thoughts to keep it away.

Wa, Wiu, and Wyna sat by the fire which had died down to coals. As I stirred the pannikin in which I had steeped the drink for Ravinga, they watched me with round green eyes. My thoughts were such that I dug my spoon deeply and hard into the mixture. For fear gnawed at me.

Suppose that Ravinga spoke the truth and this herdsman out of a barbarian land would triumph in the end. Thereafter he would face a maze trap worse than any he had known. He might be Emperor but he would speedily learn that there were powers which would stand stubbornly against him. And, with the Shadow spreading, we did not need dissension at court.

Shank-ji had a strong following, even those elders who would not welcome a break with tradition would back him if he won. His mother had been of the House Yuran, one of the oldest and most powerful. Those now bearing that name would be only too ready to support their kinsman. And if he failed, their anger would be great—

I bit my lip. They had eyes and ears in plenty in Vapala, did those of Yuran. There could be no long concealment of Ravinga's connection with this outlander. Once their suspicions were aroused—then what would follow?

Death could be the least and most desired end. Ravinga had powers, yes. I had seen them at work—but their success depended mainly on the point that she had never been questioned. That this Hynkkel had chosen to come to us—that he had been escorted hither by the guard—that he had dared to bring that beast which was the terror of legend—all this was enough to turn the wrong eyes in our direction.

Was I a coward? No, but I was one who had learned a dire lesson in the past. Where was my House now? Yet once our colors had shown proudly in the feast hall of the Emperor. Not to think of that. Yet it nagged me until, unable to sleep, I went into the shop. The grey of early daylight had become as full as it ever reached in this court. I unbarred the latch door and stepped out for a moment. Mancol had not yet come, nor had the kottis followed me. I was alone and in that moment I heard the chiming of the mobiles begin as those in the major thoroughfares were released from their night latching. Above them all sounded the louder clang of the Emperor's.

Today—tomorrow—when would they come, those others who survived the trials elsewhere? While he who slept beneath our roof—

"Bright day."

I turned swiftly. The man in my thoughts stood there, his head a little atilt as if he were listening to the incessant chimes, striving to separate one set from the other.

"Bright day," I answered him mechanically.

Then he spoke with the directness of his countrymen, so different from the courtesy-encased words of we of Vapala—

"You are no friend to me, are you, Allitta?"

"I do not know you—" I responded.

"You may know as much as Ravinga but it is not enough—"

Why he sought to tax me with this, I could not understand. Did he believe that I strove to turn my mistress against him? Yes, that I would have done long since had I been able. But my judgment had no weight for her in this matter.

"I fear you," I answered before I thought.

"You fear *me*?" He accented that last word as if he were incredulous. "Why?"

"Because of what might happen." Then all I had been thinking by the fire spilled out of me—that through him my mistress courted the danger of attracting the adverse notice of those who could and would act against her.

"I see," he said slowly. "Kynrr spoke of such things as the jealousy of the Great Houses and their secret ways of dealing with those who gained their ill favor. You think then that such might be turned upon her whom you care for, if by some unusual range of favor I do gain the crown?"

I nodded.

"The Emperor has all power, does he not?"

"Subject to the advice of the Chancellor," I corrected him.

"But he can take under his protection whomever he wishes—"

"If he may desire to do so."

"So." I had him frowning now. He favored me with a hint of wry smile. "I think you may see only shadowed future, Allitta. I have yet to claim the crown. Nor do I think that my chances are so fair. But this much I say to you: Your mistress is one who knows more than either of us. I would back her against a war band, without even a spear to hand, and yet see her a victor. She is far more than she seems."

28

RAVINGA DID NOT SHARE our morning meal nor did Allitta do me such a favor. Murri and I ate alone, and it was not an easy meal, for I waited for the summons and waiting has never been easy for me. As it never is for one who can reckon in his mind all the evils which may lurk ahead. How long that wait would be I had no way of telling.

Allitta packed two large baskets with lesser products of Ravinga's skill, or perhaps her own, and I loaded these on a hand cart for her. I would have taken my place at the push bar of that and seen her to the market but she told me plainly that it was my place to stay under cover as I had already flaunted custom by choosing to shelter with the dollmaker. My appearance as co-vendor of wares in the marketplace would only draw such attention as I must not court.

Thus I faced a long day with nothing to do. After the activity of the last period of travel and effort, that seemed a burden. The old man took over the shop and fussed about, moving Ravinga's doll people here and there on shelves and muttering under his breath, now and then peering at me from under his eyebrows as if he found me a disturbing sight. So at last I was driven into the long room which was Ravinga's workshop.

I moved about that, as careful not to touch as a child who had been sternly forbidden to do so, eyeing her work from its beginnings to the near finished figure at hand, marveling at how no two of the small faces were alike. It was as if she looked upon her art even as did my sister and had no desire to repeat any design.

There was one shelf before which I paused to give longer study to what stood there. Within me was a chill I could not account for as I looked upon the likeness of two women and a man, and beside

231

them—the snarling figure of a rat! Why Ravinga would wish to use her talent to fashion such a creature I could not imagine.

The women had the silver hair of Vapala, but their skin was a darker shade than that of those I had seen on the streets. Their garb was not ordinary robes or even court finery, but rather the scanty covering of cat dancers. Their faces were painted, and the fingers of their tiny, well-fashioned hands had the nails elongated into claws. Also they were posed as if prepared to leap forward in one of the intricate twirls of the hunt dance.

Their companion was a much more somber figure. His head was covered by a tight-fitting hood, so drawn on his skull as to suggest that no hair sprouted under it, not even the common top lock. He had been dressed in a sleeved robe which fell open on his breast and the body portion so displayed there was patterned with a device which was etched into the skin itself or so it would seem.

For the rest he had the full breeches of a Kahulawen and below those, boots fringed about the tops with black oryxen mane hair. There was no sword belt with ready weapon, no spear to hand. Rather his carven fingers were looped about the shaft of a staff of honor and that was topped by the likeness of a creature I had never seen nor heard described—but something which suggested great malignity.

The rat—it was a rat—but in scale with the three figures beside it, it was overlarge—more like one of the monsters which had been recently appearing, the like of which I had myself slain among the rock isles.

"You are interested in my people, Hynkkel?"

I was so unaware of all save the dolls that I started. Ravinga stood by my side.

"The cat dancers—I once saw a small company of those. But the man—and the rat—?"

"The man you could never have seen, nor even have heard of—not in your far outlands. There are no keepers of old knowledge there—"

"We have our Rememberers for the feasts," I protested. This implied judgment that we were indeed barbarous pricked me more than it ever had.

"Yes, and they are well trained—in the history of your people. But there were others before you, and of those none of your lore makes mention. He," she pointed to the man, "was a seeker of strange knowledge who once crossed the Plain of Desolation—before the first Emperor was crowned."

"But no man—nor beast—can dare the inner heart of the Plain!"

"The rats do," she returned. "There is much lost knowledge, Hynkkel. Some of it purposefully lost. There is also a belief that to think on things of darkness in curiosity may awaken more than one wishes. Yes—that one was a master of much power which had nothing to do with spear or sword. And the rat was his symbol!"

That any living person might use one of those loathsome creatures to stand as his House badge sickened me. Yet now I could see truly that the sign etched on what was meant to be a bare breast was the outline of a rat head, even as I wore that of the leopard on my palms.

"How do you know of him?" Perhaps the question was an impertinence but it was one I could not forgo.

"I am a Guardian, Hynkkel. From generation to generation, from reign to reign, certain women have carried the old knowledge. Perhaps not without taint or misunderstanding, for knowledge passed from mind to mind may sometimes be unconsciously altered by the very personality of he or she who holds it. I cannot be sure how true is that I myself now hold—but it is enough to warn me.

"That is Ylantilyn, once of the House of Borse." Again she indicated the figure. "His very name was a curse in its time. He reached for much, gained some, and sundered House from House, land from land, to try for more. Even the beasts, except those horrors he herded as his own, were caught up in his warring. As a result, they, too, suffered change.

"Hynkkel," now her attention moved from the figure to me and there was that about her which was like unto my father's stance when he spoke about some fault of mine, "the lives of all of us move in circles. We are born, we labor to our wills, or our needs, we come again to death. The Great Essence takes us up and once more molds us and sets the pattern afresh. Only we do not carry with us the memory of what lies behind, thus often the same mistakes are ours. Just so is the life of our queendoms, we follow patterns and in times those patterns become twisted.

"For long now have we lived in a semblance of peace. We train warriors but they have naught to raise spear against, save outlaws or the animals they hunt. We have the hardship of our lands, the sandstorms, the mountain fires, the treachery of the salt pans. Yes, all these represent danger, and many of us die of the very nature of our surroundings.

"But in the past were greater wars, and our lives were shaped by those. Such will come again, and if we are not prepared we shall be as yaksen at the coming of Murri's clan—near helpless."

That she fully believed this I could see. But from where would this danger come? Would the jealousy of the Great Houses warp and tear apart a long-held peace? Or would some danger, such as she hinted of, come from outside? And what had I, who was no warrior, to do with war?

Allitta returned home at the noon closing of the market. Her baskets of wares were depleted to be sure, but what she had brought was news and I realized that that had been her main reason in the market.

"Those of the House of Trelek have ridden out." She cupped her bowl of stew with one hand but made no attempt as yet to taste it. "Word has come that Shank-ji has completed those trials set him."

"Others?" inquired Ravinga as Allitta raised a spoon.

The girl shook her head. "No others—nor are they now expected. A courier has come to say that and the market hums with his news."

I was suddenly uninterested in my portion of the meal. No others? Two of us only for the final trial?

"They were trying to place wagers at Hawiff's booth. There were no takers—all believe that Shank-ji need only reach forth his hand to take up the Emperor's staff and it is his." Now she looked straight at me and there was plainly a challenge in her tone. "The warriors have been gathering these five days—four more House troops rode in this morning, as well as some from the outer lands. Among such is Klaverel-va-Kalikku." She repeated that name with deliberation as if to make very sure that I heard and understood.

That my brother had returned did not surprise me—this was an event which would draw many from every one of the five queendoms. All the Queens had made the journey to Vapala, ready to swear homage to the new Emperor, and in their trains there would be many of those from the principal Houses of their queendoms.

"There is talk—" Allitta paused to take up another spoonful of stew and swallow.

"Talk," Ravinga said. "Of what kind and by whom?"

"Of interference with the Customs—"

"Shank-ji must answer that then?"

Allitta shook her head. "No, the interference is said to be his."

She nodded at me. "They say that his own brother has already sworn that he was not able to win so far without aid, that he consorts with beasts more than with his own kind, that he is already outcast from his House—"

I deliberately spooned up what was before me. Could I have expected less? But what aid were they able to claim was mine? I had been escorted by the troops. In each case my coming and going had been under their surveillance. That I consorted with beasts—yes. That I was outcast—perhaps so—I had not returned to my father's dwelling after my solo, but then the manner of my setting forth for that was enough to warn me off. Could such talk keep me from the final trial, leave Shank-ji a very clear field? Though he must still face bringing out the crown from among those ever-turning, knife-edged plaques.

"And this talk," Ravinga pursued the subject, "how is it slanted?"

Allitta let her spoon splash down into the bowl and held up her fingers to count off points on those one by one.

"Firstly, there are the merchants. They want uninterrupted trade most of all—and a strong hand with the Houses. Haban-ji was of Vapala and so could muster enough good will of the Houses. The barbarians do not count for much, for the greater merchants do not trade directly with them. And they believe that an Emperor from the outer lands cannot hold a steady rein on the Houses, any more than a child upon an untrained oryxen.

"Then," she turned down a second finger, "there are the Houses themselves. They will give homage, if grudgingly, to an outlander—and intrigue behind his back. One of their own kind they believe might be influenced outwardly and quickly to understand them and their ways. They might even foresee a bending of a custom in which only the senior son of a House would be thought of for selection of Emperor trials. Shank-ji has a big following among the younger members of many Houses—he is open-handed to his friends while Haban-ji humored him and gave him much.

"Thirdly," another finger went down, "there are the people as a whole. As the merchants, they want peace and that means a strong Emperor. They do not take kindly to an outsider, especially one suspected of strange powers. That you," now she addressed me directly, "have your tie with the sandcats is a strong theme of gossip and certainly not in your favor.

"Fourth, the people of the other queendoms—there is other gossip concerning you, Hynkkel, and from those whom all would expect to wish you well rather than ill. Your brother has attached himself to Shank-ji's following. He has spoken hard and long against you and none of your own clan has answered in your defense. We have heard that only your sister Kura has kept silent and seems to have some feeling for you. However, she is but one against many and is thought to have too soft a heart."

I winced. What else could I expect from my father? If I had gone back from my solo—no, I was sure he would never have welcomed me as a full son of his.

"They talk much," Ravinga commented. "Which is only to be expected. There are always rumors upon rumors in the marketplace. When does Shank-ji arrive?"

"Perhaps two days from now." Allitta took up her spoon again and set to work on the stew.

I pushed aside my own bowl. Though I had somehow won through the other tests, I could now only hold in my mind the picture of the slash-edged mobile swinging in answer to the full arm pull of the guard, the crown resting at its very heart. Still there was nothing left for me but to face it.

"Is there a way I can see the likeness of the mobile without going into the palace square?" I asked then.

"Certainly." Ravinga raised her voice to carry into the shop. "Mancol, bring hither one of the crown mobiles. We make them in miniature," she informed me. "They are selling very well during this time. Outlanders buy them as they come here for witnessing the last test. There will be many for that, each of the Queens will bring her guards, and many of her household, while others will travel for themselves. It is perhaps only once in a generation that this happens."

The old man brought in the flashing, twisting set of plates. Ravinga stood to hook it on one of those cords, meant to hold dried fruit and meat, which hung from the ceiling. I leaned back in my seat to watch it as she set it going well with a touch of finger. At the trial time there would be steady twirling by the control ropes.

There was even a tiny crown within the blades and I regarded that without any wish to lay hands upon it. Did not death most always result from entering the mobile? I knew that it was that which was reserved for criminals whose crimes were considered the blackest. However, those unfortunates were forced in and from the start believed themselves that they had no chance.

There was a dancing light flickering on the plates as they turned. And the musical tinkle was loud in the room, though not as loud as the sound of the thing it so fully represented.

Dancing— I watched the in-and-out weave of the blades. Those real ones were knife sharp, diamond-edged, enough to slit an unfortunate into ribbons. Yet men had survived. For countless generations there had been Emperors and each of them had won his crown by passing among those blades. So it *had* been done.

Dancing— I closed my eyes against the flicker of the light and again was aware of another time and place, of dancers who were furred of hide and not slick-skinned. Behind me there was a rumble of sound—Murri had come in to lie at length at my back.

"That house in which Murri sheltered on our first visits, it is a ruin, but does not it have a great hall?"

Ravinga nodded. Allitta had returned to her dinner as if she had played her full part in the matter. She did not even seem to be listening.

"Have I your leave to go there?" I continued. "There is a need for thinking—"

"It is yours. None shall disturb you there," the dollmaker returned. Nor did she show any curiosity about what I wished. Perhaps she believed that I was about to seek out the Essence in silent meditation. Which also I was minded to do—but later.

With Murri I made my way into the ruin. It was more promising on the inside than the out. Perhaps it had once been the headquarters of a minor House. I kicked the refuse from the center floor and hung on a panel I half pulled from the wall— where I could watch it—the mobile.

I began to hum deep in my throat and a moment later heard the purring response from my companion. Though my singing in cat speech was a sorry thing, I could well recall some of the rhythm to which that tribe had danced on the isle.

Murri began the dance. He had his people's ability to gulp in air, fluff out his fur, and take to glides as long and as high as those of the sand ships of Twahihic. That advantage I lacked but I was able to leap and twist, and I found that with practice that ability grew. We wove patterns—he as graceful as all his people, I awkwardly and far behind. Yet I persisted, and as I did I continued to sing, for it seemed somehow that the sounds I made possessed a beat which inspired my feet for each leap and turn.

When I tired I dropped cross-legged on the floor and strove to empty my mind, think only of the cats as I had seen them at their festival, and I strove to somehow tap the essence of that memory and make it mine.

I spent a second day so in the hall, striving with all my energy to master as much as I could of the dance. Whether this effort would benefit me or not I had no idea but it was all which I might summon in support.

That night there was a clatter of the door mobile and Allitta let in an officer of the Chancellor's own guard. He looked at me stolidly as he said:

"Two signals before mid-day tomorrow—those who are chosen will face the task."

There was certainly nothing encouraging about that bald statement. I fancied even that he resented having to deliver it to me. However, that was the summoning and there was no drawing back.

Once he had gone I spoke first to Murri. It was only the fact that I was a candidate which protected him here—a very fragile truce which would be broken in an instant at my failure.

"You go safe, brother. Now—I cannot spread claw for you soon."

I looked to Ravinga. "Is there anything I can do to make sure that Murri does not suffer?"

Her eyes when she turned an answering gaze on me seemed cold. "Do you then doubt yourself so much, Hynkkel? Such are not the thoughts you should hold now."

"Chance really favors no man," I answered. "If chance fails me, I would have Murri safe."

She pursed her lips. "There are ties which can be called upon, yes."

I drew a deep breath. My hand went out and my fingers were buried deep in the fur on Murri's head.

"So be it. That much I ask of you."

29

As THERE HAD BEEN at the selecting of the candidates, the square before the palace was crowded—though the guard kept back the throng for a space about the mobile. On the steps behind it was the throne of the Emperor while the Grand Chancellor stood a step below that holding the staff of office, and at her feet lounged the Blue Leopard.

The mobile had been lowered closer to the ground and already those who were to keep it in motion had set those pendants clanging back and forth, the sun striking vivid colors from the plates' ever-moving surfaces. While, at the core, the crown of diamonds with its cat heads set with ruby, topaz, emerald, sapphire, those stones signifying the Outer Regions, formed a blaze of fire.

The crown hung on a chain. He who won that far must also be able to free it, then issue forth again unharmed. To pass those ever-swinging plates, the clangor of which alone was enough to deafen one, would require such agility of body that even to think of such action was daunting.

Yet we stood there ready to attempt that feat, one on either side of the mobile. Shank-ji had drawn the lot which would send him first into the whirling, cutting swing.

Stripped to breech clout he made a fine figure, surely such a one as we could want seated on the throne awaiting the winner. I knew that his body had been exercised for years in all the actions of a swordsman and a spearman of note. And he wore now the guise of one who was utterly sure of himself.

Nor were those who had escorted him hither and now behind him any less assuring. Sons and Heads of Great Houses, daughters of famous clans, they stood by custom to back him who had become their champion. Among that throng I caught sight of my brother, at the same time he was eyeing me, and there was nothing of support in the glare and sneering twist of lip he showed.

Behind me—yes, there were those showing the badges of some of the out-clans, and, closer, Murri. The people had come not because I was their choice. But Murri was there because of good will. They gave him room as he sat, his poise erect, his tail up quivering with excitement, watching the clatter of the plates in the wind as he might have eyed the scuttling of a sand lizard.

Farther back must be both Ravinga and Allitta though they were making no parade of their presence. However, I thought that Murri's good wishes were shared by the dollmaker, if not by Allitta—of whose good will I was hardly sure.

The high priest of the Vapala temple turned a fraction. One of his followers held a gong and the high priest himself had his short rod of office ready. He swung that. The gong note was loud even through the clamor of the mobile. I saw Shank-ji's body tense.

A second time the priest signaled. The warrior sprang. He twisted and turned, once nearly caught by the unexpected whirl of a plate which might have taken off his head had he not ducked in time. He had won within the inner circle, raised his hands to the crown. Then—

The mobile notes were broken by a louder sound. One of the plates turned as if it had been struck by a rod such as the priest held. There came a scream. Shank-ji rolled on the ground in a mist of spouting blood, his left hand clutching at a wrist from which the other hand had just been shorn as neatly as if the blow had indeed been delivered to prevent his taking of the crown.

There were shouts then, men of his war band surged forward. But the Chancellor had already signaled and the mobile swung upward enough to allow two of her own guards to crawl in and bring out the wounded man.

He was carried down an aisle quickly made in the crowd who had come to support him, and, from the limpness of his body, I thought that he had lapsed into unconsciousness. On the stone pavement where he had fallen there was a pool of blood and— the hand. Looking upon that I fought the sickness rising in my throat. Better death than be maimed.

Three, wearing the jeweled robes of the nobles of the first rank, had pushed forward to the foot of the steps below the Chancellor. And he who seemed the leader spoke vehemently, though the clamor of the crowd and the chimes of the mobile obscured his speech as far as the rest of us were concerned. He turned and pointed to the bloodied pavement.

Just beyond that hand there lay something else which had no place there, what appeared to be a stone about the size a man could hold in one hand. And certainly that had not been there earlier, for the ground beneath had been most carefully inspected before the mobile had been lowered.

A stone, now half in the pool of blood—and that pendant of the mobile which had jerked just as Shank-ji had reached for the crown. Those added up to—

Interference—a foul! Yet that was none of my doing and certainly I had no friends, even of my countrymen here, who would try such a trick. Whoever had flung that stone had skill—the skill of an expert slinger perhaps.

The mobile arose higher by jerks and, when it was well up, the nobles who had lodged that protest and the Chancellor herself went to the site. At a gesture from the Chancellor one of her guard picked up that stone and turned it slowly about under her close inspection.

Now one of the nobles, his face a mask of ugly malice, pointed to me. I felt rather than saw the movement of the crowd behind me. There were certainly those there who would be only too glad to drag me down as one who was unfit, who had broken honor of the outland peoples.

The Chancellor gave an order and her guard moved in behind me, forming a wall between me and the crowd. Or was it that they were prepared to take me prisoner as a traitor to custom and a perhaps would-be murderer? Murri! They would move against my fur brother also, only the thin line of a promise keeping them from already sending spear heads into his hide.

However, now the Chancellor was pointing to the plate swinging well above her and then outward at an angle into the crowd on the opposite side of the square—that from which Shank-ji himself had come. At first the nobles seemed in no mind to accept her suggestion. They still glared in my direction. Then her own staff of office swung in imperious order and I saw some of her guards begin to thread through the crowd on the other side. Though how they might discover the culprit there I could not guess.

The intrigues of the Great Houses were so well known that this could have been aimed at Shank-ji out of jealousy or spite. Doubtless he had, as we all do, those who would wish him ill.

The Essence knew that there were enough gathered here this day who had no kind thought for me. Someone must have feared Shank-ji's ascent to supreme power and what it might mean to himself or to his House. I could see no other answer.

Though my mind did go back to those points Allitta had made of those who saw in my winning trouble to come. Was there a mind behind all this which courted trouble? A picture flashed through my mind then of the figure in Ravinga's house—he who wore the stinking rat for a badge. But that one was long dead. No, this must be the result of some House intrigue.

Those under the mobile withdrew to the steps and the Chancellor gave a second wave of her staff. Once more the mobile creaked downward. I ran my tongue across lips suddenly dry. So it would go forward and now the trial was mine. It would be difficult enough to keep my mind strictly on what I was doing.

I did not hear it, I could not have with the continual chime of the mobile and the uproar of the crowd about me, but I sensed it— that song which came from behind me—Murri's song. It moved me to answer, and it was with that humming through my whole body, possessing me, that I moved forward.

The flicker of the panels before me was near blinding. My right hand sought, without any conscious order, that pendant mask upon my breast and I made my first move. There were no true paths there and no planes; rather I faced the twisting, turning bodies of cat people rapt in their own mystery into which they had drawn me.

In—out—to the left—to the right—I leaped and turned, twisted, stooped, to leap again. And in my mind I held tight to that picture of cats, dimly knowing that that was my only hope now.

How long did that dance take me? There was no reckoning for me now. Only a blaze of light before me and that was what I must secure. Suddenly that illusion of the dancers was gone. I had reached the core of the mobile while overhead swung the crown, the glitter of the gems in it enough to blind one who looked directly at it.

I stood so for a breath and then I sprang. The treasure I would hold was attached to a chain. My left hand closed about the chain and I swung, feet off the ground, as with my right fingers I strove to unhook my trophy, only too aware now of the menacing sway of the panels about. None of them had yet crashed against the chain to which I so desperately clung though one spun perilously close.

The crown was mine—at least it was in my hold, free from the hook which had held it. I dropped to the pavement, one foot slipped, and I went belly down on the stone, an outflung hand being no help as it, too, slid along a sticky surface. With the scent of blood about me I realized that I had fallen into the spot where Shank-ji had finished.

There was a vicious swing near my head and I ducked forward. I was sure now that the wind had truly risen and that my present position was near fatal. Nor could I wriggle on my belly, for at least two of the panels were only finger heights above the pavement and swung back and forth in threat of slicing open anybody striving to pass beneath them.

I could no longer summon up again that vision of the dancing cats which had led me here. There were only those knife-edged panels a-swing. Yet the crown lay heavy within the crook of my arm and I dared to raise my head a fraction to view all I could of the swinging death about me.

Now I got to a crouch, having taking the chance that the two nearest of those panels, no matter how far they swung, had a space between them. From that crouch I reached my feet. Before me directly now was another panel helping to form the ring just before the innermost one which now imprisoned me. To clear that I must spring and twist at the same time. I tensed and moved.

Then the wind of one panel passing nearly sent me sprawling straight into the last and most vicious outer line. My head jerked at a pull upon my up-knotted hair. I could not remain where I was to be cut down on the next swing. Once more I leaped, having only seconds to judge the wheel of body to carry me past.

I sprawled face down on the pavement, the noise of the mobile near deafening me. Or was it altogether that? There was something else, voices raised in such an uproar as to drown out the metal's clamor. Jagged locks of hair whipped at my face as I crawled forward a space, fearing any movement to feel the knife edge of a panel slitting across my body. Then, hardly believing it, I knew I was free of that devilish thing and I rose unsteadily to my feet, stooping to pick up the crown I had brought with me.

There was softness of fur against my body, a rough tongue lapped across my ribs. I gripped Murri's heavy shoulder hair and held that as if the touch alone would make me believe I had really won.

At last I turned, in time to see the mobile rise again. Beyond it waited the Chancellor and the priest, beside them the Blue

Leopard of rulership. Yet I did not yet go forward; rather I rubbed my hand across Murri's broad head. And I said:

"Only by your favor, brother," knowing well that I spoke the truth. There were none here—unless Ravinga was somewhere in the crowd behind me—who had wished this finish—none save Murri.

"By your will—" he made me answer.

I loosed my hold on him to turn the crown around in my hands, perhaps to assure myself once more that I indeed held it. The gems made a flashing show which were in contrast to my blood-stained body. Though by the greatest of favors none of the red painting came from my own veins.

The mobile was well up. I could cross that stretch of pavement to the steps without fear now. The end of strain had left me weak, light of head, so that the figures of Chancellor and priest wavered in my sight.

However, I set one foot before the other, until I realized suddenly that Murri was no longer by me. Some stubbornness within me would not allow me to advance without him. The roar of the crowd was even louder. Were they trying to howl down in anger my triumph, or were they cheering me for my success? I did not know.

When I looked around for Murri I saw only open mouths and waving arms, the guards with spears lowered across their bodies to form a barrier to keep this bit of pavement clear.

I could not linger, though my concern for Murri—if the crowd was truly united against me his danger was very great. Still if I was Emperor, then let me claim my victory and show these that a "barbarian" took what he had fought for without awkwardness of bearing.

I came to the steps. To the priest I offered the crown. Though I had truly and honestly won it, it would not be mine until the official coronation. Though at this moment I was indeed Emperor—something I found very hard to adjust to.

The Chancellor held forth the royal staff of office, the leopard crouched and rumbled something not far from a purr. I knew that I must now turn to face this unruly mass of my subjects, that rod in hand.

I climbed a step and then two. The high throne was still empty at my back but I made no move to seat myself there. Somewhere, perhaps on the roofs about, was that slinger who had accounted for Shank-ji. It could well be that some bitter House intrigue would see fit to dispose of one they considered an upstart to allow another trial—with new candidates—such was not beyond reason.

Then I saw the crowd waver, draw apart. Over one of those spear barriers leaped Murri, soaring as he had in the dance. He carried in his mouth a rod the end of which glittered in the sun.

The priest stumbled back, clutching the crown, his face showing his fear. However, the Grand Chancellor stood her ground, her hand going to the Sword of Presence at her belt, even though that weapon of ceremony might be as nothing against this raider from the outlands.

In a single bound Murri reached me and I took from his jaw hold the sandcat-topped staff Ravinga had wrought. Though I did not relinquish the other which bore the leopard symbol.

On my left side the Blue Leopard, belly down, ears flat to skull, sounded a hiss. At my right Murri stood tall, his yellow eyes round on the beast who disputed his coming, showing no fear, no sign of warning of battle to come.

With the two beasts and the two staffs, I faced the people, whose shouts had died away, and who were staring back at me as if amazement had struck them dumb. An age had ended, a new one begun. In one hand I held the ancient symbol of the past, in the other I gripped that which had come to me by my own efforts. What the Essence would demand of me in the future I had no way of foreseeing, but it was true that I must be my own man, that much I had learned. At that thought, near bare of body, stained with blood, the hair released from my shorn topknot tossed by the wind, I claimed what was mine and what I would hold, even as my fur brothers claimed and held what they had won.

Epilogue

RAVINGA HAD LIT only one of the lamps, but by that I could see well her face, and I recognized the strength of purpose in her expression.

"He has won," I said. That that win had astounded me was a simple way of expressing how I felt. This Hynkkel, what had he in him anyway? To be made to twist my thoughts of him in another pattern was difficult to accept.

"He but begins," Ravinga corrected me.

"They must accept him—it is custom—" I caught part of her hint.

"You speak so, knowing what you know, what you yourself have endured, girl? Do not play the simpleton. Shank-ji may have lost a hand, he has not lost a head. There is a slinger to be accounted for—that need is immediate. Beyond lies much more—"

Her gaze swept beyond me to that shelf on which stood the figure of Ylantilyn.

"Therefore," now she spoke briskly as one who had finished one task only to turn to another, "we move again. You, Allitta, have now the right to claim your heritage. Custom decrees that what one Emperor has done, a new one may undo. The last of your House shall do homage with all her peers, shall claim all rights and privileges due her line—*all* rights." She repeated that as one who could not be crossed.

Past bitterness arose in me so strong I could almost taste it. "No!" Still—a second thought—was this not what I had once dreamed of? If strange circumstances brought it about, why should I throw it away?

"Yes!"

247

I could not stand against her. I could not even stand against that part of me which wanted what she took so easily as a fact. A new life—a dangerous one—but I had lived with danger for many seasons—it would not be new or daunting for me.

"We move," Ravinga continued. "Even as the mobile swings, we begin to move."

LIZZY HARRISON LOSES CONTROL

Lizzy Harrison isn't a romantic heroine. She is in no way hopelessly scatty and disorganised — her life is in perfect order. Okay, she hasn't met the right man yet, she's too busy with her job in PR, her packed schedule of improving activities and her diary planned for months in advance. But after her best friend, Lulu, challenges her need for control, it's not long before Lizzy is thrown into the arms of her boss's top client, Randy Jones. Reluctantly, she relaxes her hold on routine and discovers that losing control could win her more than she had ever imagined.